The Suitors in the *Odyssey*

Hermeneutic Commentaries

Pietro Pucci
General Editor

Vol. 2

PETER LANG
New York • Washington, D.C./Baltimore • Bern
Frankfurt am Main • Berlin • Brussels • Vienna • Oxford

Martin Steinrück

The Suitors in the *Odyssey*

The Clash between Homer and Archilochus

PETER LANG
New York • Washington, D.C./Baltimore • Bern
Frankfurt am Main • Berlin • Brussels • Vienna • Oxford

Library of Congress Cataloging-in-Publication Data

Steinrück, Martin.
The suitors in the Odyssey: the clash between
Homer and Archilochus / Martin Steinrück.
p. cm. — (Hermeneutic commentaries; v. 2)
Includes bibliographical references and index.
1. Homer. Odyssey. 2. Homer—Characters—Bachelors.
3. Archilochus. 4. Epic poetry, Greek—History and criticism. I. Title.
PA4167.S675   883'.01—dc22   2008036483
ISBN 978-1-4331-0475-6
ISSN 1043-5735

Bibliographic information published by **Die Deutsche Bibliothek**.
Die Deutsche Bibliothek lists this publication in the "Deutsche
Nationalbibliografie"; detailed bibliographic data is available
on the Internet at http://dnb.ddb.de/.

The paper in this book meets the guidelines for permanence and durability
of the Committee on Production Guidelines for Book Longevity
of the Council of Library Resources.

© 2008 Peter Lang Publishing, Inc., New York
29 Broadway, 18th floor, New York, NY 10006
www.peterlang.com

All rights reserved.
Reprint or reproduction, even partially, in all forms such as microfilm,
xerography, microfiche, microcard, and offset strictly prohibited.

Printed in the United States of America

To the friends who helped:
Janika Päll, Piero Pucci, Regina Portenier, Maria Vamvouri-Ruffy,
and anonymous ones

Table of Contents

Foreword: Reading the *Odyssey* against the grain 1

1 Preface 3

2 Iambus 7
   2.1 Aggression in iambus 7
   2.2 Hypothesis: young men as the audience of the iambus 9
      2.2.1 First argument: attacks against fathers 11
      2.2.2 Second argument: aggression against girls 12
      2.2.3 Homophily of husbands versus heterosexuality
          of unmarried young men 14
      2.2.4 In battle, the death of young men is prettier
          than the death of husbands 14
      2.2.5 The theme of colonization 15
      2.2.6 The gods invoked in the iambus are the gods of the νέοι 17
      2.2.7 Polemic intertext between iambus and epic 17
   2.3 The eighth evidence 20

3 Composition 27
   3.1 An ambivalent glance 27
   3.2 Narrative patterns and the ambivalence of in and out 29
   3.3 Marriage, the death of young men and Zielinski's rules 31
   3.4 Two meanings of *return* 36

4 Fathers 43
   4.1 Foxes 43
   4.2 Eagles 45
   4.3 Odysseus among the fathers 47
   4.4 Father Zeus 52

5 "Calves" 61
   5.1 Oxen 61
   5.2 Young men 63
   5.3 A bipartition 67

6 Stories 75
   6.1 The pattern of erotic adventure 75
   6.2 First example: Circe and better a young man 81
   6.3 Another intertext: oar breaking and stag-hunting 82

6.4 Hermes and Athena: plain and inverted iambic stories 84
6.5 Knocked-out teeth 86
6.6 Bellies 89
6.7 Punishment 91
6.8 Baldness... 94
6.9 Allysis: a possibility 96
6.10 Herakles 98

7 Point of view in the *Odyssey* 105
7.1 Objectivity versus identification-readers........................ 105
7.2 *tomorrow* 108
7.3 Control and freedom of character-speech....................... 109
7.4 Point of view of individuals: πόσις 112
7.5 The point of view of the group: ἄναξ 115
7.6 A counter-example: ξένος 120
7.7 Hindering perspective: the Suitors 124

8 Results and remarks 131
8.1 Summary 131
8.2 A colonial viewpoint 133

Bibliography 139

Index 145

Foreword
Reading the *Odyssey* against the grain

Readers of the *Odyssey* have always realized how puzzling are the characterization, the role and the destiny of the Suitors in that poem. These noble young men are seen constantly enjoying parties, drinking, eating and dancing, and yet they are never characterized by some gastêr-connotations that would debase them to a social inferior status; their aristocratic nature and role is always beyond suspicion, but no iliadic model resemble them, though they are young, unmarried fellows and when they fight they are shown to be not coward. Their generation, with Telemachos, does not belong any longer to the Heroic Age: Odysseus closes it. In their pleasant and erotic pursuits, the Suitors ressemble the Phaeacians, but while the Phaeacians are viewed with a positive and sometimes admiring light by Odysseus and his Narrator, the Suitors, on the contrary, are worthy only of contempt and charged with such negative traits and deeds to justify–though not for a modern sensibility—their massacre.

To this contradictory or enigmatic picture of the Suitors it should be added that the narrative keeps them ignorant of all that is happening around them in the house of Odysseus: they do not suspect Odysseus, the false beggar, for they are not allowed to see him; and inversely the readers can never see the Suitors through their eyes.

Who are, then, these Suitors? The puzzle is resolved in this book by its Author' very ingenious critical insight: the Suitors correspond to the generation and audience of the Iambus; this means that their artistic preference, style of life, and pursuits are inscribed in the poetics of Archilochous, Hipponax and Semonides .

But as soon as this solution is offered to the readers, the questions, the doubts the puzzles, the enigmas begin to assail them. For indeed the situation is complex: on the one hand the ideological ethical stance of the Narrator and of his returning hero are directly opposed to that style of life and to that poetics; but on the other there are iambic features in the *Iliad* and in the *Odyssey*, and there are clearly iambus stories and themes in the *Odyssey*, though they most be read so to speak against the agenda and inclination of the poem. The stories of the miser fathers refusing their daughters, of the young men sent to found colonies, the themes of the bellies, of baldness, of the knocked-out teeth, etc. form a long series of iambic presences that Martin Steinrück reads in the reverse side of the the Odyssean page.

This form of reading appropriates some of the strategies of the deconstructive approach but essentailly depends on the tremendous virtuosity of the Author who is a master of all the textual, narratological devices, schemes, and tricks beginning with the meters, the narratological patterns, the ring-composition and ending with the accurate reading of the focalizing strategies. In his reading Steinrück evokes the presence of the iambic the elegiac and epic poems putting them in a constant comparison.

An original and suggestive image of the *Odyssey* emerges from these pages: an *Odysssey* whose ingenious labor has been not only that of carrying home its hero, this husband and father, but also of containing, putting into a negative light, and repressing the, attitudes, spiritual and social needs of a generations that was finding its mirror in the iambus. Steinrück allows the Iambus and the Odyssey to function as mirrors that represent the real sociological situation of the new aristocratic generation. In this mirror scholars have read also the onset of colonisation and of a new mercantile (bourgeois) society (Horkheimer, Adorno). In Steinrück's analysis, the mirror remains essentially a poetic one, not a mere document.

The *Odyssey* that comes to light is a poem that a Narrator holds under his iron ideological control, denying many characters, the Suitors included, any focalisation, i.e. any indirect representation of their own views, indipendently from the context of the story. In this strong assertion and demonstration, Steinrück rightly contests some readings concerning focalisation proposed by De Jong.

The Odyssean Narrator may well have produced his story as a story that should enchant his readers, but between the two poles that I have shown to be opened in the supplement *"thelgein"* ("to charm") , Steinrück puts the accent on its negative pole, that of the loss.

The act of producing a poem that enchants implies the awareness of what its seductiveness must cover up and hide. In my work, I have suggested that the charm silences man's fear of death, the improbabilities of the return to the same, and the tricky cleverness of its narrative/writing: now the charm seems needed to hide also the modes of life of a sacrificed generation.

Luckily, however, and for excellent reasons, the charm of the poem saved it and has seduced generations of readers with its delightful, ironic allusions to the Iliadic sublime, with the stories of Penelope's weaving, Telemachos' trip to Sparta, Odysseus' and Athena's *metis*, Ares and Aphrodite, the Cyclops, Circe and the enigmatic Sirens.

Pietro Pucci Cornell University Ithaca, NY

1 Preface

The mere fact that there are iambic features in epic is not new. Gregory Nagy, Anne Sutor, and Evelyne Scheid-Tissinier have shown that we can find them in the *Iliad* and in the *Odyssey*[1]. This book is rather concerned with the way we read these passages. I shall follow an intertextual approach.

I would like to deal with two points of view that are socially and methodically complementary. There is one view on the Suitors displayed by the audience the *Odyssey* is aimed at. This rather polemic glance can be explained, described enlarged by some plasticity if we use its intertext with the Iambus. For, although we cannot be confident in romantic definitions and set out to compare simply the iambic genre to the epic genre, the usual audience of a series of texts given the same name (iambic) has proved to be a good criterion. We will discover that not only iambus and together with it its audience are poking fun on the *Odyssey* and its audience, but inversely, the *Odyssey* represents the very specific iambic audience by the young men who call themselves the Suitors. The epic audience seems to be almost pleased by the epic justification of their slaughter. Epic and iambic audiences as well as theirs glances at the Suitors can be defined by an intertextual approach[2]. Furthermore we have to display a counter-proof. An analysis of what we call the epic illusion will help to answer the second question: Are the Suitors simply not aimed at or are they really excluded from an Odyssean audience? Or in other terms, the young men who often attend to Archilochus' parties and who can find themselves in his texts, can they go as well to a feast of the epic audience, at their parents for instance and project their sorrows into the bard's song on the Suitors. Can they listen to the *Odyssey*[3]?

While working on the audience of the iambus- regardless of epos at the beginning—I became aware that there was a special social relationship between the iambic audience and the epic audience and that there are constant mutual attacks in both discourses. The iambic audience has been more completely described in another place[4]. In this book I will focus on the *Odyssey*. The tools of intertextual reading follow Pucci's proposition of a polemic rather than homologue dialogue between texts[5]. Applying them I will show, that the audience of the iambus is socially identical with the Suitors. Chapter 2 summarizes the evidence for young men being the iambus' audience. Chapters 3-6 establish the identification of this audience with the Suitors by describing both the iambic attack against epos and the epic attack against iambus. From chapter 7 on we shall discuss the function of intertext as a perspective, as the Suitors' viewpoint *in* or *at* the *Odyssey*.

Notes

[1] Nagy G., *The Best of Achaeans, Concepts of the Hero in Archaic Greek Poetry*, Baltimore 1979, 228-232 and Suter A., "Paris and Dionysos, iambus in the Iliad", *Arethusa* 26 1993, 1-18, Scheid-Tissinier E., "Télémaque et les prétendants, les νέοι d'Ithaque", *AC* 62 1993, 1-22, observed a *classe d'âge* and points out that struggle of νέοι against returning kings were a topos in Plat. *Legg.* 682d.

[2] At this point another problem emerges. The relationship between iambus and epic has been described with Aristotle's definition of iambus. Aristotle represented the iambus in an agonistic pattern. According to him, iambus is blame-poetry that defines itself by contrast to praise-poetry. Therefore he could interpret the recall of iambic scenes in the *Odyssey* as the contrasting way Homer defines this epic as praise-poetry. It seems that this anthropological interpretation can be justified. For reading archaic Greek texts we have to leave behind our own beginning 21th. century ideology which we could very roughly sketch as a concern for invisible norm and its visible deviation, in other words as a relation between a pure *unmarked* field and a spot that deprives it of purity and is, consequently, *marked*. Early Greek readers, as it appears, were rather trained in opposition than in privation. This is also the impression we get from the Presocratic philosophers of the 6th century or by studying the agonistic economics of honor that we find in Homer's narratives. Most of Homer's (modern) readers, however, live in a system of (western) thought, where normative patterns are dominant, and sometimes we tend to project these patterns on the one we find in early Greek texts. In a rather small number of cases (cf. the concept of "thémis" versus that of "díke") this is probably justified, but in general mere oppositions prevailed from archaic until Hellenistic times. In the case of the Aristotelian couple of concept "blame - praise" we often have some difficulties to understand praise not as an affirmation, but as a discourse that is supposed to be as strong or as performative as blame is to our ears. We see for instance narrative iambus as a comic or critic deviation from the norm, but adversely cannot understand epos as an aggressive text against deviation from the norm promulgated by the epos. And yet, within a system based on oppositions defining each other, we should expect the *Odyssey* to develop a sort of anti-blame against the iambic blame. Even if we try to avoid this possible hermeneutic circle, the ritualistic reading of Aristotle's pair of notions will renew the problem. Thinking that iambus is basically a ritual exhaust valve of bad temper or social stress, therefore part of the establishment, means not to take the couple of notions seriously as an opposition, but, again, as a pattern of *norm vs. deviation*. I will try to take it as the expression of "real" social problems and as a dialogue between two texts of their own right. Nevertheless, I am aware that the difference between "our" and "their" system is a matter of "more or less" rather than an exclusive.

[3] Thalmann, in his work on slavery in the *Odyssey* already went this way, suggesting that this text is a manifest of an aristocratic restoration (Thalmann W., *The Swineherd and the Bow, Representation of Class in the Odyssey*, Ithaca London 1998.). My interpretation will not contradict his thesis, but stress a different aspect that is less concerned with the struggle of aristocracy against other social groups, but, instead, will concentrate on the social/gender-oriented order within it (a definition of the concept in Lerner G., *The Creation of Patriarchy*, New York Oxford 1986, 10: "Gender is the cultural definition of behavior defined as appropriate to the sexes in a given society at a given time. Gender is a set of cultural roles; therefore it is a cultural product which changes over time. ").

[4] Steinrück M., *Iambos, Studien zum Publikum einer Gattung in der frühgriechischen Literatur*, Spudasmata 79, Hildesheim 2000.

[5] Pucci P., *Odysseus Polytropos, Intertextual Readings in the Odyssey and the Iliad*, Ithaca London 1987.

2 Iambus

2.1 Aggression in iambus

The etymology of the word "íambos" is still being discussed, but the meaning the word evokes today is most likely that of a rhythm. Majakovskij, Whitman and Racine used and knew an alternating verse that already in the 5th century BC was called "iambeîon" (Aristophanes, *Frogs* 1133). Yet, the corpus of texts the Greeks designated with the word "íambos" consisted of many rhythms, not only of the "iambeîon". Even a speech in rhythmic prose could be entitled "íambos" as late as the 4th century AD[1]. It appears that the "iambus" did not get its name from a verse called *iambic* ("iambeîon"), but, inversely, the verse often used in the iambic texts got its name from the iambus, whatever this word might have meant[2]. The only known occurrence of the word before the 5th century BC vacillates in sense between "a sort of text" and "party" (Archilochos fr. 215 W) [3].

Καί μ' οὔτ' ἰάμβων οὔτε τερπωλέων μέλει
"and I have no interest in iambi or amusements" (Gerber)

Isolated, this verse could mean, what the Byzantine scholar Tzetzes reads (γράφειν μὴ θέλων ὅλῳ), i.e. that Archilochus is no longer interested in composing iambi and in fun[4]. Yet a parallel suggests a different interpretation. In an elegiac text that was probably sung during a symposium, Archilochus uses a similar formulation (Archilochus fr. 10.10f. W):

οὔτε τι γὰρ κλαίων ἰήσομαι, οὔτε κάκιον
θήσω τερπωλὰς καὶ θαλίας ἐφέπων

"I cannot make (the friend's death) better by weeping
nor worse by heading for amusements and dinners."

"I cannot make (the friend's death) better by weeping nor worse by heading for amusements and dinners". If the first passage refers to the same situation, then "íambos" means rather something (but not exactly the same) like θαλία, the soirée, a party seemingly full of fun where these texts are performed. Both interpretations, however, remain hypothetical.

We are interested in the people who frequented these parties and listened to the iambi being performed. The first hint is given by the history of transmission of these texts, by the Alexandrian "edition" of the iambographers[5]. Not all iambi were composed in iambic verse (iambeîa), nor were all texts composed in iambic verse considered iambi. Authors of the 7th-6th century BC such as Solon, Mimnermus, Ananius, Anakreon, Xenophanes, and possibly Sappho[6], left a considerable number of iambic verses, but the Alexandrian editors of the 3d century BC did not include them in the canonical group of iambographers. It seems that only three authors fitted the criterion of what they called writers of iambi: Archilochus of Paros, Semonides of Amorgos and Hipponax of Ephesus. Their criterion was hardly a mechanical one as for instance that only these authors exclusively composed iambi, whereas other poets had a larger repertoire. Archilochus and Semonides left elegies too, and Hipponax even composed hexametrical texts. All these circumstances indicate a qualitative criterion for choosing iambi. We can try to reconstruct it in gathering the qualities common to the three iambic poets.

> a) All three were victims of political expulsion (Hipponax) or of colonization-enterprises (Archilochos, Semonides), which, as Plato says, is almost the same. In a text on the ideal colony (*Laws*) he points out, that the occasional use of the word "colonization" was only a euphemism for the expulsion of a group of misfits[7].
>
> b) All three iambic poets seem to come from rich families, but at least two of them complain about their social status[8].
>
> c) According to both, ancient and present day readers, the texts of all three iambographers differ from that of other poets by an extremely aggressive style. Ancient readers associated the same story of a poet who kills by text with both Archilochus and Hipponax[9].

The last criterion makes the context of their performance difficult to imagine. What audience would want to listen to such texts? Why are the iambographers so angry? How can this behavior be integrated into a social system? Up to now, the following three answers have been given.

> a) The aggressive style is simply the expression of an aggressive character. Yet this biographistic explanation can be applied to one but not to all three authors[10].
>
> b) The theory is popular according to which in archaic times aggressive behavior had its place in aggression-rituals[11]. Anthropological parallels exist, and it should not be neglected that some rites are mentioned in the texts in association with the iambus. In my view, however, the argumentation (aggression from aggression-rites?) is too foggy and in a scholastic way circular.
>
> c) Using Aristotle's discourse-opposition ψόγο and ἔπαινο West seems to apprehend iambus as an institutional and socially integrated literary form not only being performed for and before the same audience, but also treating the same subject as elegy. In what follows, I shall offer some evidence against this idea: iambus appears to be destined to another audience than elegy, and even within the limits of a subject common to both (such as "love") very sharp distinctions need to be made[12].

It is striking that all explanations tend to minimize or to trifle aggression, although for ancient readers this was the prominent feature of these texts. Modern approaches refuse to consider iambus an expression of a "real" conflict in ancient Greek society. They prefer to look for a harmonizing system instead that might explain aggressive texts not as the result of conflict but as a cathartic prevention of misbehavior (institution, rite) or as accidental exceptions (character). My aim is to take this aggression seriously and to understand both iambus and epos as traces of a programmed, but unresolved conflict in the structure of Greek society. In order to describe the audience of the iambus, i.e. people, who (according to the texts) seem to approve of its very critical position, I am interested in the biography not of individuals but of a group, i.e. a typical and programmed yet unsatisfactory perspective of life, that would be reflected by all three iambographers. For clarity's sake, however, we shall not adopt this inductive approach, but a deductive one. Therefore the 2nd chapter will describe a mere hypothesis of who they were. Afterwards a catalogue of arguments will justify the hypothesis.

2.2 Hypothesis: young men as the audience of the iambus

According to our working hypothesis, the audience of the iambus consists of unmarried young men who are in between the two major states of Greek tribal initiation: boys and ephebes (paîdes, meírakes, and épheboi) on one hand and husbands (ándres or gérontes) on the other. Sometimes they are called νέοι, which is a very broad determination that occasionally also covers ephebes or husbands (cf. *infra* chapter 5.2). Nevertheless, in the 4th century they formed distinct clubs. Socrates attempts to define their age by 20-30 years[13]. But as shows the case of the very young Diomedes, being a "neos" is less a matter of age than of social status. In the *Iliad* Diomedes belongs to the group of the "gerontes" because he is married, whereas Achilles who is roughly the same age but has no wife is described as a "neos". In the texts of Archilochus or in the *Odyssey* the term used for unmarried young men sometimes is *néoi ándres*, "young men". Both νέοι and "young men" will also be used in this study.

Within the male, but also within the female ancient Greek system, the male unmarried status is not entirely acknowledged as a gender of its own right. Even in the 4th century, when νέοι were organized in clubs, they became a current subject of laughter in Attic comedy[14]. One of these comic νέοι describes his status with the word *atimía*, "being deprived of honor", which basically means exclusion from public functions[15]. The pressure seems to have been even worse in Sparta, where they were forced to undress themselves at public festivities and sing mock-songs about themselves[16]. These and other texts show that the νέοι were not considered "accomplished men", and that they were unwillingly bachelors. Why would now such a fairly large group of unwilling young bachelors exist? Three reasons can be claimed.

    a) The father of a bride had to pay an enormous wedding-gift, which often he could not afford[17]. Moreover, there were several legends that provide examples of a very close relationship between father and daughter. A father, therefore, had no good reason for giving his daughter away to a bridegroom.

    b) A girl did not gain many rights by the wedding-rite. On the juridical level she remained a child depending on a kúrios: husband or father were her "kurioi". She changed only the father. Within her social life (unlike that of boys), wedding did not mean a new status. She did not become adult but by giving birth to children, and this rather within the female society. Hence, it would be reasonable, that some girls attempted to remain unmarried as long as possible and to enjoy what was probably the only time of freedom in their lives (for boys the inverse was the case).

    c) Another reason for the status and the number of bachelors could be a custom that quite understandably would have left only a few trails in literature[18]. Demographic records (from necropoles) show that an average Attic family of the 5th century BC had two sons but one daughter only. One can draw the conclusion from it, that maybe some or all of the missing girls could have been exposed, in order to avoid too expensive wedding gifts, to respond to an economic crisis or as a consequence of a general misogyny[19]. We have, of course, only small evidence that this has really happened. Yet the statistics cannot be ignored and the epic stories show that there is no reason that this would have been different in the 7th century BC[20]. This would mean that the first statistical (in general the first born) son not only inherited the father's land but also married the neighbor's only daughter. The second son, however, would remain without many goods and much hope to become an ἀνήρ, a husband.

If this scenario is correct and be it in some points only, then there existed a fairly large group of young men who remained, 20 years after their birth, without much social perspective. They all shared the difficulty to find a bride and to claim the rights of their adulthood for one thing because there were fewer girls, for the other because neither the fathers nor the girls were too interested in marriage. This superfluous generation was considered an ἄχθος ἀρούρη a weight of the arable soil, in a time of agrarian crisis (7/6th. centuries)[21]. To avoid them becoming a political problem, they were sent either to the front in order to die in the first rank (thus protecting others) or to found a colony. Now, we have reasons to think that there was a larger group of bachelors. Why, then, should they be the audience of the iambus? To answer this question, one must compare the ideology of this group, their desires, hates, fears and preferences with those that can be found in the iambic texts.

2.2.1 First argument: attacks against fathers

One would expect such a group's enemy number one to be the fathers who refused to give their daughters into marriage and also the husbands who had won for marriage the girl (which means as well: the father) desired by another. This is exactly the main topic in Archilochus' and Hipponax' fragments. It appears from the reactions of the ancient readers that the ancient edition of Archilochus' texts arranged the attacks against father Lycambes into a biography of the author. This "story" gave rise to a quarrel among modern biographists and scholars who prefer to explain texts as the result of poetics[22]. If our hypothesis, however, is correct, we should not care whether the father Lycambes and the daughter Neoboule were real persons or turn out to be poetic stock-characters[23], or whether the claim of Hellenistic legends that Lycambes was a good friend of Archilochus' father is more than a romanticizing reading of the Alexandrian edition[24]: the iambic audience shared (with Archilochus and his texts) the experience that fathers refuse them their daughters. Therefore, be it a real person or a poetic stock-character, every young man in the audience would have perceived in Archilochus' Lycambes his own "Lycambes". The Byzantine lexicon *SOUDA* considered Lycambes to be similar to Orodocides in the iambi of Semonides or to Bupalos in Hipponax' texts. The only thing we know about Orodocides is that he was supposed to be the first iambic target that had a name. We ignore, however, whether or not he was also a father Semonides had to fight with. At least, Semonides was known for his catalogue of wives, which represents the only iambic text transmitted in its full or almost entire size. In this very aggressive iambus Semonides denies the possibility of happy marriage in present time. We know some more about Hipponax enemy Bupalos but not enough to establish beyond any doubt whether he is a father who has an incestuous relationship with his daughter or the husband of a woman, loved by "Hipponax". Other solutions such as the relationships of this woman with a brother or her son seem less satisfactory. The texts, however, clearly describe a rivalry that gives the institutional power to Bupalos, but the erotic superiority to Hipponax. This is the first evidence why the audience of the iambus would correspond to a group of young unmarried men. These iambi were especially aimed at an audience who enjoyed (τερπωλή) attacks against reluctant fathers of nubile girls or against husbands of young wives. We will see some example-texts in the chapter 6.1 comparing the *Odyssey* and the iambus.

2.2.2 Second argument: aggression against girls.

If our hypothesis concerning the iambic audience is correct, the second enemy of young men is a girl who refuses to get married. They also would be attacked in the iambus. And yet, this attack does not go without an ambivalent attitude mixing up both, desire and refusal as a reaction to being withdrawn by these girls[25]. According to a Byzantine reader, extreme aggression against girls who refuse marriage was one of Archilochus' main topics[26]. Sometimes the attack against girls is just a way to hurt their fathers. This is also reflected by the texts that have been transmitted to our times, rather in papyrus than in indirect tradition. In Hipponax' texts a girl seems to be plotting together with the young man against her father or husband. The Cologne-Epode of Archilochus shows an adventure in which a young man sleeps with a girl against her intention[27]. In both cases the young man seduces, overwhelms the girl and publishes his doings in order to hurt her father.

Today, the ambivalence of the iambic hero's attitude would be expressed by an image that is not as anachronistic as it might seem at first sight. The young man is like the fox in the fable who cannot reach the grapes and, not to lose face, pretends that the grapes are too sour. This image goes back to the end of the 7th century BC, to fables ascribed to the slave Aesopus. In this version, the word for grapes is ὄμφαξ which means both unripe grapes and, very often in Greek literature, girls who are not yet nubile[28]. Perhaps Aesopus' tale is not just a simple description of a certain character, as in La Fontaine's version, but a mock description of aggressive young men who, in fact, desire what they reject[29]. Sappho's answer to this male refusal, though she uses a slightly different image (not unripe/ripe grape but unripe/ripe apple)[30], shows that this theme is a well-known element of the gender polemic and not simply a general consideration about human feelings[31].

Further, the very misandric iambus *Margites* refers to a fox that knows many things and a hedgehog that knows only one yet important thing. The same iambic verse is explicitly attributed to both the *Margites* and Archilochus[32]. One can project a gender opposition into the defense of the hedgehog (who knows only one yet important thing = giving birth?) and the attack against the fox who knows many, but less essential things[33]. In archaic Greek poetry, the "wisdom of the manifold ways", the μῆτις, is associated with young warriors rather than with adult hoplites[34]. Therefore a 7th century audience might see the image of the fox especially, though not exclusively, as a reference to young men.

Semonides' long iambus seems, at first sight, to be concerned with married women, not girls[35]. But in the context evoked above, his text too turns out to be an attack against girls who would never meet the requirements of good wives even if they wanted or were forced to marry a young man. The *Margites*, which appears to be a female answer to such mockery, describes a young man as unable to fit marriage rites, inferior to the wisdom of the girl's mother, and with a lot of vain ideas (called μῆτις) in his mind[36]. Accordingly, in Semonides' iambus the girls would not be appropriate to marriage because they have no children, no family and what is even striking is that they are all associated with animals (pig-woman, dog-woman, fox-woman...). This might remind us of modern gender-polemics such as *men are pigs*. But another association determines the sense of this animal image in a society where young girls of more affluent families spend an initiation-year as bears, dancing and singing for Artemis[37], and where stories are told of girls like Mestra who repeatedly escapes from the status of a wife by transmogrifying herself into an animal[38]: the wives are not real wives but still animals which means still girls, even if the catalogue does not explicitly allude to a special initiation-dance group but distorts their customary initiation-names (horses, bears, doves, maybe bees?, even apes[39]) into that of weasel-woman, donkey-woman and so forth. Perhaps, the catalogue contains even a sort of attack against texts such as the *Margites* and the place where they might have been performed[40]. Semonides sketches the picture of one good, but unreal wife, the bee-woman (who has children and is loyal to her husband but does not exist anymore). That she does not go to the all-women parties where sex-stories (ἀφροδίσιοι λόγοι) are told is one of her appreciated qualities: she does not do what the male audience of Semonides does, another hint to the fact that the audience is supposed to consist of young men, not husbands.

The connections between female rites and iambus are based on the Hellenistic legend about Archilochus as well as on the *Homeric Hymn to Demeter*. It seems to be a widespread opinion already in Antiquity that there was a female iambus (such as, I think, the *Margites* or at least to what it alludes). The third iambographer, Hipponax, mentions a word meaning "house of women", the δοῦμος, where such performances might have taken place[41]. It answered the attacks of the male iambus perhaps more moderately as is said by later readers about Sappho's iambi[42]. However, a look into Sappho's songs confirms this intertextual division of gender. On the male side the distinction between married and unmarried is much stronger and more precise than on the female side. Girls and married women can feast together, and sing together. There is no attack against unmarried or married women neither in Sappho nor in the *Margites*-scraps. The male iambi, however, are marked by both the opposition against married men (never against ephebes) and the hatred opposition against married women and girls. In the archaic gender-system, this double intertext leaves only one social category for the audience of the iambus: that of young unmarried men.

2.2.3 Homophily of husbands versus heterosexuality of unmarried young men

If our hypothesis is correct, then we expect the iambi to carry some signs of an unmarried status. Such a sign can be found when comparing iambus to elegy. In his book on Greek elegy and iambus, Martin West points out that elegy and iambus have in common the audience because the subjects are the same, for example "love"[43]. But in archaic Greek culture "love" does not mean the same practice for unmarried young men and for husbands. Adult males had the institutional and socially accepted possibility to fall in love with non-initiated boys and to live this romance, whereas no text speaks about homophile relationships between uninitiated men[44]. This distinction appears to be reflected in elegy and iambus: Theognis of Megara, Simonides of Teos, Solon of Athens only scarcely mention heterosexuality; they never mention their wives, as Sappho's fragments are silent about any possible husband. Almost all erotic elegies of these authors concern the boys they desire. This type of sexuality is not found in iambus, and the allusion to homosexuality among peers is scarce. These male authors and their audience seem to be exclusively obsessed by heterosexuality and marriage. This complementary relation between iambus and elegy gives little support to a hypothesis according to which the same audience could have listened to both iambus and elegy at the same occasion. Instead, we find an argument in favor of a hypothesis according to which the audience of iambus consisted of unmarried men, the one of elegy of adult and married men.

2.2.4 In battle, the death of young men is prettier than the death of husbands.

We find more evidence for the type of audience in the way iambus deals with the theme of war. Archilochus and, in a similar way, Semonides contest the common opinion that death in battle brings glory and public love[45]. If we look for the texts that iambographers could refer to, we find, again, elegy and epos. As Vernant puts it, the *Iliad* promotes the ideology of beautiful death. Not only does the Iliadic aesthetic admit the description of beauty only when something is destroyed, but in addition the death of a (typical) unmarried young man is also called "beautiful". Achilles has the choice between a long life in the darkness of oblivion and a short life that carries glory. He becomes a model for young men, because he prefers to die and receives glory through the *Iliad*[46].

Tyrtaeus in Sparta and Callinus in Colophon adopt this pattern for elegies that they probably did not dare to sing in front of young men, but in the tent of the king or during the symposia of married men[47]. For both elegists have the same pattern: the elegy is divided into two halves circumscribed by ring-composition[48]. Both use very different tone and argumentation when they inspire husbands to fight and when they incite the νέοι. In one of these halves, they remind the married men of their children and wives in a rather polite comprehensive tone, in the second part, they use a considerably harsher language when persuading explicitly the νέοι to die in the first rank of the battle formation in order to protect the older married men behind. Young men, Tyrtaeus says, may be handsome in the eyes of married women and impressive in the eyes of married men, but become beautiful only in battle death. Both Callinus and Tyrtaeus point out that death is the means of obtaining from the city what young, superfluous men are most short of: glory and love. This ideology might provoke nodding heads in the tent of the Spartan king or in the symposia of the fathers, it might even seduce some young fellows, as Leonidas sarcastically remarks, but Archilochus' answer is unmistakable: "Do not believe them! For to be loved, you have to be alive, and nobody ever won glory by death"[49]. "They even forget him very quickly", adds Semonides (frr. 2-3 W). Therefore, the audience of the iambus should be identified with the νέοι who are to die soon in the first battle-rank rather than with the married men who like to incite them to die this way.

2.2.5 The theme of colonization

Plato, in the *Laws*, says that the superfluous sons are doomed to found a colony[50]. This remark is supported by recent work on the metaphors, used by the Greeks in order to describe colonization: sending out young unmarried man (often without girls and without the right of immediate return) into another land, ἀποικία, is considered a sort of wedding with the new land[51]. Inversely, Euripides can call ἀποικία the bride's wedding-rite journey from her father's house to that of the bridegroom[52].

Most real marriages were virilocal (the girls went to the boy's family)[53]. The Greeks must have understood a depreciatory shade when the image of marriage was applied to the involuntary journey of young men. In the colonization-image of wedding it is not the bride, i.e. the land that comes to the bridegroom, but we find the reverse pattern. A bridegroom who takes over the part normally belonging to the bride, and goes to her father's house, has less control over his intended wife[54]. Whereas in virilocal marriage the wife has the status of her husband's "daughter", in uxorilocal marriage, the husband holds the position of her "uncle" and cannot take the full paternal control over her. However, the colonization-metaphor is based on the uxorilocal wedding. Perhaps this is one of the reasons why the colonization-legends often contain an element of female domination[55]. In the foundation-legend of Rhegion, for instance, the colonists are expected to look for a place "where the female takes the male as wife" (ὀπυίει)[56]. The male takes the female's part, and the female the male's. Even by a symbolic marriage, young men would reach a lower status than proper husbands.

We find this same pattern on another level of the Greek code of images. The archetype of a hero, Achilles, seems to be considered one of these young men (cf. *infra* 5.3). He is one of the young who fight in the first rank to protect other warriors[57]. He is the prototype of the young man who accepts to die a beautiful death, but it also appears that, on the cosmic level the whole heroic generation represents a young men's generation. Their "father" Zeus decides to annihilate them[58] by wars because the "mother" Earth "cannot carry them longer", an expression often used for too heavy young men (they are the "earth's burden"[59]). It is interesting to see that father Zeus does not really want to kill them directly; he banishes them on an island, the Isle of the Blessed, where they continue to live. Zeus transforms his death-sentence, the Trojan War, into a colonization sentence[60].

As for the iambographers, they are all in connection with exile or colonization enterprises. According to a notice of the Byzantine lexicon *SOUDA*, Semonides could have been the leader of one group of Samian colonists in Amorgos[61]. Archilochus' texts apply wedding-metaphors (the same as the ones we find in Semonides) to the island of Thasos, where the city of Paros sends him with others, as it seems, again without girls[62]. Tyrants have expelled Hipponax from Ephesus. This is not a real colonization, but he behaves like Archilochus or Semonides in attacking Klazomenai, the city where he lives during his exile[63]. He does not seem to be the only one expelled and his audience could consist of other foreigners in Klazomenai. All these links and oversetting of images can explain why Hipponax attacks fathers or husbands as if they were tyrants[64].

There is one more element of the colonization code, shared by the iambographers: there were much to be said for young men fearing seers and priests who could send them away from their family. Especially the seers or priests of Apollo were entitled to pronounce an oracle for colonization. In almost all the foundation legends an Apollonian oracle tells the colonists either to go or where to go. This might explain why iambic texts attack seers (Batusiades in Archilochus, Kikon in Hipponax[65]).

2.2.6 The gods invoked in the iambus are the gods of the νέοι.

If the iambic audience consisted of adult, married men, we would have to expect Apollo, god of men and of male initiation, to be at least one of the most important gods appearing in the iambus. But he is summoned only once, by Archilochus, and this in a very ironical but also fearful passage (not to kill him and his group)[66]. This silence is counterbalanced by a strong predilection of the iambus for Hermes and Herakles. Hermes is not only the god who, in the *Odyssey*, would like to be an illicit lover of Aphrodite, Hephaestus' wife. He is not only the god whom satyrs are looking for when they are called νέοι ἄνδρες, he is also one of the two gods adored by the 4th-century corporations of νέοι[67]. Herakles is a hero or a god who has, like Hermes, a young-man-biography: second by birth, he has to work for the first-born brother, he often wants to marry and his behavior reminds us of the violent character of young men. Archilochus composed one "rhapsody on Herakles" for sure, and a *Hymn to Herakles* has been attributed to him by Pindar or the Alexandrian editors[68]. If the prevailing gods in the iambus are the gods of the νέοι we should deduce from it that the audience consisted of young, unmarried men.

2.2.7 Polemic intertext between iambus and epic

Archaic epics seem to be composed mainly for an adult and mixed audience[69]. It is interesting to see that iambus often contains mock-allusions to epic language, even to Homeric or Hesiodean tradition. The most striking example is probably Semonides' catalogue of wives: It appears to be a parody of the *Catalogue of heroines* or *Ehoiai* we know from the Hesiodean tradition[70]. In addition, there are many allusions to expressions we read in Hesiod's works. The catalogue of Heroines that the *Odyssey* gives in the 7th century shares some verses with the pseudo-Hesiodean one[71].

Now these catalogues celebrate women of the Heroic Age and end with the end of Heroic Age, with the Trojan War and Zeus' plan to abolish this generation. Semonides, however precisely begins where the *Ehoiai* (and the Odyssean catalogue) end: after the Trojan War. The women he counts up are wives, and bad wives because, first, they are still girls and, second, the times are bad. Whereas heroines are praised for giving birth to heroes[72], the girlish wives of Semonides' catalogue have no children. Marriage-rites as a whole are represented as an invention of Zeus destined to avoid the repetition of the catastrophe that finished the Heroic Age: men can no more gather around one single woman because they are attached to one wife each.

We have seen that the heroes are associated with unmarried young men. The transition from the Heroic Age to the Iron Age is -not only in Semonides- considered a sort of wedding. The Iron Age seems to be the age of husbands and wives. All this shows how iambus is connected to epic which exclusively tells stories of the Heroic Age to an audience mainly made up of husbands and wives, whereas iambus not only tells stories about what happened after the Trojan War, i.e. during the *hic et nunc* of the Iron Age, but also tells them to an unmarried audience. This cross-pattern reflects the desires of the audience: for wedded people the unmarried time or the lost youth, for unmarried people what they aspire, the time of marriage. Semonides apes Hesiod and, as we will see, in a certain way the *Odyssey*: "If composing a catalogue of the real time, of the *here and now*, look what is coming out!"

Archilochus' allusions to the epic discourse were already the subject of Hellenistic books. Such a catalogue of similar verses by both Homer and Archilochus was still in use during the 2d century AD (Clemens of Alexandria)[73]. Some modern readers even believe that Archilochus had an impact on the *Odyssey*. Our inquiry, however, does not aim to discuss chronologies, but to illustrate a dialogue between the discourses of two groups. We cannot decide whether Archilochus knew the *Odyssey* or not or inversely, whether the aoidos of our (or nearly our) *Odyssey* knew Archilochus' *texts*, but we can show that each of them knew the others *discourse* very well and that they answer each other in a very ironical and sometimes aggressive way. We have seen how Archilochus answers to the Iliadic ideology of beautiful death (see below 5.3). In addition, one of the best examples might be fr. 185 W., for it shows that Archilochus is a dangerous enemy, not because he denounces what fathers, girls or mighty people have done or said, but because he is a master of showing how they speak.

ἐρέω τιν' ὕμιν αἶνον, ὦ Κηρυκίδη,	ἀχνυμένη σκυτάλῃ.
πίθηκος ᾔει θηρίων ἀποκριθείς	μοῦνος ἀν' ἐσχατιήν.
τῷ δ'ἄρ ἀλώπηξ κερδαλέη συνήντετο	πυκνὸν ἔχουσα νόον.
I shall tell you people a fable, Cerycides -	with a grieving message stick,
A monkey was on his way alone -	in the outback apart from animals
when a crafty fox met him -	with guileful mind (after Gerber)

Aristotle pointed out that Archilochus has this capacity, namely to imitate and to jeer at a father's discourse, the ethos[74]. In fr. 185 W he attacks epic language, in three ways: by means of the semantic structure, the prosodic-metric structure and the tone. As for the semantic structure, the reader can cover the right side of the fragment with his hand, and he will discover that nothing important is lacking in the structure of the story: the second part of each verse does nothing else but repeat part of what has already been said in the first part. The expression μοῦνος ἀν' ἐσχατιήν is only the epic expression of what has been said, by ἀποκριθείς, in an iambic, every-day language. The same relation can be found between πυκνὸν ἔχουσα νόον and κερδαλέη. It is epic discourse that we find here clearly quoted in the second verse-part and its first qualification is emptiness: it does not mean more than everyday-language. The only reason of the repetition is to obtain a stylistic difference. This difference is underlined by the metrical and prosodic structures of the verse: the first part can be called an iambic trimeter, which later got its name from the iambus, the second part is a hemiepes, the first half of an epic hexameter[75]. Since there is not only a difference of rhythm but also a difference of vocabulary between the two parts, we can say they are suitable to oppose iambic style to epic style. And this is "staged" by a pause stronger than in other Archilochean verse-blends. The audience thinks, that the verse finishes with the iambic trimeter, but a little verse colon comes after unexpectedly[76]. This procedure stresses the mocking function of the little hemiepes. Its high heroic style, pronounced a second afterwards and very quickly, cannot be taken seriously by the audience.

There is a third indication in the text itself of how the after-verse was pronounced. In the first hemiepes, the Narrator promises a story with a lamenting message-stick (ἀχνυμένῃ σκυτάλῃ). The exact meaning of this expression is still a matter of dispute among scholars but the lamenting tone was associated with the heroic-epic discourse[77]. Ancient commentaries to Homer say that the people of the heroic times were more inclined to tears than nowadays[78]. So perhaps Archilochus ridiculed epic style not only by an ironic repetition of the same thing in epic rhythm and vocabulary, but also in exaggerating its longing tone in a late-coming verse, too short for real epic style.

Hipponax criticizes the *Iliad* and the *Odyssey* more precisely (fr. 128 W). By mixing the proems of both of them he points out the ridiculous side of the epic discourse. And, what is more, he does not only use the stock formula in an improper context, but he also distorts the meter, by padding the caesura with a long patronymic (Εὐρυμεδοντιάδεα) that reminds us of the beginning of the *Iliad*. But this Iliadic quotation is swallowed by an Odyssean one, a poetic figure that can only underline the sense of the verses: they speak of an enormously hungry belly:

> Μοῦσά μοι Εὐρυμεδοντιάδεα τὸν ποντοχάρυβδιν,
> τὴν ἐν γαστρὶ μάχαιραν, ὃς ἐσθίει οὐ κατὰ κόσμον,
> ἔννεφ'ὅπως ψηφῖδι <U-> κακὸν οἶτον ὀλεῖται
> βουλῇ δημοσίῃ παρὰ θῖν'ἁλὸς ἀτρυγέτοιο.

Muse, of Eurymedontiades, the sea swallowing,
of his stomach carving, of him who eats in no orderly manner
Tell me, so that through a baneful vote determined by the people
he may die a wretched death along the shore of the undraining sea!
(after Gerber)

The patronymic *Eurumedontiadea* does not only remind us of the heavy synizesis of the patronymic Πηληιάδεω in the first verse of the *Iliad* but beats its length by two syllables and, furthermore, points out its monstrosity in filling the usual middle caesura of the hexameter. This belly-monster grows and is intertwined between Μοῦσά μοι and ἔννεφ' which does not go without reminding (ἄνδρα) μοι ἔννεπε Μοῦσα, the beginning of the *Odyssey*[79]. To refer to the belly is a typically iambic way of humiliating important people. And yet, as it appears, iambus does not attack Achilles, not the heroes in general save one, who is a sort of antihero, a renegade among young men: a husband. We find several texts of Hipponax that directly parody Odysseus and the *Odyssey*[80]. Odysseus' love for Calypso for instance becomes the victim of a sexual pun, becomes "Kypso" in fr. 129 W[81].

> πως παρὰ Κυψοῦν ἦλθε
> somehow he came to Cypso

If epic is destined to an adult, married and mixed audience, and iambus attacks the epic discourse in general and the *Odyssey* in particular, there is an argument in favor of our hypothesis according to which the audience of iambus is a non-mixed, non-adult or unmarried audience.

2.3 The eighth evidence

Our sketch of the iambic audience might have shown, that it consisted of young unmarried men. Maybe their death were the answering pattern of the female babies exposed after birth; maybe this is only the male version of archaic (but not unparalleled in our times, if we look to the war in Tchetchenia, to the wedding-rules in India) sort of postnatal birth-regulation (by war and colonization), maybe not. Perhaps there is another explanation for the unfortunate situation of young unmarried men, but the polemic discourse between epic and iambus shows that iambus had another audience than epics. Young men met each other on parties, upraised themselves, attacked the aggressors, and defended themselves against attacks. This would presuppose that there are attacks, not only from the female side (Sappho and perhaps the *Margites*) but also from the husbands' side. Does Homer attack young men? We have seen that the *Iliad* can be interpreted as a masterpiece of propaganda for the death of young men. But why Hipponax (and some said Archilochus too) attack the *Odyssey* and especially Odysseus? The eighth evidence will, thus, be the rest of this book, an inquiry on the Odyssean attack against young men, the attack which iambus answers.

This inquiry is justified. From the beginning on, the *Odyssey* speaks about young men, and at its end all three types of young men, the warriors, the colonists, and the dangerous groups at home will be discussed and judged. Two of them are condemned to death, one to oblivion. There are the Phaeacians, colonists and young men forever, who resolved the slave-problem (almost entirely) by robots and are addicted to dance and song. Their society, as that of other colonization-stories, is marked by a certain inversion of gender-power. The queen speaks to men and has a seat in the assembly of the old. Men refuse war and are bad warriors. Their king and their queen are related in the same way a husband is to his wife living in the house of her father: he is her uncle (not her father). This group is judged to be the better of the three, but when Odysseus leaves them, any access to their land is interrupted and the *Odyssey* uses the same formulas to describe this end as for telling the ends of the other two groups.

There are warriors too, Odysseus' companions. They all are dead at the end, whereas the beginning of the text underlines that they died by their own foolishness, that Odysseus "lost" them. But it has been shown that the expression "to lose someone" has, in the *Odyssey*, a very ambiguous ring[82]. It means as well "to kill", and this is exactly what their fathers say in the end of the story: Odysseus killed the young warriors and their brothers, half of young men of Ithaca.

This steady Odyssean self-justification for killing young men, more than the preceding two, concerns the third group, which strangely resembles the iambic audience of Archilochus: young men having escaped battle and colonization, possessing no land but coming from the best families and having but one thing in mind: to get married. They wear the title of Suitors even where they are no more associated with their wish of marriage. It is the title not of narrative agents, but of a social unity, the 108 for-ever-suitors[83]. This characterization not only justifies their steady and loud laughter, their pleasure in dance and song, but also makes them very suitable to tell each other their own stories just like the audience of the iambus. Like the iambic audience they love erotic adventures, hate seers and husbands, fear fathers like Icarius, the father of Penelope. Like them they have to fear Apollo. The list of the sons of one Ithacan (Aigyptios) defines their social situation in the same way as we did for the iambic audience. Aigyptios has four sons; two of them inherited the father's land and work there. They are not among the Suitors, and we can assume that they are married. Two are still bachelors. One of them has been conveyed with Odysseus into the Trojan War. He survived to the Trojan spears, but not to the Cyclops's teeth. The other of the two bachelors is a "Suitor", a young man such as the one who listened to Archilochus. They are of course associated with Hermes and Herakles.

If this identification of the Suitors with the iambic audience is right, then we have to change a little bit our image of the calmly telling "biotic" *Odyssey*. Then the *Odyssey* not only justifies the status of husbands and wives, of the epic audience, by telling one of their (re-) foundation legends, but also attacks those who are not married, by justifying their elimination[84]. This would be the attack, Hipponax, Semonides', and Archilochus' iambus answers, and this hypothesis will be corroborated in the following three chapters. They explore the intertext from the point of view of the *Odyssey* according to the criteria "composition", "stories", and "images".

Notes

[1] Cf. Lacombrade Ch. ed., *L'Empereur Julien, oeuvres complètes* II 2, *Discours de Julien l'Empereur*, Paris 1964, 156-157 (367a1-368b6).

[2] The refutation of this point of view by Lennartz K., "Zum erweiterten Jambusbegriff", *RhM* 143, 2000, 225-250, is very useful, but, it seems to me, relies on a circular argumentation.

[3] The metrician Diomedes (1, 477, 9 Keil) quotes two verses of Arctinus, who is believed to have composed the *Ilioupersis*, in the archaic period (= fr. 16 Bernabé). The two verses are called "iambus" and could describe the way an iambic is danced. Nothing, however, proves that the title is as old as the verses.

[4] Tzetzes *Alleg. Hom.* Il. 24.125ff. Kantzis I., *The Trajectory of Archaic Greek Trimeters*, Boston Leiden 2005, 2ff. follows Tzetzes and rejects West's interpretation although without real arguments. A priori, the connectors καί ... οὔτε ... οὔτε could imply both synonyms and antonyms. But the context shows that both elements share the element of leisure opposed to grief as in *x καί y* of fr. 10.10 West.

[5] In Archilochus' case four books (elegies, trimeters, tetrameters and epodes) by Aristophanes of Byzantion or Lysanias of Cyrene. Similarly in the Hipponax-edition cf. Pòrtulas Miralles, 1988.

[6] Cf. Terent. Maurus 2456ff. *Gramm.Lat.* 6.398, Hor. *epist.* 1.19.26.

[7] Plat. *Legg.* 736a1f.

[8] Cf. Semonides frr. 1.17ff., 3, 25 and Hipponax frr. 32f., 36, Archilochus fr. 109, 114 and cf. Rankin H. D., *Archilochus of Paros*, Park Ridge NJ 1977.

IAMBUS 23

[9] Pseudoakron (1.404 Keller) ad Hor. *epod.* 6.11 ff., cf. also *epist.* 1.19.23ff., *AP* 7.351, 7.71, Meleagr. *AP* 352, Eusebius, *Praeparatio evangelica* 5.32.2.

[10] For the biographistic position Rankin 1977.

[11] Brown Ch. G., "Iambus", in D.E. Gerber ed., *A Companion to the Greek Lyric Poets*, Leiden New York Köln 1997, 41.

[12] For iambi of (αὐτοκάβδαλοι) professionals in Sparta, Brown 1997, 31. Miralles C. Pòrtulas J., *Archilochus and the Iambic Poetry*, Roma 1983 and id., *The Poetry of Hipponax*, Roma 1988, give some evidence for the iambographer as wolfish trickster. Nearest to the hypothesis I propose is Pellizer E., "Per una morfologia della poesia giambica arcaica", in K. Fabian E. Pellizer G. Tedeschi edd., *OINHPA TEUXH*, Alessandria 1991, 15-29 (who sees something "childish" in the iambus).

[13] Socrates' definition of νέοι in Xenoph. *Mem.* 1.2.35 (under thirty?). Usually the νέοι are to be settled between the παῖδες or ephebes and the ἄνδρες or γέροντες cf. Forbes C. A., *Neoi, A Contribution to the Study of Greek Associations*, Middletown 1933, 2.

[14] Cf. the play *The youngsters* of Antiphanes fr. 164 K.-A.

[15] Alexis fr. 264.1-7 K.-A.

[16] Cf. Brelich A., *Paides e Parthenoi* 1, Roma 1969, 125f.

[17] Cf. Eur. *Med.* 232f. and on the dowry Leduc C., "Comment la donner en mariage? La mariée en pays grec (IXe-Ve siècle av. J.C.)", in P. Schmitt-Pantel ed., *Histoire des femmes* I, *L'Antiquité*, Paris 1991, 259-316.

[18] Cf. Men . *Sam.* 389 or Aristophanes' ἐγχυτρισμός *Vesp.* 289, *Ran.* 1190 and the Schol.

[19] Cf. Gallant Th., *Risk and Survival in Ancient Greece*, Stanford Cal. 1991, 21. Pomeroy S. B., *Families in Classical and Hellenistic Greece, Representations and Realities*, Oxford 1997, 55, however, points out that there is no evidence for Spartan infanticide.

[20] Single Nausicaa and her brothers, Odysseus' sister seems to have lost her sisters, the six Aeolids survive because they get married with their brothers, on the other hand, in a non-Greek land Dolon's too expensive sisters, 50 daughters of Danaus in Egypt, 50 daughters of Priamus in Asia, Agamemnon's three daughters might be explained as sign of the very rich king.

[21] On land-shortage Plat. *Legg.* 708b. On the reasons of the population-explosion during the 7th century Snodgrass A., *Archaic Greece, The Age of Experiment*, London 1980, 22 and Ruschenbusch E., "Überbevölkerung in archaischer Zeit", *Historia* 40, 375-378.

[22] Cf. Dover K.J., "The Poetry of Archilochos", *Entretiens Hardt* 10 1963, 205ff. who thinks that even Lycambes might be a stock-character. Cf. the etymological transparency of their names (the father who "walks like a wolf" and the daughter who "wants" always "new or young" men).

[23] Pòrtulas Miralles 1983, 65, 138.

[24] P. Dublin inv. 193a, col. I 2-7, Hor. *epod.* 6.11 ff., *epist.* 1.19.23ff. cf. *AP* 7.351, 7.71, Meleager *AP* 352.

[25] On these mechanics Quincy L., *The Poetics of Disappointment, Wordsworth to Asbury*, Chalottesville 1999, and Wray D., *Catullus and the Poetics of Roman Manhood*, Cambridge 2001, 113.

[26] Cf. Euseb. *Praeparatio evangelica* 5.32.2. On iambs against girls waiting a long time before marriage cf. Anaxilas fr. 67 K. -A.

[27] Hipp. fr. 84, 104 W, Archilochus fr. 196 + fr. 196a W.

[28] Aesop. fab. 32 (I) Hausrath and *AP* 5.19, 12.205 cf. Alcaeus fr. 119.16 Voigt; on the oriental back-ground of these traditions West M.L., "The Ascription of Fables to Aesop", *Entretiens Hardt* 30 1983, 127.

[29] In a similar way German unmarried girls of the 17th century had to defend themselves after carnival (the usual wedding-time) for not having accepted marriage proposals (cf. Schindler

N., *Widerspenstige Leute, Studien zur Volkskultur in der frühen Neuzeit*, Frankfurt/Main 1992, 175ff.).

[30] Fr. 105 a Voigt: οἶον τὸ γλυκύμαλον ἐρεύθεται ἄκρῳ ἐπ' ὄσδῳ,
ἄκρον ἐπ' ἀκροτάτῳ, λελάθοντο δὲ μαλοδρόπηες-
οὐ μὰν ἐκλελάθοντ', ἀλλ' οὐκ ἐδύναντ' ἐπίκεσθαι.

[31] Like Page D.L., *Sappho and Alcaeus*, Oxford 1955, 121.

[32] On the iambic-comic tradition and the *Margites* Jakob D., "Die Stellung des Margites in der Entwicklung der Komödie", *Hellenica* 43 1993, 275-279. Not only are the grapes a very precise picture, but the image of the fox might also mean something more than just a resourceful human character. In later texts the fox becomes the animal stock-character of the wise. The names, however, boys were given during their initiation-time in Sparta refer to the fox, the fables of Archilochus often designate a young man as fox. Cf. *infra* chapter 4.1).

[33] Bowra C.M., *On Greek Margins*, Oxford 1970, 59-60 (Archilochus is the fox and the hedgehog), Bodson L., "Le renard et le hérisson (Archiloque, fr. 201 West)", in *Stemmata, Mélanges de philologie, d'histoire et d'archéologie grecques offerts à Jukes Labarbe*, Liège Louvain-la-Neuve 1987, 55-66, and Treu M. ed., *Archilochos*, München 1959, 239 (Archilochus only is the hedgehog).

[34] On the *métis* Detienne M., Vernant J.-P., *Les ruses de l'intelligence, la Métis des Grecs*, Paris 1974.

[35] As a poem produced during the Gamelia, Schear L., "Semonides Fr. 7: Wives and their Husbands", *EMC* 28 1984, 45.

[36] Cf. Eust. *In Od.*1.395.17 (1669.48) = fr. 4 W; for the presumably gynaecocentric point of view within the *Margites* cf. Steinrück 2000, 93ff.

[37] Schol. Aristoph. Lysistrata 645. On Mestra as a fox Hes. fr. 43, 31, on the uncertain doves Alcm. fr. 1.60 Calame, horses in Alcm. fr. 1.50, 59 Calame. On the gender-polemic-interpretation cf. Lloyd-Jones H., Females of the Species: Semonides on Women, London 1975, or Loraux N., "Sur la race des femmes et quelques-unes de ses tribus", *Arethusa* 11 1978, 57, for Brauron Kahil L., "L'Artémis de Brauron, Rites et mystère", *AK* 20 1977, 86-98.

[38] Cf. also the "nymph" Psamathe transmogrified into a seal in order to escape Aeacus in Schol. Eur. Andr. 687, Apollod. 3.12.6 or the "nymph" Nemesis in a similar situation of "marriage" transformed into a goose in *Cypria* fr. 9. Bernabé.

[39] A grotesque ape-woman persecuting a man on a Cabirian skyphos of Thebes (priv. coll. cf. *JHS* 84 1964, pl. 5-6).

[40] About the connection between iambus and female culture cf. the role of the maidservant Iambe in the female feast of the Thesmophoria *HCer* 202-204 and Brown 1997, 16-25, and Calame C., "L'hymne homérique à Déméter comme offrande: regard rétrospectif sur quelques catégories de l'anthropologie de la religion grecque", *Kernos* 10 1997, 11-33. Herondas, in his first Mimiambus, seems to represent either female or male pets under the mask of women using choliambics (1.70). The same context brings the heroine Mise in, which seems to be an Asian variant of Iambe.

[41] Cf. Hipp. fr. 30 W= Hesych. 4.2256.

[42] Otherwise Sapphic iambus could mean her attacks against her brother (fr. 5 Voigt, but we cannot be shure of this), against husbands like Menelaus or the indifferent husband, which does not die of a glance on his wife (fr. 31 Voigt), or against what she takes for masculine aesthetics (fr. 16 Voigt). However Catullus uses thrice the word *iambus* to refer to the phalaeceans, an Aeolic meter.

[43] West M.L., *Studies in Greek Elegy and Iambus*, Berlin New York 1974, 18: "Virtually every type of subject can be matched from melic or iambic poetry .... We have seen that

elegy is actually a variety of melic poetry... ". On the concept of *genre* Calame C., "La poésie lyrique grecque, un genre inexistant? ", *Littérature* 111 1998, 87-110, esp. 89 f.

[44] On homophile phantasms Calame C., (Lloyd J. trans.), *The Poetics of Eros in Ancient Greece*, Princeton NJ 1999 (Roma Bari 1992), 68 (διαμηρισμός), with another interpretation Halperin in D.M. Halperin J.J. Winkler F. Zeitlin edd., *Before Sexuality. The Construction of Erotic Experience in the Ancient Greek World*, Princeton 1990, 30, but cf. Solon fr. 25 W; ἔσθ'ἥβης ἐρατοῖσιν ἐπ' ἄνθεσι παιδοφιλήσῃ, μηρῶν ἱμείρων καὶ γλυκεροῦ στόματος.

[45] Archilochus fr. 133 W, Semonides frr. 2-3 W.

[46] Critics of Vernant's thesis Assunçâo T. R., "Nota critica à la 'bela morte' vernantiana", *Classica São Paulo*, 7-8 1994-1995, 53-62, Finkelberg M., "How Could Achilles' Fame Have Been Lost? ", *SCI* 11 1991-1992, 22-37.

[47] Tyrtaeus fr. 10 W and Callinus fr. 1 W.

[48] For the semantics of Homeric ring composition Lohmann D., *Die Komposition der Reden in der Ilias*, Berlin 1970, and Stanley K., *The Shield of Homer, Narrative Structure in the Iliad*, Princeton 1993, on typology and diffusion in Steinrück M., *Kranz und Wirbel*, Hildesheim 1997, applied to an elegy West M.L., "Simonides Redivivus", *ZPE* 98 1993 1-14.

[49] Arch. fr. 133 W and about Leonidas: Plut. *Cleom.* 23 [2].4.

[50] Plat. *Legg.* 923.

[51] Cf. Dougherty C., *The Poetics of Colonisation: From City to Text in Archaic Greece*, Oxford 1993, Calame C., *Mythe et histoire dans l'Antiquité grecque, la création symbolique d'une colonie*, Lausanne 1996, and Detienne M., *Apollon le couteau à la main*, Paris 1998.

[52] Eur. *Hippolytus* 629, on ἀποικία as "departure" Casevitz, M., *Le vocabulaire de colonisation en grec ancien*, Paris 1985, 128.

[53] The preponderance of virilocal marriage in Pomeroy 1997, 27f.

[54] Hesiod, *Op.* 406, a suspected line, already warns against a wife that would not be "owned".

[55] On the childlike status of wives Leduc 1991, 259-316.

[56] Cf. the foundation of Rhegion in Diodorus Sic. 8fr.23.2. Plat. *Legg.* 776ab links, it is true the word ἀποικία with a—at first sight virilocal wedding (so Dougherty 1993, 61), but the family concerned has two houses, one that continues to belong to the parents and one of for the newly married. That means that also the bridegroom has to leave the parental home. Plato's image is an exception but does not contradict the rule.

[57] After Achilles' refusal to fight, Nestor must reorganize the army in a way that demands victims of all contingents, which was not the case during Achilles' participation.

[58] They are considered as illegitimate sons, as *nothoi*.

[59] The Suitors use the metaphor when speaking of the beggar (*Od.* 20.379), but as we shall see, the viewpoint of the audience applies it probably to themselves.

[60] Cf. the disappointed (unknown) son of Zeus at the end of the pseudo-hesiodean *Catalogue of women* (fr. 204.120 M-W).

[61] *Suda* 4.360.7 Adler.

[62] Archilochus fr. 21-22 West.

[63] *Suda* 2.665.16 Adler and fr. 1 West.

[64] Incest not only was believed to be a custom of Persian rulers, but its image was also connected to Greek rulers who behaved in a non-Greek, Asian way, tyrants such as Oedipus or Hippias. In the context of wedding as image for colonization, marrying one's own mother would mean something like not to go for the colony but to return to the mother-city. This is what tyrants really did after expulsion.

[65] Batusiades in Archilochus fr. 182-184 W, Kikon in Hipponax fr. 4 W.

[66] Arch. fr. 26 W.

[67] *Od.* 8.338ff. and Soph. *Ichn.* 366f.
[68] Cf Archilochus fr. 286 West. Schol. Pind. Ol. 1.9 quotes the text of the hymn.
[69] Doherty L. E., "Gender and Internal Audiences in the 'Odyssey'", *AJPh* 113 1992, 161-178, points out that Penelope and Arete can represent a real female focalization of a female audience.
[70] The pseudo-Hesiodean *Ehoiai* are dated of the 6th century, but West M.L., *The Hesiodic Catalogue of Women*, Oxford 1985, thinks that the tradition goes back to the 7th. On catalogues Minchin E., "The Performance of Lists and Catalogues in the Homeric Epics", in: I.Worthington ed., *Voice into Text, Orality and Literacy in Ancient Greece*, Leiden New York Köln 1996, 3-20.
[71] Especially the verses on Tyro in *Od.* 11.235ff.
[72] This act is comparable in archaic ideology to male battle-fight. The killing-catalogues of the *Iliad* are poetically, in both the use of the traditional phrase and the narrative structure the model of birth-catalogues (cf. Steinrück M., "Comment faire l'éloge d'une femme?: tuer et mettre au monde dans les Ehées", *Métis* 11 [1996] 2000, 25-36.
[73] Cf. P. Dubl. 193a = T 10 Tarditi (Tarditi G., *Archiloco*, Roma 1968.).
[74] Aristot. *Rhet.* 1418b28.
[75] On the meter of the trimeter in Archilochus' time Steinrück M., "Sur le parfum tragique des côla métriques chez Aristophane", in C. Calame ed., *Poétique et langue d'Euripide en dialogue, Etudes de lettres* 4, 2004, 59-70, and Steinrück M., *A quoi sert la métrique?interprétation littéraire et analyse des formes métriques grecques:une introduction, avec la collaboration d'Alessandra Lukinovich*, Grenoble 2007, 20ff.
[76] Later metricians (cf. Heph., *De Poem.* 7.2 (p. 71 Consbruch) or Marius Victorinus, *Ars grammatica* IV, 141ff. Keil VI.) called the verse *sung afterwards* (stikhos epoidos).
[77] West S., "Archilochus' Message Stick", *CQ* 38 1989, 42-47.
[78] Schol. Il. 1,349 and Schol. Il. 19.5.
[79] As for the person Eurymedontiades, the interpretations diverge: A Giant of this name is mentioned in the Odyssey as an ancestor of Arete, the Pheacian queen. Since the "queen" of Hipponax' heart is called Arete, too, some think he attacks a woman. But we have no witness of scapegoat-rites directed against women, and it would be the only text against her. Yet, if Arete is, as it might be, the daughter of Hipponax usual or stock-enemy Boupalos, then he has even more right to be called descendant of Eurymedon. And he is steadily threatened by the scapegoat-rite in Hipponax' texts (cf. Miralles Pòrtulas 1988, 46).
[80] Rosen M.R., "Hipponax and the Homeric Odysseus", *Eikasmos* 1 1990, 11-25, defends a similarity rather between Hipponax and Odysseus.
[81] An allusion to fellatio? Cf. Marzullo B., "Archil. fr. 42 W (Reversa Neobule?) ", *MCr* 30-31 1995-6, 37-66.
[82] Pazdernik Ch. F., "Odysseus and His Audience: 'Odyssey' 9.39-40 and its Formulaic Resonances", *AJPh* 116 1995, 347-369,
[83] For the already fixed use of μνηστήρ in the *Odyssey* Schubert P., *Noms d'agent et invective: entre phénomène linguistique et interprétation du récit dans les poèmes homériques*, Göttingen 2000, 50.
[84] The verses Homer's biography attributes to him are very clear about young men and the husbands (Ps.-Hdt. *Vita Hom.* 30): κλῦθί μευ εὐχομένῳ, Κουροτρόφε· δὸς δὲ γυναῖκα/ τήνδε νέων μὲν ἀνήνασθαι φιλότητα καὶ εὐνήν /ἡ δ' ἐπιτερπέσθω πολιοκροτάφοισι γέρουσι/ ὧν ὥρη μὲν ἀπήμβλυνται, θυμὸς δὲ μενοινᾷ.

3 Composition

3.1 An ambivalent glance

One of the strangest phenomena in ancient Greek enthusiasm for epic is its ambivalence. On one hand, the audience enjoys the stories of the past because they help forget the present. Epic tradition re-creates again and again a new past necessarily different from the present and defined by Herodotus, for instance, as the age of the gods or, by others, as the age of the heroes. This past is separated from the present by a precise event, the Trojan War, an "engine" Zeus invented to abolish the heroic generation. On the other hand, there is a sort of cosmic biography. In his version of the legend of ages, Hesiod defines couples of ages—first the Golden and Silver ages of the babies, the Bronze and Heroic Ages of adolescents—as age of men who live a long youth. The fifth age, the age of iron knows old age, it is the time of husbands and wives. The second part of this third couple is still to come, the "age" of old age, when babies are born with gray hair. The *Odyssey* articulates the transition between youth-ages (bronze and heroes) and adulthood-ages (Iron and old age) by an event that could be described as a second wedding of a husband with his wife. The Ps.-Hesiodean *Catalogue of heroines* also introduces the catalogues of suitors (of Helen and of Oenomaus' daughter) at the end the Heroic Age (and of the text). Semonides defines marriage as a trick Zeus invented after the Trojan War.

Epic, therefore, creates a past through an event that separates time into "before" (the past) and "now" (the present), a turning point the Greeks took for granted as we do in the case of the French revolution or the Renaissance. This division is not only connected to the cult of heroes and implies, thus, that the audience honored and admired these old ancestors, but it also reflects the opposition between young (heroic) and adult (married). There is, however, a certain contradiction in this double opposition. In one opposite pair the heroes are the old, admired ancestors who grant power to certain families, in the other opposition, the same heroes are young non-adult men and, we have to infer, the non-adult has no power in the world dominated by male adults. In this second opposition the epic tends to justify the present as the better world, the world of marriage of adults. In a system where nothing determines social power more than the sharp limit between unmarried non-adults and married adult males[1], the audience's glance becomes ambivalent when the singer passes from their adult Iron Age back to the heroes.

Seemingly, ancient epic audiences have been eager to hear the stories of the past. The comparison of the audience with the Lotophages (a narrative echo of the Sirens) is probably right. It is not the sentimental glance often attributed to romantic literature, but the veneration of heroes that starts in Greece from the 8th century on, the nostalgia of lost youth constantly found in Greek elegy (not iambus), in an exclusively adult audience. The misogamist gender polemics in Hesiod and Sappho, Stesichorus' tales and vase-painting or Pindar's odes which liken the present to the past, also attest to the popularity of the heroic youth in adult audience and show that Homeric texts were embedded in a narrative tradition able to help forget the sorrows of age by stories of (one's own) youth.

But crossing the barrier from old present to young past, guided by a dihegetes (which is to be translated by *crossing guide* or *Narrator*), also means defining or creating one's own age in contrast to another virtual age. One's own life cannot be defined but by opposing it to another, all the more in an ideology that seemed to be based on a marked-marked-system (and not so much on a marked/unmarked conception of what we call normality or normativity: see introduction). This might be the reason why the theme of the ending Heroic Age is so popular with epic (Theban and Trojan wars). Like, in the fifth century, when Attic theater-audience affirmed its democracy from time to time by looking at failing (heroic) kings, the adults of the 8th and 7th centuries listened to Homer in order to affirm their own age (in both meanings) by the end of the age of youth: when, by Zeus' own will, everlasting and happy youth must disappear, Iron and adult age is justified as reality that has been left and not yet failed. Ideologically, this justifies the hard Spartan initiation of adolescents, the power of "achieved men" over "half men", and the domination between wives and husbands[2]. It also justifies the critical attitude towards youngsters we find in different texts: in the elegies raising up young people to war, in Critias' blame of Archilochus or of the successors of the iambographers Socrates and his young men (Alcibiades)[3], in the pejorative representation of the Suitors in the *Odyssey* who are said to be responsible—themselves—for their own death and in the *Laws* of Plato, who says that the city expels angry young men pretending that there are colonies to be founded.

The relationship the epic audience entertains to the heroes is as twofold as to the kings acting on the Attic theater. People love them, admire them, but at the end of the play they are glad they are not like them. This going and returning, going back to youth and heroic past and then returning to adulthood and Iron present, this repetition and, thus, affirmation of the own initiation failed once: in Phrynichus' play on the sack of Miletus, which did not allow to return to the present as another time. Phrynichus paid for it.

"Inventing the past" (Ford), then, means to invent the present by contrast and causes the kind of ambivalence husbands and wives probably felt towards Homer's stories. We must be aware of this attitude when reading the *Odyssey* as an attack of adult ideology against youngsters[4].

3.2 Narrative patterns and the ambivalence of in and out

Three elements of the *Odyssey* seem in particular to reflect the audience's attitude towards the epic text: the image of Odysseus' fellows, the image of Odysseus himself and the narrative pattern employing these images.

Odysseus' return is embedded in a narrative pattern whose traditional nature emerges not only from its formulaic diction or from the repetition of the same pattern within the *Odyssey*, but also from its recurrence in other epic traditions. Serbian or Usbekian epic stories of return sometimes agree with disarming faith to detail (the husband at his wife's wedding, bow-contest, disguise as an old slave, romance with unmarried girls which enable the protagonist to escape, slaughter of the young man who took the place and the wife of the returning king). Both traditions sometimes repeat both variants of this theme, the plotting of the couple (husband *and* wife) against the Suitor(s) and the indeterminacy-version, where the wife acknowledges her husband on an unconscient psychic level, but without recognizing his identity. The Usbekian *Alpamysh* for instance offers both versions in the same epos, just as the *Odyssey*[5]. In the first variant of this narrative pattern we can roughly distinguish three phases[6]:

   1) A lady in distress (or her friend) writes a letter (or sends a messenger) to her boyfriend (or husband).
   2) The husband/boyfriend is in prison and receives the message.
   3) The daughters of the king help but delay the departure. His escape and return.

We shall suspend the analysis of the *Alpamysh* for a while and concentrate on the *Odyssey*: Its beginning exposes Penelope's and Telemachus' desperate situation which corresponds to the first narrative phase. Odysseus' liberation from Calypso by a messenger very clearly corresponds to the second phase. If the third phase is applied to the first half of the *Odyssey*, many episodes—the Laestrygons, the island, the cave, and the eye of the Cyclops, the Sirens, the Planctae, Calypso's island, her clothes, the Pheaecians with their cloths and their harbor which shall be barred by Poseidon—can be understood as scenarios of imprisonment and escape, as a series of successively closed spaces that the protagonist has to open (first the eye, then the cave and then the flight from the island of Cyclops).

This is only the first half of the epos. If, as we think, the second half is really constructed according to the same pattern, how can we relate the two halves? Ahl and Roisman have given one possible answer[7]. They read Odysseus' ram-trick as an ironical inversion of the sack of Troy. It may be difficult to show that the Homeric audience did as well, but it is true that the trick of Odysseus "destroyer of cities" plays a major part in the second half, where the protagonist no more has to escape but to enter a system. Lambin and Latacz pointed out that the trick of the wooden horse is the intertextual correspondent of the beggar's disguise trick[8]. To understand this, we should keep in mind that the lesson Odysseus learns in the first part and teaches in the second is to be quiet. When he grasps Eurycleia's throat (in order to hinder her telling his identity to Penelope), this scene refers to a similar scene that happened in the wooden horse (and was told during the first phase of the first part). In this scene, Helena imitates the voice of the wives of the warriors hidden in the horse. One of them, Anticlus, loses his countenance and tries to answer—but Odysseus grasps his throat and saves the Greeks from being discovered.

Up to this point the Serbian, Usbekian and ancient Greek return-epics share the liberation/irruption themes, but it is not yet obvious that both halves, liberation and irruption, use the same narrative pattern. There is one problem in particular: How can an irruption be told by a liberation-pattern? We have seen that the irruption of the "silent" beggar into Ithaca might be associated with the irruption of the silent warriors into Troy. Yet both themes also show the situation of imprisonment. On the other hand, the eruption theme in the cave of the Cyclops might contain an allusion to irruption (opening the eye, the ram as realized metaphor of a battering ram used to open the walls of a city). As Segal and others have seen, the convertibility of the two directions (in-out) becomes very clear when Odysseus summons the singer Demodocus to tell the story of the wooden horse[9]. Demodocus sets out to sing, but Odysseus reacts to his song by weeping—not like a destroyer of cities as in the song but as compared to a victim, a woman who has lived in the sacked city and lost her husband. Entering Troy, escaping Calypso, escaping the past, entering the present, entering the Ithacan system, is not quite the same but somewhat of the same event, the transition from one age to another. Thus escaping or getting out, also mean entering, irruption. We will continue to look into this relationship in the next chapter by focusing on the role young men play in this twofold pattern.

3.3 Marriage, the death of young men and Zielinski's rules

The passing over from one age to another told as a transition from a non-adult, heroic status to that of a married, adult one, has been maintained by Papadopoulou-Belmehdi[10]: Odysseus comes from νύμφαι to a γυνή. The word "nymph" has two meanings in this context: first, that of a goddess such as Circe or Calypso, and, second, that of a young girl before marriage or even a married girl before giving birth to a child, a girl such as Nausicaa. With Circe, Odysseus meets the first νύμφη. He is in love with her for one year, after which his fellow warriors finally remove him. The opposition between girlfriend and fellows points out the strength of this first love. When the second romance begins, all fellows are already dead. But even if they were alive, they would not have the same function, because even though Calypso, the second νύμφη, holds Odysseus longer than Circe, the seven years that he spends with her, show a change: in the beginning Odysseus likes her and wants to stay, but in the end his only wish is to leave her. The relationship with this νύμφη is weaker than the preceding one. The third νύμφη, Nausicaa, earns a clear refusal from the beginning. Non-married girls characterize the world Odysseus wants to escape from. The world he enters is marked by marriage, even if it is only a confirmed marriage. The more Odysseus rejects the νύμφαι, the more the fellows die, and the closer Odysseus comes to his wife. We understand that in the beginning of the tale, Odysseus is not the "old man" (γέρων) he is in the *Iliad*, but still a young unmarried man, a real hero. However, as Segal points out, Odysseus does not want to stay a non-adult hero, he wants to become adult, human or what the first word of the *Odyssey* announces as main theme, an ἀνήρ, i.e. a husband[11]. Remarrying his wife means to him changing between ages.

Odysseus' fellows are not only an Iliadic background for this process, they play a major part in it. The temporal structure of the narrative is one of the features that show how important their death is for the audience. This structure is already prepared in the first lines of the text and consists of an inversion of the chronology. The textual image of the singer, or what has been called the énonciateur / Narrator 1, this voice that uses the first person of singular, sets out to explain to the muse what will be the starting point of her narrative[12]: not after the Trojan War, not during the journeys which make Odysseus lose his fellows, the "Narrator 1" summons the muse to start with the moment where all fellows are already dead and Odysseus himself is a prisoner on the island Ogygia.

In Homeric poetics, such a determination defines clearly which hitherto are the temporally limited subjects the Narrator[13] (or as some say *Narrator 2* or *narrateur*) and the characters can chose to tell in an autonomous way. In the beginning of the 20th century Zielinski formulated a "law" of concomitance in Homeric narratives[14]. It has been modified recently, but, basically, it still represents a valuable tendency[15]. One can deduce from the Homeric representation of two concomitant actions the rules for the relationship between the reality described by the Narrator and the description a character gives of this narrative reality in direct speech.

The muse, i.e. the blend of a singer-mouth and a goddess-voice we call *Narrator*, has the copyright on all that chronologically follows the imprisonment of Odysseus on Ogygia. The Narrator can freely narrate from the Calypso-episode on. What *freely* means, emerges from the way the characters speak about this same lapse of time. The Narrator seems to control these character speeches so that they cannot tell things the Narrator has not already told[16].

This control disappears when the character-speech concerns events that happened before the crucial beginning of the Narrator or muse's narrative. Inversely the Narrator avoids to make an analepse and to tell what happened before, whereas character-speech freely tells "external analepses" on events that happened before the Narrator's outset of narration, things the énonciateur or Narrator 1 summoned the muse to keep silent about[17].

Accordingly, all that happened before the beginning of the Narrator's tale belongs to the character. It is up to Odysseus to tell what the Narrator 1 summoned the muse to keep silent about: the journey during which his fellows die. Yet at first sight, the Calypso episode (C2 in the following scheme) does not seem to fit the rule.

A1) Ismaros, the Lotophages, the island of the goats, the Cyclops, the island of Aeolus, all those events reduce their number,
    B1) but the real catastrophe is the final point of this first series of adventures: The Laestrygons kill the young companions of Odysseus like tuna fish, only one ship escapes.
        C1) The rest on Circe's island gives them a break for one year,
A2) then they go on to the second series: the descent to "hell", the Sirens, Scylla and Charybdis and, finally,
    B2) they sacrify the oxen of Helios on his island. This religious fault causes their total extinction in a tempest.
        C2) ?

Odysseus' tale ends with the death of the young men, before the sojourn on Calypso's island, i.e. before what the audience might expect as part C2 in the parallelism described above. In later times, readers and poets did not agree with this end. In what is probably the first film on the *Odyssey*, 3 1/2 minutes filmed by Georges Méliès, the long journey shrinks to two events. The adventures with Cyclops and Calypso are both located on the same island. Gabriel Germain might have seen this movie as a boy. However when he wrote his analysis of the journey as an enormous ring composition, he arranged the text in order to make the Cyclops-episode at the beginning correspond to Calypso-episode at the end[18]. This fits with the chronology of the adventures but by no means with Odysseus' tale: Odysseus stops sooner and mentions Calypso only in a negative way. He says he will not tell the Calypso-episode to his audience because he has done so already. However this is only half the truth.

It is true that when he first met the king and queen two days ago, Odysseus had already drawn up a report on the tempest, the arrival on Calypso's island until the departure from Ogygia, then the second tempest and the arrival on the Phaeacian island (*Od.* 7.241ff.). However, it is not true that "the audience" of his long report of the journey heard that part: Odysseus told it alone to the king and queen since the other Phaeacians were already gone. If the internal audience of Odysseus were really the criterion of telling the Calypso-episode or not, he would have had to tell it. The only audience that can be meant here is the external one, the singer's audience. In this context the poetic rules of who can tell what are clear: the character Odysseus would not be allowed to tell what the Narrator (or the muse) must tell, if the Narrator did not already tell at least the basics of it. But since the Narrator has already told the story of Calypso, the character is free to retell it whenever he wants to, i.e. for instance after the account of the journey. Odysseus not only would have to, he would also have the right to it.

The exclusion of the Calypso episode, therefore, is not the result of narrative constraints, but a thematic choice. The fact that Odysseus distinguishes and separates what he "has the right" to tell in the Narrator's "licence" (Calypso) and what he is free to tell in his own right (the journey) shows us that Odysseus not only respects the limit given in the prooemium, but also that his tale only includes events related to what is called "the death of the fellows" in the prooemium.

Odysseus' tale appears to focus mainly on the death of his fellows—not less than on Odysseus' endurance or on the customs of foreign countries and cities. This result of the inquiry into the poetic rules is confirmed by a broader analysis of the composition. Here, "composition" does not necessarily mean the structure the audience understood. It is more the singer's tool and answers the question of the Russian Formalists: How is this work (for instance Gogol's *Cloak*) "made"? Thus, it is a matter of the aesthetics of production. Since the publications of, for example, Arend, Powell, and Louden we know that around the world traditional singers use already existing narrative patterns, which can even be repeated within the same epos[19].

The Usbekian epos *Alpamysh* already mentioned is one of the best examples. It is both surprisingly similar to the *Odyssey* and completely independent from the Odyssean tradition. In order to compose the *Alpamysh* the singer Yuldash Fazyl used the narrative pattern "a husband returns to the wedding of his own wife" twice. Yet the audience does not necessarily have to understand this poetical device as "narrative structure". Fazyl introduced so many variations into the two realizations of the same pattern that one gets the impression of two different and successive parts, although sometimes one feels narrative echoes without always knowing to what. This also seems to be the case in the *Odyssey*, where the same pattern is used twice. As Krischer points out, the story we read after the Calypso episode is surprisingly similar in its events to what happens on the island of Ithaca[20]:

On both islands, Scheria and Ithaca, a stranger arrives who does not know the place and conceals his identity. On both islands, he enters in conflict with xenophobic young men, eager to get married and who like nothing more than dancing, singing, listening to a singer and making jokes. In both sequences the stranger is a potential rival for local suitors. The young men jeer his lack of aristocratic values, but enter in a contest with him where a bow plays a major part. The stranger, however, finds his place in the new society by becoming a singer or almost a singer: only then does he reveal his identity. Among the Phaeacians, Odysseus starts to tell his story by designating himself as the story's hero and going on with a relative clause: "I am Odysseus who...." " The second time, again after a sort of wedding-contest, when he makes himself a singer, he uses the metaphor of the bow as Phorminx (*Od.* 21.430), the traditional string-instrument of the singer. He promises the Suitors to tell them a story during their dinner. As he touches the string of the bow it sounds like a phorminx, and, as the first throat of a Suitor is pierced, he reveals his identity: "I am Odysseus whose glory... ".

Phaeacians	pattern	Ithaca
Od. arrives on Scheria	X arrives on an island	Odysseus arrives on Ithaca.
Od. does not know where he is	X do. not kn. where he is.	Od. does not recog. Ithaca.
Od. does not say his name.	X does not say his name.	Od. does not say his name.
young men think he is a rival.	Conflict with young men	Conflict with the Suitors.
in a possible wedding.	X is a rival in a wedding.	Od. is a rival in a wedding.
Young men mock him	Young men mock him	Suitors mock him.
dialogue with Arete and Alkin.	dialogue with the queen	dialogue with Penelope
Contest with allusion to a bow	Bow-contest	Bow-contest
Od. reveals his identity	X reveals his identity	Od. reveals his identity
is compared to a singer	is compared to a singer	is compared to a singer
tells the death of the fellows	Death of the young men	kills the Suitors

On the (productive) level of composition, therefore, the murder of the Suitors is an equivalent or a variation of the story Odysseus tells the Phaeacians about the "death" of his fellows. Not only are these Troia-warriors the social equivalent of the Suitors, but they are also represented as their elder brothers. The murder of the Suitors and the death of Odysseus' fellows are in a close relationship[21]: Odysseus says he lost his fellows because of their own fault, but the Greek verb "to lose", ὀλλύναι, also means "to kill, to make perish" and sometimes in the text we have the same impression as the fathers of the fellows and the Suitors: that Odysseus "killed" them both[22].

We could now continue to confirm our thesis of the ambivalent view at epics by focalizing on the parts we left beside, the story of what happens before the Phaeacian-episode (books 1-5) and between the Phaeacians and the episode in Odysseus "palace" (books 13-16). Both start and end with a council that is followed by the sending of messengers. In both cases these messengers display a departure/escape-scenario with scenes of loquacious hospitality. But we are not looking for a perfect parallelism since we do not think that the aesthetics of production simply coincide with the audience's (and, in a way, the singer is part of it) interpretation. Thus, the differences between the two halves of the *Odyssey* are not less important and even more with regard to the reading of the audience.

The first half is concerned by escape-stories, which means that Odysseus separates himself more and more from his fellows. The wider the gap Odysseus feels between himself and the heroes, the more he minds his fellows. The less Odysseus likes the nymphs, the more the fellows die. With Circe Odysseus still behaves like his fellows, he is even more a typical young man than they are. He falls in love and stays with the nymph until a certain rivalry between the masculine group and Circe puts an end to this relationship. Like the fellows of the legendary Kazak leader Stenka Razin in a popular Russian song, they want their leader back—after a year. Like Stenka Razin, Odysseus decides in favor of the young men and against the nymph (or Stenka Razin's case: the bride). And yet, this confirmation of his original status as a quasi-young man might be the first germ of the detachment from the young men because it implies a first detachment from the nymphs, which already means a certain closeness to marriage[23]. Both the nymphs must be left and the young men must die before Odysseus is able to return to Ithaca and to marry his wife "again". When Odysseus arrives on Calypso's island all fellows are dead and after some years Odysseus himself starts to refuse this second nymph's love. When Odysseus tells this story before the parents of the third nymph (in the sense of *young girl* or *bride*), which is Nausicaa, he underlines his eagerness to leave Calypso. So, from the beginning on, he makes sure that he will not stay with the Phaeacians nor marry "the nymph". At this state of extreme refusal, Odysseus fellows have already been dead seven years, but they reappear in the long tale about their inevitable death. The death of two types of young men, the Suitors and the warrior fellows, is a central feature of the *Odyssey*.

3.4 Two meanings of *return*

On the level of the narrative structure (the variation of the composition pattern which is perceptible for the audience), the fellows are part of the prison from which Odysseus wants to escape, while in the second half of the *Odyssey* the Suitors form the fortress he has to enter. This ambivalence between composition and structure creates a strange opposition of the themes of escape and entering, a couple that also has qualities of equivalence. But might this not be simply the contingent effect of a traditional type of poetics or of a possibly farfetched reading? As we have seen, this coincides with the overall theme of transition between two ages, which is really a blend of escape from one age and intrusion into another. This ambivalence might explain why, in spite of the justification of the murder of the Suitors, the *Odyssey* sometimes nearly apologizes for it and in that way admits the possibility that its protagonist is a murderer. In order to pass from the state of a hero and young man to the human husband, Odysseus has to abandon his ancient world, i.e. his fellows. This transition-theme does not really fit what scholars of traditional epic around the world perceive as a common theme of the "husband-on-the-wedding-of-his-own-wife" texts: the theme of return.

Looking at the returnee image in the *Odyssey* we usually discover themes of endurance, of joy, of trickery too, but there seems to be a lack of critical voices. In order to see if there are any, we will compare the *Odyssey* to the returnee image that young men were suitable to use in their texts and minds. Since Malkin and others read the *Odyssey* as an epos on colonization we can start by looking at young men involved in colonization[24].

In order to understand the point of view of these sent away people, we have to recall the code of images underlying the colonization matter, the language of colonization. Doherty has shown that the image of marriage is one of the most important images of such an enterprise[25]. As in the first state of an Attic wedding-rite, a bride-father "gives" his daughter into the hands of the future bridegroom by pronouncing the formula "as ground to cultivate". Inversely, sending unsuccessful young suitors into a new land to cultivate can be described by the metaphor of marriage. Yet, as we have already seen in the iambus-chapter saying that colonization was a kind of wedding-substitute for bachelors does not seem very precise.

It is probably true that they often set out for a colony without girls or women and that they found a wife among the indigenous people, or that, at least metaphorically, they "marry" the land by cultivating it[26].

But the image does not entirely fit the social conditions: there is an important difference between the widespread virilocal type of marriage that provided the husband with almost all the paternal control over his wife and the rather seldom uxorilocal marriage, where the boy stays in the house of the bride-father. De facto the father keeps the status of the κύριος, the bridegroom becomes the brother, and in some juridical circumstances, the uncle of his wife. He does not control her and she could even control him either herself, or through her father. In comparison with the virilocal marriage, the roles are reversed. We have also seen that this reversal left traces in the foundation legend of Rhegion (see 2.2.5). The same inversion is found in the *Odyssey*, when Odysseus comes to the colony of the Phaeacians. Before Odysseus or the audience might meet the Phaeacians, the Narrator tells their foundation legend. In what follows, however, Odysseus understands more of the customs of this city: Not only is the intrusion of women into the decision-process of men a normal feature on Scheria, and the kinship between king and queen could reflect the economics of power in an uxorilocal colonization-marriage, the king *is* the queen's uncle. To conclude this modification: Colonization is a marriage substitute for bachelors but it is not as good a solution. No wonder the colonization oath of Cyrene forbids immediate return to the mother-city[27]. In addition to the desire to become an ἀνήρ, Odysseus has a good reason not to marry on this island;

Plato says that colonization is expulsion. Being sent out by the city without much hope for return is the young men's destiny[28]. From this point of view the word *return* rings differently from consolation, joy or desire because it is the return of another man. To return means not only to be a traitor of the mother city, but also a traitor of his old friends, i.e. the fellows who remain in the colony.

From the point of view of the city, expelled people who return are often perceived as "tyrannoi". In the 4th century AD this image was still in vigor: Prohaeresius, the Armenian professor of rhetoric begins to have too much influence in Athens. People call him the king because he has more students than other professors. Some of his enemies obtain his expulsion from the city by bribery or justice. Later some of his friends obtain permission for his return. But when Prohaeresius comes back, people give him another title: he is not a "king" anymore but a "tyrannos" because he returned in the same way as Pisistratus and Hippias, tyrants of Athens during the 6th century BC[29].

We cannot infer from this story that all "returnees" were tyrants in the eyes of the Greeks[30]. But it seems that young men like Hipponax associated tyrants with returnees, people who did not accept marrying another land but married the mother-city instead. Perhaps it is because the Greeks believed that Asian rulers, i.e. tyrannoi, slept with their mothers, that Sophocles calls incestuous Oedipus a tyrannos. When the Athenian tyrant Hippias was chased out of Athens and wanted to come back, he dreamt that he slept with his mother[31]. If, in the logic of the colonization metaphor, a foreign country is like a bride, then one's own country, i.e. the mother-city, can be associated with the mother. When the iambographer Hipponax attacks husbands, he associates them with people who, like tyrants, sleep with their mother[32]. A possible trace of this Greek vision of Asian rulers can also be found in a text that is contemporary to the *Odyssey*. When the iambographer Semonides attacks the horse-woman a type of wives who never consents to sleeping with her husband, he only sees two suitable husbands: eunuchs who cannot and "tyrannoi" who do not want to make love with their wives maybe because they were considered preferring their mothers[33]. The Greek rulers, people called *tyrannoi*, do not seem to have minded this image. They even confirmed it in their propaganda, with the image of fertilization of the mother-city or the mother Earth. They promote irrigation, a technique rather neglected before in Greece: Theagenes of Megara, Polycrates of Samos, Periandros of Corinth, the Peisistratids of Athens and possibly the tyrants of Sicyon realized plans of fountains, of channels, of canals, of tubes of ceramic and pipe-lines of leather[34]. The Greek verb used for this technique *okheteúein* is open to all the puns on *okheúein*, "to make love"[35]. Yet often the people seem to have appreciated these concrete politics and preferred it to the more ritual power of the basileîs or what convention translates by "kings". More than other tyrants, Pisistratus created the image of a wedding with the mother-city Athens. The first time he came back from exile he rode on a chariot like in the wedding-rite with a tall girl disguised as Athena. He connected the *Odyssey* to this image in including the recitation not only of the *Iliad* but also of the whole *Odyssey* at the Panathenaia in his program. Cook and Schubert have shown that, in the Athenian reading of the *Odyssey*, Odysseus became the image of the good returnee, whose bad evaluation could only be defended by the bad guys, the Suitors and their fathers[36]. Now the *Odyssey*'s tendency of representing a good returnee becomes apparent, and we can confront it to his bad image. We shall look for the remains of it in the *Odyssey*, for the gestures and figures that clearly not only describe a good returnee, but avoid the image of a bad one and, thus, attest the existence of another viewpoint, of ambivalence.

Odysseus would fit the image of a returning "tyrannos", but only from the point of view of an audience consisting of young men or Suitors. This would explain for instance why the returnee's mother must already be dead. The fact that Odysseus meets his mother among the dead, allows avoiding a recognition scene with his mother on the island of Ithaca and the image of a young man returning to his mother. Nor is Ithaca itself represented as a mother. Odysseus kisses the ground once he has recognized the island, as he kisses Penelope, once she has recognized him. He comes back to his wife and therefore Ithaca is more associated with his wife than with his mother. Furthermore, the bad image is reflected in the Suitors' reaction on the possibility of the king's return. They are ready to kill him.

But the *Odyssey* changes the possible image of the dangerous returnee into that of a good one. Odysseus does not dig channels. He has not been chased out of Ithaca. He is called a father and a king. To be sure, Odysseus is not a tyrant. He may be a traitor of his own "hetaîroi", of the Heroic Age, but the text justifies this in celebrating the fact that Odysseus becomes an ἀνήρ.

We have seen in this chapter that the Odyssean intertext left some marks of at least two different viewpoints at the *Odyssey*. The glance at the Suitors is clearly negative inasmuch as the narrative pattern used in the production twice links this slaughter to the perspective of a husband and a singer. The repetition of the theme (instead of a variation) make the fact clear that in the eyes of the audience the rule has to be accepted, according to which young men (Suitors/fellows) must die or disappear far from the "andres" (cf. the Phaeacians) when marriage nears. There are, however, some, though hidden, elements that indicate that another audience, for instance the Phaeacians, could contest this ideology. When Odysseus tells his story to them he has to excuse himself for "losing" his fellows. This is less necessary in front of the "real" audience when the Narrator (and not Odysseus) tells (the compositionally correspondent episode, i.e.) the slaughter of the Suitors.

We are starting to understand that looking for the Suitors' viewpoint in the *Odyssey* mostly means a reading "a negativo". We are looking for avoiding patterns. The ambivalence we found in the integration of intrusion and leaving into one and the same process of transition might be its mirror. We might not need to assume that only young men could understand or have this other view. The audience composed of wives and husbands is itself ambivalent in its glance and can understand what the main ideology is avoiding. The presence of the fathers and their critical judgment of Odysseus' deeds also show that the audience needs the ideological corroboration by the epic. For they are their fathers, mothers, brothers and sisters themselves. They love these losers of the system and need some excuses for suppressing them. This is why we will take a closer look at the underscored image of the father in the *Odyssey* in the next chapter.

Notes

[1] It appears that even the domination of wives by husbands is organized by this opposition of adult - non-adult. Cf. Leduc 1991.

[2] This is also very obvious in some of Pindar's odes, where the admiration of the winner compared to a hero turns into a warning to consider this status as higher than the present. Often, when the winner is very young and the father has not won any prize, Pindar attributes the glory of the victory to the father (e.g. *Nemean* 7). On the "mute" condition of the Spartan boys Xenoph. *Resp. Lac.* 3.4. Cf. Brelich 1969, 125.

[3] Critias 88b44 D.K, cf. Plat. *Symp.* 212d3ff. and Crit. fr. 4 West..

[4] For it underscores a particular feature of the *Odyssey*. Its protagonist transgresses the borderline between heroic past and matrimonial present during the epos, and in a way returns together with the audience to the Iron Age. However, discovering an Odysseus being a reader is not a random interpretation but simply fits the pragmatics of the *Odyssey*.

[5] Therefore, we have no reason to follow the analytic and neo-analytic assumption according to which there was once a plotting-version of the *Odyssey* transformed later and for other purposes into an occasional indeterminacy-version. Both versions were traditional and existed together; there is no necessity to assume an evolution.

[6] On the basis of the text offered by Zirmunskij V. ed. L. Pen'kovskij trad., *Alpamys po variantu Juldasa Fazyla*, Moskva 1958, and Chadwick N. K. Zirmunskij V., *Oral Epics of Central Asia*, Cambridge 1969, 293. Cf also Baldick J. *Homer and the Indo-Europeans. Comparing Mythologies*, London New York 1994, and West M.L., *The East Face of Helicon, West Asiatic Elements in Greek Poetry and Myth.*, Oxford 1997. Very similar are the Serbian songs cf. Danek G. "Die Apologoi der Odyssee und 'Apologoi' im serbokroatischen Heimkehrerlied", *WS* 109 1996, 11, 16

[7] Ahl F. Roisman H. M., *The 'Odyssey' Re-Formed*, Ithaca New York 1996.

[8] Lambin G., "Le cheval de Troie", *Gaia* 3 1998, 97-108, Latacz J. Holoka J.P. vert., *Homer, His Art and his World*, Ann Arbor 1996.

[9] Segal Ch., *Singers, Heroes and Gods in the 'Odyssey'*, Ithaca London 1994, 25ff.

[10] Papadopoulou-Belmehdi I., *Le chant de Pénélope. Poétique du tissage dans l'Odyssée*, Paris1994.

[11] Segal 1994, 62 et passim.

[12] On this distinction Calame C., *Le récit en Grèce ancienne*, Paris (2)2000, 12f.

[13] For the relation between Narrator and Locutor cf. *infra* p. 126 n. 5.

[14] Zielinski T., "Die Behandlung gleichzeitiger Ereignisse im antiken Epos", *Philologus Suppl.* 8 1899-1901, 407-449.

[15] Steinrück M., *Rede und Kontext. Zum Verhältnis von Person und Erzähler in frühgriechischen Texten*, Bonn 1992., Rengakos A., "Zeit und Gleichzeitigkeit in den homerischen Epen", *AA* 411995, 1-33, (underlines the importance of the "desultorian" Method of Homer). Nünlist R., "Der homerische Erzähler und das sogenannte Sukzessionsgesetz", *MH* 55 1998, 2-8 (considers *Il.* 14.428-432, *Il.* 15.458, *Il.* 13.183-187, *Il.* 13.650-652 as exceptions), Seeck G. A., "Homerisches Erzählen und das Problem der Gleichzeitigkeit", *Hermes* 126 1998, 131-144 (there is no direct, but maybe indirect expression for "at the same time"). Danek G., "Darstellung verdeckter Handlung bei Homer

und in der südslawischen Heldenlied-Tradition", *WS* 111 1998, 67-88 (Homer avoids concomitant actions).

[16] Steinrück 1992.

[17] These terms are defined in Genette G., *Figures* III, Paris 1972, 82-105 (Engl. *Narrative Discourse*, Ithaca New York 1980).

[18] Germain G., *Genèse de l'Odyssée, le fantastique et le sacré*, Paris 1954.

[19] Arend W., *Die typischen Scenen bei Homer*, Berlin 1933, Powell B., *Composition by Theme in the Odyssey*, Meisenheim am Glan 1977, Louden B., "Pivotal Contrafactuals in Homeric Epic", *CA* 12 1993, 181-198, and id., "An Extended Narrative Pattern in the 'Odyssey'", *GRBS* 34 1993, 5-33.

[20] Krischer T., "Die Bogenprobe", *Hermes* 120 1992, 19-25.

[21] Pazdernik 1995, for the guilt of Odysseus also Ahl Roisman 1996.

[22] Cook E.F., *The Odyssey in Athens, Mythes of Cultural Origins*, Ithaca London 1995, 21f.

[23] The series of the three nymphs: Papadopoulou-Belmehdi 1994.

[24] Malkin I., *The Returns of Odysseus, Colonisation and Ethnicity*, Berkeley 1998.

[25] Dougherty 1993, 4. on the case Cyrene Calame 1996, 109, and on Apollo's function Detienne 1998.

[26] Cf. Hdt. 1.146.2. Plat. *Legg.* 923. But Graham A.J., "The 'Odyssey', History, and Women", in B. Cohen ed., *The Distaff Side, Representing the Female in Homer's 'Odyssey'*, New York Oxford 1995, 3-16, believes that the colonist's wives were Greek at least ideologically. The Greek words in Pollux, *Onom.* 3.34ff. A short abstract in Haase M., "Hochzeitsbräuche und -ritual", in *Der Neue Pauly, Enzyklopädie der Antike* 5, 652-654, cf. also Contiades-Tsitsoni E., *Hymenaios und Epithalamion, das Hochzeitslied in der frühgriechischen Lyrik*, Stuttgart 1990 and Mösch-Klingele R., *Die loutrophoros im Hochzeits- und Begräbnisritual des 5. Jahrhunderts v. Chr. in Athen*, Bern 2006.

[27] On this oath - be it an original or later historicism - cf. the texts collected by Létoublon F., *La ruche grecque et l'empire de Rome*, Grenoble 1995, 166f.

[28] Plato, *Plt.* 293d says that a ruler must keep constant the number of inhabitants and clear the city of bad elements, even if he has to kill citizens to send them like bee rows into colonies.

[29] Cf. Giangrande I. ed., *Eunapii Vitae Sophistarum*, Romae 1956, 10.3.16.

[30] On the concept of the tyrannos Berve H., *Die Tyrannis bei den Griechen*, München 1967 and Andrewes A., *The Greek Tyrants*, London 1980 and Ogden D., *The Crooked Kings of Ancient Greece*, London 1997 (king or tyrannos is only a matter of the imaginary, of the point of view). On "kings" Drews R., *Basileus, the Evidence for Kingship in geometric Greece*, New Haven London 1983, 101ff. or Deger S., *Herrschaftsformen bei Homer*, Wien 1970, (the sacral king 69f.). Against: Carlier P., *La royauté en Grèce avant Alexandre*, Strasbourg 1984, 142 and 204 N. 325.

[31] Cf. Hdt. 6.107.2

[32] The word is *metrokoítes* fr. 12.1-2 and cf. fr. 70.7ff. W. It is a wide spread image in imperial Greek literature Clem. *Paed.* 1.7 (55.2), Ael. *N.A.* 6.39.8, Eust. *In Od.* 1.363.38

[33] Semonides fr. 7.69 (West or Pellizer-Tedeschi).

[34] Lang F., *Archaische Siedlungen in Griechenland, Struktur und Entwicklung*, Berlin 1996, 125, on the link to the Pisistratids.

[35] Cf. Steinrück M., "Roi et tyran dans l'imaginaire grec archaïque", *Gaia* 3 1998, 27-35.

[36] Schubert P., "Le palais d'Alcinoos et les Panathénées", *REG* 109 1996, 255-263, and Cook 1995, passim.

4 Fathers

4.1 Foxes

Segal has shown that Odysseus uses different narrative styles in the first and the second halves of the *Odyssey*[1]. He tells the truth to the Phaeacians yet lies to his Ithacan audiences. But, the different styles he uses suggest the reverse: the "truth" is told in a fairy tale style, the lies are marked by realism. Furthermore, these realistic lies sometimes seem to basically tell the same stories as the "true" accounts. On the island of Ithaca Odysseus disguises himself as a beggar and pretends to have led the life of a young man very similar to that of unmarried Eumaeus and of the Suitors. He introduces himself as the son of a mighty Cretan and his concubine (*Od.* 14.185-359). His more legitimate half-brothers have divided the heritage among them. So Odysseus represents himself not as a member of the Heroic Age, but as what corresponds to this in the Iron Age, i.e. as a young man who is deprived of heritage, but reaches some wealth and a wife as a merchant, by piracy, and war. But he has lost everything because of a fault of his fellows: they slaughtered oxen they shouldn't have. When the beggar re-tells more or less the same story to Penelope, he even invents a name: Acthon, son of the Cretan Idomeneus and his concubine. There is a lot of literature about this story[2]. Here, the name needs special concern: in the legends, for one, *Aithon*, "the intensely brown or burning red", is the name of a famous and very hungry father who does not want to give away his daughter; for the other, it is one of the names for "fox"[3].

As we have seen, the fox appears in the iambus, the anti-discourse of the epos. In Archilochus' epode of the fox and monkey (fr. 185 ff. W), the monkey wants to be the king of the animals[4]. The fox meets him:

τῷ δ' ἄρ' ἀλώπηξ κερδαλέη συνήντετο,
a crafty fox met him –

Then he promises him a treasure and leads him to the place where it is supposed to be hidden. But the treasure, whatever it was, is in a trap. The sly (κερδαλέη) fox outwits the king. There is no doubt about what the fox represents: young men fighting against people who do not deserve their position.

Another verse, perhaps in the context of mutual gender-polemics, allows us to understand the intelligence of the fox more precisely. The verse according to which a fox knows many things, the hedgehog only one thing, but an important one, is attributed to both Archilochus *and* (not *or*) the *Margites*. In the *Margites*, whose fragments are composed from a female and very critic point of view (and maybe even by women) against unable husbands, the verse seems to describe the manifold and constantly changing ideas of a young man who does not fit marriage. It is a critique of the *mêtis* of young men. The hedgehog on the contrary might represent birth giving and demonstrate female superiority and stability[5]. Archilochus might have used the same verse in associating female ideology of (matrimonial) adulthood with aristocratic establishment. This amalgamating of female and aristocratic positions is a critical tendency we also find in Semonides' texts, in the tales on Pittacus, in ironical attacks of Anacreon or, later, in comedies such as the *Clouds* of Aristophanes[6].

Archilochus often represents young men as foxes. We have already seen that this image fits the image of Spartan uninitiated adolescents during the hard time they spend outside of the community as "foxes"[7]. Eusebius tells us that Archilochus attacked in his texts the girls refusing to marry him[8]. Archilochus pretended that these girls were too young or too old for him, but in fact he longed for them. This ambivalent relationship is also described by a fable that is attributed to the slave Aesopus who criticized Ionian society. A fox cannot reach the grapes but pretends to refuse them because they are not yet ripe. During the long process of transmission from Aesopus to Socrates, to Phaedrus, Babrius, to Lafontaine, Krylov, Lessing or Thurber, the image of the fox might have been given another meaning according to different societies. But the Ionian context of the beginning of the 6th century BC makes it possible that Aesopus mocked at the ambiguous attitude of the young men.

One text gives the fox Archilochus meeting the girls' father. Fr. 172 West[9] starts with "Father Lycambes, who changed your mind though sane before?" Lycambes has broken the oath to give one of his daughters in marriage to Archilochus. The text continues with the story of the fox that made a deal with an eagle not to eat each other's children. The eagle feeling too safe on his high rock breaks the oath. The fox invokes Zeus who helps. This is another image of the father marked by eagles. The eaglets are driven out of the nest by a fire. They fall down and the fox eats them.

4.2 Eagles

Eagles are associated with fathers in their relationship to children during the whole Antiquity and in the beginning of the Middle Ages. According to Aristotle they can expulse their children when there is a nutrition shortage[10]. Or they select their children and accept only the one able to look directly into the sun[11]. The Archilochean image of the eagle desperately looking for his children reemerges when Aeschylus tells us how parents, especially fathers feel when they lose their children. The chorus of the old men in *Agamemnon* (v. 49) uses this image to describe Agamemnon who sacrifices his daughter Iphigeneia in order to assure his power as a Panhellenic king. During the whole play, the image is reused and also modified: sometimes the chorus does not speak of eagles but of *aigypioi*, vultures. Old men and young men seem to use the same image for the father, but it would be surprising if Aeschylus really adopted the image from an enemy of the fathers such as Archilochus. Aeschylus is a very close reader of Homer, especially in the *Agamemnon*, and, if the *Odyssey* is really composed for husbands or fathers, we should find the image of eagles and, eventually of vultures, in this epos, too.

Thus it is not surprising that the first time eagles appear in the *Odyssey*, the text treats the theme of the father. In the second book, Telemachus tries chasing the Suitors during an assembly, but the political means fail. The necessity of the father's presence is demonstrated by the fact that the Suitors have too much influence. The *demos* does not dare to reject them. This is what we would call the construction of a need in the semio-narrative syntax of Courtès-Greimas: Odysseus in his quality as Telemachus' father is missing[12]. In the center of the assembly, and in the center of the first long ring composition of the *Odyssey*, when Telemachus abandons all hope to manage the situation without his father, two eagles fly straight ahead to the assembly, draw two circles looking and shouting grimly, then they fly away[13]. But the text itself provides us with a clue for the fact that this divine sign deals with eagles and with the number 2 of the two circles. The seer Halitherses, a person the Suitors fear and hate of course, interprets the sign as the imminent return of the father Odysseus after 20 years. The eagles are associated with Odysseus when he is needed as a father[14].

Moreover, this meeting is introduced by one of the elder Ithacans, a man characterized by the Narrator as a father. He is described through the status of his sons: two own still the inherited fields, one has been sent to the Trojan War (Polyphemus devours him). The fourth son is one of the Suitors. The father's name is *Aigyptios*. Modern commentators explain it as the nickname of a man who was in Egypt. But in the context of the Aeschylean eagle- or vulture-image for the father, it is likely that Homer's audience could not oversee the association with the Aigypios, the vulture as the image of a father who loses his children[15].

The next eagle is a sea eagle or beard-vulture, a φήνη. Perhaps this is just one of the multiple puns of Athena: she transforms herself into a "phene" (an "apparition bird" from φαίνομαι?) when Telemachus, once again, loses courage. With Athena disguised as Mentor, he goes to ask Nestor what he knows about his father. Nestor's long answer suggests that Odysseus has sailed directly into "the dark clouds of evil"[16]. Telemachus is disappointed, even rude with his host, and refuses to think of his father anymore. Athena, still disguised as the mortal Mentor, must do something if she wants the adolescent to continue his quest. She "appears" as a "phene", again linked to the theme of the absent but necessary father. Nestor interprets the sign and explains that, before, Athena appeared only to Odysseus in this frank manner. Once again, an eagle seems to be associated with the theme of the father. In Aristotle's reading the *phene* is the type of eagle accepting children of eagles which their father has driven out of the nest[17].

After this divine narrative device Telemachus continues to Sparta in his quest. He asks king Menelaus. Menelaus tells him a story that gives the boy courage and makes him decide to wait for his father at Sparta,—but Athena comes back to tell him lies about his mother: that she is willing to accept one of the Suitors as her husband. Telemachus, thus, turns his horses homeward. At this moment an eagle appears and throws a goose in front of the chariot. "What might that mean?" Helena asks her husband. Before Menelaus can realize that this is a rhetorical question, Helena cuts him short and offers the interpretation herself: the eagle is of course Odysseus, the goose means the Suitors[18].

In this context one might wonder whether the eagle simply signifies Odysseus and not necessarily the bird of father Zeus or the father as a social position. But in the forth eagle-sign, we see that an eagle in opposition to the goose simply stresses another view of the father. The goose is Aphrodite's animal, and four books later (*Od.* 19.536ff.) Penelope tells the beggar (Odysseus) that she dreamt of an eagle that slew her 20 geese. During the dream, the eagle reveals to the queen, that he is her husband Odysseus. He even continues his interpretation and the beggar confirms it: according to them the 20 geese are the Suitors. If so, the image of Aphrodite's birds might reveal the queen's hidden desire, and Odysseus, still a beggar, would tactfully pass over. But it often happens in the Homeric interpretation of divine signs that interpreters do not say the whole truth, whereas the audience is probably aware of this silence. In a similar way, the audience and Penelope perfectly know that 20 geese cannot mean 108 Suitors. Maybe Aphrodite's bird means a member of this over-sexualized group of young men, but the number 20, rather signifies, as Pratt saw, the 20 lost years of matrimonial life[19]. Whereas Halitherses could easily pretend that 2 circles of two eagles mean 20 years, Odysseus, as a beggar and a husband, keeps silent about this long absence.

There are still some eagle-images to come. The very last of them occurs in the last line but ten of the *Odyssey* (*Od.* 24.538). The Suitors are already buried and the army of their fathers tries to take revenge on the Laertiads: Odysseus, Laertes, and Telemachus. There begins a battle between fathers having lost their children and fathers who are going to lose them. With the help of Athena, the side of the Laertiads wins. Odysseus is shouting and sets out to persecute the fathers *like an eagle*:

οἴμησεν δὲ ἀλεὶς ὥς τ'αἰετὸς ὑψιπετήεις,

he pounced on them like a swooping eagle

But Zeus stops his daughter Athena with a thunderclap, Athena stops Odysseus: he is not to persecute his enemies.

4.3 Odysseus among the fathers

This seems a very abrupt end for the *Odyssey*. Moreover the Scholiae on *Od.* 23.296 seem to agree on this impression. In *Od.* 23.296, Penelope has already recognized and accepted her husband and they pass the first night together after 20 years. This fact would not necessarily constitute a very pathetic theme during archaic or classical times when husbands and wives spent every day life in separate realms. But when gender rule changed into the togetherness of matrimonial life, in the Hellenistic age[20], the theme probably became more significant and might have been a goal. The Alexandrian editors and commentators of Homer, however, perceived this scene as the τέλος or the πέρας of the *Odyssey*, words some modern scholars would like to translate by "the end" of the *Odyssey*. Yet it is very unlikely that Zenodotus or Aristarchus found copies of the *Odyssey* that materially ended with *Od.* 23.296, and it is improbable, that Aristarchus believed this verse to be the very end of the text because he continues to distinguish between authentic verses and later additions even after this τέλος. What could it mean to him then? Erbse has shown that the Homeric scholars, Aristarchus and Aristophanes of Byzantium, used Aristotelian concepts[21]. In

Aristotle's terminology, the τέλος of a story does not necessarily mean the end of the text, but simply its narrative goal, when the hero has reached what he was struggling for[22]. Afterwards the so-called narrative sanction-phase can still happen, the moment we know from television serials, when the rewards are given and the reestablished order is highlighted. According to Erbse, then, the Scholiae want to say that (in Hellenistic eyes) *Od.* 23.296 marks a narrative goal. This might be an explanation for the the use of the word τέλος. Nevertheless, the word πέρας does not fit the idea of a narrative goal.

In order to find a possible meaning of πέρας we need to reenter the problem of composition, but composition here as the structure the audience perceived: the different ends of the threads the *Odyssey* is woven of. The composition, i.e. the production of the text involves, as we have seen, two layers of the same pattern but with variant realizations.

	I	II
messenger	Athena/Telemachus	Athena/Odysseus
stories	Nestor/Menelaus	Eumaeus
messenger	Hermes/Odysseus	Athena/Telemachus
palace/wedding	Phaeacians	Ithaca
contest	bow	bow
teller	Odysseus tells	Odysseus "sings"
death of young men	the death of his fellows	the death of the Suitors
difficult recognition	Ithaca	Penelope

We could of course take a further step to distinguish narrative phases such as manipulation (sending messengers), competence (knowledge), performance (trading stories for return/ killing enemies for power), and sanction (reward: the land/the wife). But those structures are less clearly perceived. Let us look for the structural level the audience is expected to understand. The first verses of the *Odyssey* clearly indicate the two main layers: first the return to Ithaca, then the adventures on the island of Ithaca itself (καὶ μετὰ οἷσι φίλοισι). Furthermore the criterion of space makes us distinguish between a Telemachus-story and an Odysseus-story within the first layer. We then have three parts. The ends of these bigger narrative units are marked for the audience by short recapitulations. At the "end" of the "Telemachy", i.e. at the end of his journey, a reluctant Telemachus is forced by his mother to make a report (17.107ff.). At the end of the revenge-story, the Suitors must tell the other dead heroes what happened (24.121ff.). Yet, at the first end of the third narrative unit, the journey of Odysseus, a summary would be absurd because Odysseus has spent the last three books making a long report. Furthermore his story only ends when he has re-gained

Penelope's trust. Only then, during the couple's first night, a reluctant Odysseus gives the summary Penelope and we are waiting for. This reflection enables us to change the focus in the sentence of Aristarchus: Not "here is the *end* of the Odyssey" but "*here* is the end of the *Odyssey*". Not only does Aristarchus (with *Odyssey*) refer to one of the three narrative units (the second one), but he also highlights the fact that this abstract comes late.

In a similar way, Proclus, when commenting the *Iliad* by telling what happened before and after, presupposes that, in fact, his readers perfectly know the *Iliad*. So he comments the events of the *Cypria* that chronologically precede the *Iliad* but are mentioned within the *Iliad* by the same type of syntax: *here* the snake-wonder happens (of which the *Iliad* reminds us) or *here* the death of Palamedes happens[23]. Similarly, the readers of Aristarchus of course knew the text of the *Odyssey* and the story of the journey from comedies and satyr-plays. Aristarchus, thus, could have said that the narrative unit *Odyssey* they know does not end where they think, i.e. after the Phaeacians, but later.

The revenge story ends with its own summary a few verses later, at the beginning of the 24th book. All three layers are, thus, ended, but not what the Narrator (énonciateur) summoned the muse to tell: ἄνδρα μοι ἔννεπε μοῦσα. Odysseus was able to get rid of his peers, he even killed their brothers, and he married a second time,—all-important stages on the way to becoming an ἀνήρ, but one poetic and ideological problem still remains. Odysseus refers to it when introducing himself to Penelope and, in a way, it underlies the whole *Odyssey*: young men are the enemies of *men*, but they still are the children of fathers, and therefore of men, too. The remaining problem seems to be that the society cannot accept Odysseus as a husband *and* father as long as the fathers are his enemies. Perhaps this is why we are guided, after the three main layers of the *Odyssey*, into the realm of the fathers:

> 1) Odysseus repeats the recognition game with his father Laertes.
> 2) Father Zeus appears, for the first time in the text, to be superior to his daughter. Athena (the first time in the *Odyssey*) does not know how to resolve the problem.
> 3) Then, the Suitors' fathers assemble to make decisions concerning Odysseus' punishment. Part of them form an army and go against him and his family.
> 4) The battle formation gives an opportunity to take a family picture: Laertes enjoys it (24.514f.):
>
> τίς νύ μοι ἡμέρη ἥδε θεοὶ φίλοι ἦ μάλα χαίρω·
> υἱός θ'υἱωνός τ'ἀρετῆς πέρι δῆριν ἔχουσι.
>
> "Dear gods! What a day this is to warm my heart!
> My son and my grandson are competing in valor." (Rieu[24])

The whole male lineage of the Laertiads fights together against the enemies. But only Laertes has the "social" or poetic right to kill someone. Athena puts the other fathers to flight. When Odysseus, like an eagle, sets out in their pursuit, Athena, according to Zeus' order, has to stop him. The father-context enables us to put forward the hypothesis that the reason is to be found in Odysseus' new status. A father should not kill other fathers. Laertes can kill one of the younger generation, but Odysseus, being an eagle now, is one of the father generation. He has finally become what the eagle-sign announced[25].

This transition from heroic status (of young men) to that of husbands and fatherhood represents a main theme of the *Odyssey*. The *Iliad* only knows an Odysseus who takes part in the council of the old. When the *iuventus* leaves the army letting the corporations of the old die, a quarrel-scene ensues that must both remind the audience of iambic themes and illustrate the crisis of the adult army. In this situation the Iliadic Odysseus only knows one way to make clear on which side he is standing: he defines himself as the father of Telemachus, not as the son of Laertes (*Il.* 2.260). In the *Odyssey* he becomes at the end, what he is in the *Iliad* from the beginning on.

All this is to say that on the thematic and narrative level, the end of "our" *Odyssey* is consistent with the remaining corpus of the *Odyssey*. However this is not the only level of the text that causes problems. There is no need of excessive sensitivity to feel what many readers say, namely that the underworld-events, the story of how Laertes recognizes Odysseus, the following scene among the gods, the assembly on earth, Laertes taking his bath and, finally, the battle scene, are a whole set of events which are told in a hurry and presented as in strange mix. Here seems to be a problem of composition. Neither a rhythm of themes, nor a small ring composition is discernible, as if the goal were to get rid of some remaining problems very quickly and not to stage a conclusive ending by tying up the threads of the story. This description is very typical of a certain type of passages. Such negative judgments appear in the commentaries[26] where thematic analysis localizes the second half of a longer ring composition.

The trouble of ring composition is not a matter of acceptance by classical scholars. There is an impressive list of respectable philologists who perceived this onionskin structure in Homeric texts during a whole century[27]. But the first hard evidence for an anthropological relevance of this feature, and this means, for the fact that the audience heard this thematic rhythm, is the surprisingly constant possibility to read complex ring compositions in or into the *Odyssey* (or the *Iliad*), whereas it is rare or impossible to find the same complex pattern in texts of other traditions[28]. This evidence of coherence can be supported, secondly, by recurrent seemingly self-referential metaphors in the center of Homeric ring compositions[29]. Thirdly, there are passages such as in the name catalogues, where the reader simply is forced to follow the symmetrical order *abcd....dcba*.

However, if the pattern of ring composition was used in Homeric composition, this would explain the commentators' observations about the inconsistency of its form. Concerning the end of the *Odyssey* Bertmann, for instance, read it as the second part of a ring composition on a higher scale[30].

combat with the Suitors a	a' combat with the fathers
council about the fathers b	b' council of the fathers/Zeus
Odysseus' bath (beauty) c	c' Laertes' bath (beauty)
recognition (sign, wife) d	d' recognition (sign, father)
summary (Od.) e	e' summary (Suitors)

One could object to this proposition that the events follow each other in a surprisingly abrupt way. However, Homeric ring composition could be an explanation inasmuch that as they differ from the slowly and carefully arranged ring compositional patterns of Thucydides or Pindar which are "written" texts from their composition on: they show the same formal structuring in the first as in the second half. When, for instance, a smaller ring composition fills the first half out we find another ring composition in the second half. In the supposedly oral composition of the *Odyssey*, the Narrator starts, ideally, with a small ring composition. This small pattern is then integrated as the first half into a second ring composition of a higher scale. And this pattern again forms the first half of a new construction. This principle can be repeated up to five times. But every time it will be less easy to combine local and larger structures. From a certain level on, the second half does not show a local structuring anymore, but only respects its higher level. In other words, the scenes which answer the scenes of the first half are no more structured in themselves, they are a mere series. For example, Odysseus and Telemachus' relatively brief discussion concerning the fathers of the Suitors would be echoed by not one, but even two discussions in the 24th book: one among the fathers, the other between Zeus and Athena. With such a criterion in mind, a well-formed end would even make us more suspicious (of interpolation) than a simple catalogue. At least the weak composition cannot be used as evidence against the authenticity of book 24.

The other problem raised by the thematic correspondences (b - b') is whether or not Zeus can really play the role of the father. We know, of course, the standing expressions Ζεῦ πάτερ, *Iuppiter,* and the formula πατὴρ ἀνδρῶν τε θεῶν τε, but whether this is more than a honorific title, an epithet of power, whether or not we have the right to assume that eagles are father-birds because they are Zeus' birds is not obvious. Nevertheless, the intertext not only of the eagles, but also of Zeus seems to confirm the hypothesis according to which Zeus epithet *father* was understood in a very literal sense in the 7th century.

4.4 Father Zeus

According to Aristotle, Archilochus' fragment 122 W is a good example of "ethos", the rhetoric use of discourses for characterizing characters[31]. This text indeed begins with a special discourse the audience knows very well: the discourse of fathers. This text implies the bad experiences of young men eager to marry a girl but unable to find a wife because they always hear the same answer: "We regret to inform you that.... " The father whose discourse is enacted by Archilochus takes pleasure in a rather perfidious explanation, why he will not be able to give his daughter in marriage. It is not excluded, he says, that there will be marriage (and marriage-gifts), because nothing is excluded, if day becomes night. The father is referring to one of the eclipses of this time. If "adynata", "impossible things" are possible, marriage is too. But since, we have to supply, adynata are generally impossible, the young man will not get his daughter. We can find the same topos as late as in Menandrus[32]. With this preamble let us read the beginning of the iambus:

χρημάτων ἄελπτον οὐδέν ἐστιν
   οὐδ' ἀπώμοτον
      οὐδὲ θαυμάσιον,

Nothing is to be unexpected
   or sworn impossible
      or marveled at ... (Gerber)

Three times the father claims the same thing in a litotes: there might be a possibility of marriage, but, unfortunately, nothing can be taken for sure. This triple repetition of the same emptiness is a typical device of 7th-century ἦθος[33] and it always stands for the same thing: the contrary. Aristotle mentions another text as example of "ethos": in fr. 19 West the credibility of the carpenter Charon is undermined by his triple affirmation that he is not interested in other people's wealth. The poem begins with Charon's words: "I am not concerned by Gyges' gold". 2) I do not envy Gyges 3) I let him have what a god gave to him. Hardly anybody in the audience would believe him[34].

When Hermes, 200 years later, in the *Homeric Hymn to Hermes*, steals the gods' cattle and has to answer Apollo's uncomfortable questions, the thief's reaction is very similar: he never saw the cattle[35]. This lie is again marked by the performative contradiction of the triple series. The swineherd Eumaeus of the 7th-century-*Odyssey* also uses this feature, when he does not understand what is going on anymore. His host does not behave as a beggar should (although Odysseus accepts to work for Eumaeus, he refuses after having made his plan with Telemachus, things the Swineherd ignores), but Eumaeus indicates his confusion by a fruitless attempt at concealing it (*Od.* 16.136):

Γιγνώσκω
    φρονέω·
        τόδε δὴ νοέοντι κελεύεις.

I see,
    I can understand,
        I got the message!

The fact that we are not only dealing with a simple formulaic traditional phrase used and reshaped many times before but also with what Russian Formalists call "skaz" or Aristotle apprehended by the concept of "ethos" is shown when Odysseus repeats this verse in order to hide his social identity. To be accepted as a member of Eumaeus' class, he imitates his discourse (*Od.* 17.193, 282).

In the eyes of rich young men, such a language is ridiculous. And not only Archilochus' audience laughs, when he imitates the seer's discourse[36] but the Suitors laugh at the same matter. In *Od.* 20.351 the Apollinian seer Theoclymenus is upset about the behavior of the young men and tries to deter them by what he is seeing. But his discourse makes them loose all countenance.

"ἆ δειλοί, τί κακὸν τόδε πάσχετε· νυκτὶ μὲν ὑμέων
εἰλύαται κεφαλαί τε πρόσωπά τε νέρθε τε γοῦνα,
οἰμωγὴ δὲ **δέδηε**, δεδάκρυνται δὲ παρειαί,
αἵματι δ' **ἐρράδαται** τοῖχοι καλαί τε μεσόδμαι·
εἰδώλων δὲ πλέον πρόθυρον, πλείη δὲ καὶ αὐλή,   355
ἱεμένων Ἐρεβόσδε ὑπὸ ζόφον· ἥλιος δὲ
οὐρανοῦ **ἐξαπόλωλε**, κακὴ δ' **ἐπιδέδρομεν** ἀχλύς"

"Unhappy men, what blight is this that has descended on you?
Your heads, your faces, and your knees are **veiled** in night.
There is mourning burning in the air; I see cheeks wet with tears.
And look the panels and the walls are splashed with blood.
The porch is filled with ghosts. So is the court –
ghosts hurrying down to the darkness and to Hell. The sun
is blotted out from heaven and a malignant mist has crept upon the world."
(after Rieu)

What strikes first is the number of perfect-forms. Theoclymenus speaks in the present-tense as his colleagues often do, as if what he sees in the future is happening in the present. But then he even overturns his vision in presenting the slaughter as an accomplished state of affairs. This choice of reduplication-forms is linked to another typical feature of oracular discourse often parodied in comedy (cf. the oracular hexameters of Cleon in the *Knights*): sound repetition or "parechesis". Note for instance the repetition of 6 /d/ in the 9 syllables of δὲ δέδηε, δεδάκρυνται δέ, always in the initial position of the syllable. Finally the metaphors, a pathogenic bias according to Aristotle's *Rhetoric*, go beyond painthreshold. That "heads are rounded by darkness" might be acceptable for an *Iliad*-audience, that "knees are wrapped in darkness" is harder to conceive, but when the voice of lamentation becomes "a torch in the dark", the field of the comparisons Homeric audience is accustomed to has been left so far behind that the audience cannot but understand the Suitors' laughter.

ὡς ἔφαθ', οἳ δ' ἄρα πάντες ἐπ' αὐτῷ ἡδὺ γέλασσαν.

"Those were his words. They laughed at him delightedly, with one accord;"
(after Rieu)

They pretend to take the present and the perfect tense seriously and send the seer to the market place because he sees darkness in the reduced daylight of Odysseus' palace[37].

This excursus on the iambographers' and their audience's pleasure of ethos was necessary for understanding the fr. 122 W of Archilochus. His audience recognized the sarcastic discourse heard many times before for real, the discourse of a father who likes to tease suitors: of course there shall be no wedding-gift, no marriage, but who knows, maybe...

"χρημάτων ἄελπτον οὐδέν ἐστιν οὐδ ἀπώμοτον
οὐδὲ θαυμάσιον, ἐπειδὴ **Ζεὺς πατὴρ** Ὀλυμπίων
ἐκ μεσαμβρίης ἔθηκε νύκτ', ἀποκρύψας φάος
ἡλίου λάμποντος, λυγρὸν δ' ἦλθ ἐπ' ἀνθρώπους δέος."

"Nothing is unexpected or sworn impossible
or marveled at, now that Zeus father of the Olympians
has made night out of noonday, hiding away the light
of the shining sun, and clammy fear came over people." (Gerber)

The father, presumably Archenactides, explains his decision through father Zeus' decision. If father Zeus can change daylight into darkness, then maybe father Archenaktides is able to do it, too.

"ἐκ δὲ τοῦ καὶ πιστὰ πάντα κἀπίελπτα γίνεται   5
ἀνδράσιν· μηδεὶς ἔθ'ὑμέων εἰσορέων θαυμαζέτω
μηδ'ἐὰν δελφῖσι θῆρες ἀνταμείψωνται νομὸν
ἐνάλιον, καί σφιν θαλάσσης ἠχέεντα κύματα
φίλτερ' ἠπείρου γίνηται, τοῖσι δ' ὑλέειν ὄρος."
[   ]Ἀρ]χηνακτίδης   10
[   ]ήτου πάις[
[ἐρη]τύθη γάμων[
[   ]..αινε..[
[   ]νεῖν·
[   ]   15
[ἀν]δράσιν·
[   ].[].[]

From now on (you) men can believe and expect anything
let none of you any longer marvel at what you,
not even if wild animals take on a briny pasturage
in exchange with dolphins and the crashing waves of the sea become dearer to them than
the land, the wooded mountain dearer to dolphins.
                      Archenactides
                      child of (vert. Gerber[38])
                      retained from the wedding
                      ....
                      ....
                      ....
                      husbands/men

    We should not make ourselves the fools of this paternal discourse. Neither Archenactides nor Archilochus live in the heroic time where an eclipse provoked by Zeus made the hero Ajax pray for light[39]. The Suitors and the audience of the *Odyssey* do no more believe anymore in the divine origin of eclipses than Thales and his precursors in Ionia or Mesopotamia did. Like Theoclymenus, Archenactides is not only characterized by his foggy style but also by the arrogant attitude of an adult speaking to children in fairy tales. In the *Iliad*, Agamemnon once uses a similar discourse (I do not believe you can brush your teeth/fight like an man) towards Odysseus, a grown up man and a member of the elders-council, and earns a very angry answer[40]. Maybe this is why Archilochus calls the suitors ἄνδρες, male men (not "humans" or "men" as some have translated). For us, the identity of the *andres* with the Suitors becomes clear through the syntactical relation of this word with the second person of the plural "you (the suitors of my daughter)".

    However, the element of the paternal discourse we are interested in is its justification by "father Zeus", not in the sense of the honorific formula "father of gods and men", but in the narrower sense of a father-god. We can compare it to the use the author of the *Homeric hymn to Aphrodite* makes of it[41]. Firstly, he represents Zeus as the youngest son of Cronus who swallowed his elder brothers and sisters, first of all his sister Hestia. But Zeus forces his father to give them back. In a way, "he gives birth" to them a second time and in the inverted order. Cronus becomes, thus, a mother and his womb is called a *nedus,* which otherwise describes female wombs. This story explains why Hestia, who was the oldest daughter, became the youngest, and why accordingly Zeus is called *father Zeus* by the formula the Narrator uses after this story (v. 27). This text has a chance to date of the 7th century BC and re-actualizes the unconscious catachrestic use of the formula as a sheer title by an etiological story that offers a new etymology.

The formula does not appear in the iambic "catalogue of wives" that Semonides of Amorgos composed in the 7th century. But there is no mention of any human parents either. Instead Zeus is considered the bride-father of these girls, he and the Olympians "give" them to the husbands[42]. In a similar way Zeus sends a robot-girl to the husbands (*ándres*) according to the *Works and Days* of Hesiod, also composed during the 7th century[43]. This image of Zeus as a higher instance of the fathers seems to be reproduced in fr. 179 W of Archilochus, an iambus on failed marriage:

Ζεῦ πάτερ, γάμον μὲν οὐκ ἐδαισάμην,

Father Zeus, I did not arrange a wedding, (but...)

When Archilochus represents a young man who tries to invert the arm of the fathers and to gain power over father Lycambes by invoking the god of fathers, we find the same formula. The fox betrayed by the eagle prays to Zeus in fr. 177 W[44].

ὦ Ζεῦ, **πάτερ Ζεῦ**, σὸν μὲν οὐρανοῦ κράτος,
  σὺ δ' ἔργ'ἐπ'ἀνθρώπων ὁρᾷς
λεωργὰ καὶ θεμιστά, σοῦ δὲ θηρίων
  ὕβριός τε καὶ δίκη μέλει.

Zeus, father Zeus yours is the rule in heaven
  you oversee men's deeds
wicked and lawful, and both
  the violence and the justice of beasts are your concern (Gerber)

The fact that the fox suddenly leaves the fiction of speaking animals and appeals to Zeus' reliability to both domains, animal *and* human, makes the fox' speech a prayer of Archilochus himself. As we have seen, the image of Zeus as a father is not restricted to the iambus, though one could say that the hymn to Aphrodite and especially Hesiod are sometimes polemic towards the *Odyssey.*

The following example that does not represent the male point of view only is less suspicious: In Alcman's fr. 5.2 II 22 Calame (= fr. 81 Campbell) it is a girl who seems to believe that an invocation of Zeus could influence her father's choice:

Ζεῦ πάτερ, αἰ γὰρ ἐμὸς πόσις εἴη·
Father Zeus, if only he were my husband! (Campbell)

The beginning of another 7th-century epos, the *Cypria*, represents a dialogue Zeus has with Themis about the heroic generation[45]. Mother earth complains that they are too heavy an ἄχθος, expression of a real or forged agrarian crisis[46]. Zeus has to act although, according to the *Works and Days*, he is the Ζεὺς ... πατήρ of the heroes. Therefore, he acts like a human father: he chooses to kill them in two long wars, but then he prefers to change the procedure and sends them to a sort of colony on an island near the Oceanus.

We have seen that at least in the 7th-century tradition not only in the iambus but also in the epos the expression Ζεὺς πατήρ is not a simple honorific title, but focuses on Zeus as a paternal god reliable for all that makes fathers. The *Odyssey* shows the same irony or reenactment of the formula when Zeus' daughter accuses her father (Ζεῦ πάτερ *Od*. 5.8) with the words "be no more king kind like a father (as Odysseus was)" implying that Zeus as god of the fathers does not protect him. Zeus seems to feel the irony, at any rate he retorts with irony ("wasn't it you who had this idea? "). Alcinous too prays to Zeus (Ζεῦ πάτερ *Od*. 7.311), when he wants Odysseus to be his daughter's bridegroom. Hephaestus calls his father-in-law Ζεῦ πάτερ, in Demodocus' song (*Od*. 8.306). Laertes prays to Ζεῦ πάτερ, knowing that the slaughter of the Suitors will provoke their fathers to revenge (*Od*. 24.351). The *Odyssey*, thus, takes part in the ironic reenactment of the honorific title *father Zeus*, and we can say, after all, that the associations of Odysseus with Zeus and the eagle corroborate Odysseus' image as a father. When Zeus the "chief" of all fathers, intervenes in the last scene of the *Odyssey* to stop Odysseus the eagle (*Od*. 24.539), he does not try to avoid war in itself but war between equals, between fathers. Odysseus has, thus, become a father, a husband, and an ἀνήρ.

By reading in the intertext, we saw the same strange convertibility of images we can also observe in the gender polemics between girls, wives and young men. The *Odyssey* and the iambus use both the same images "eagle" for *father*, "fox" for *young man*. The polemic does not emerge from different vocabularies or from a different set of images, but from the different use of the same images. The "fox" is negative in Homer (he lies), positive in Archilochus (he wins), an eagle is negative in the iambus (he loses) but positive in the *Odyssey*. In the same way, even the belly stands for husbands in both, iambus and epos. If the iambic audience was composed of well trained young men who mocked at the husbands because they did not continue to frequent the gymnasium, the audience of the *Odyssey* could not invert the meaning but the value: the belly becomes a sign of realism and of the Iron-Age-knowledge about needs, whereas young men such as Achilles are represented as frantic "idealistic" warriors who forget that soldiers have to eat before battle. With this observation on the way this polemic intertext works we will read, in the fourth chapter, the iambic stories "staged" in the *Odyssey*. But first we have to look for the words and the images of "the young".

Notes

[1] Segal 1994, 165ff.
[2] Bona G., Il νόος e i νόοι nell'Odissea, Torino 1966, 52, Reece S., "The Cretan 'Odyssey': A Lie Truer Than Truth", *AJP* 115 1994, 157-173. On the Colour brown cf. Russo J., *Commentary on Homer's Odyssey* III, Oxford 1992, 86.
[3] Hes. fr. 43a.41-43 M.-W.
[4] The king-motive in Aesop. *fab.* 83 (I) Hausrath.
[5] The hedgehog might be an image of female sexual parts (cf. Hipponax fr. 70.8 W): is Archilochus' text an argumentation of giving birth to children as female power? On the whole interpretation of the Margites as displaying a rather female point of view cf. Steinrück 2000, 92-97 and id., "Polémique de gender dans le Margites?", in *Polémique, critique, allusion, intertexte dans la philosophie, l'histoire et la littérature grecque du VIème avant notre ère* on http://www.unine.ch/antic/parsa/parsa03.htm. The main arguments are: every time we are told a story on Margites (in the bed-chamber, during the wedding-rites, asking who engendered him, the father or the mother), only female observers are supposed to be present (his mother-in-law, his wife, his mother, never his father, never a male friend. The mocking ressembles the way Semonides attacks women who are not adult wives, but girls still longing for their youth. A text produced for a male audience would maybe mock at men as well, but provide it with more male point of views within the text.
[6] On Pittacus cf. Plut. *De tranqu. an.* 471B1ff, the relevant text of Anacreon in fr. 13 Gentili (= 358 PMG), and Aristoph. *Nub.* 1ff.
[7] Cf. Burkert W., *Greek Religion*, Cambridge Mass. 1985, 262.
[8] Euseb. *Praeparatio evangelica* 5.32.2.
[9] West M.L. ed., *Iambi et elegi graeci ante Alexandrum cantati*, voll. I+II, Oxford 1971, I 1992.
[10] Arist. *Hist. an.* 619a 27-31, 619b 26-31 cf Pl. *NH* 10.6
[11] Arist. *Hist. an.* 620a 1-5, Plin. *NH* 10.10, Cf. Lucan 9.902-906.
[12] Greimas A./J. Courtés J., *Sémiotique, Dictionnaire raisonné de la théorie du langage II*, Paris 1986, s.v.

[13] *Od.* 2.151: Their moving in circles, the δίνη occurs elsewhere in the midpoint of bigger ring compositions. Maybe the audience associated this with the screwing movement of the text (compare the δίνη in the center of the Polyphemus composition).

[14] When Plato, in the *Laws*, interprets the story of the Suitors as that of the νέοι, he probably uses iambic features when saying that they wanted to kill the home-comers after the Trojan War. But they "did not receive them as suitable": οὐ καλῶς ἐδέξαντο. This expression is nowhere to find within the iambic texts, but Callimachus, at the end of the second iambus seems to imitate it: He tries to concentrate iambic speech about Aesopus (2.17) οὐ καλῶς ἐδέξαντο.

[15] Aesch. *Ag.* 48ff.:
μέγαν ἐκ θυμοῦ κλάζοντες ''Αρη /τρόπον αἰγυπιῶν,/ οἵτ' ἐκπατίοις ἄλγεσι παίδων/ †ὕπατο† λεχέων στροφοδινοῦνται/πτερύγων ἐρετμοῖσιν ἐρεσσόμενοι.

[16] Cf. *Od.* 3.162ff.

[17] Arist. *Hist. an.* 592b 5-6, 619b 23-25, Plin. *NH* 10.13.

[18] *Od.* 15.141ff.

[19] Pratt L. H., "'Odyssey' 19.535-50: On the Interpretation of Dreams and Signs in Homer", *CPh* 89 1994, 147-152.

[20] Cf. Foucault M., *Histoire de la sexualité* II, *L'usage des plaisirs*, Paris 1984, 205-269.

[21] Erbse H., *Beiträge zum Verständnis der Odyssee*, Berlin New York 1972, 97-109, 166-244, on Aristarchus' anthropological point of view Lehrs K., *De Aristarchi studiis homericis*, Leipzig (3)1883, 191-196 and Schmidt M., *Die Erklärungen zum Weltbild Homers und zur Kultur der Heroenzeit in den bT-Scholien zur Ilias*, München 1976, 75ff.

[22] However, readers of other times and other ideologies such as Dante or Commencini remarked more clearly that the first night of Odysseus and Penelope takes place when Odysseus is already through with his husbandry and announces his soon departure. This cannot be called an end or goal.

[23] *Cypria* 23 and 48.

[24] Rieu E.V., *Homer, The Odyssey*, Baltimore 1946.

[25] When in the *Iliad* Zeus sends a sign to the Trojans where an eagle holds a snake, Homer's audience accustomed to snake-hero-similes could understand that this sign signifying first that the husband and father Hektor will be victorious over the heroes announced in fact the Trojans' defeat: For the snake bites the eagle in the chest, and he must let fall his victim and probably die. But as seers do in Homer, the Trojan interpreter keeps silent about this detail.

[26] Cf. Hainsworth J.B., *A Commentary on Homer's Odyssey vol.* I, *Books* V-VIII, Oxford 1988. on *Od.* 6.186ff. till Odysseus enters the city. Hainsworth quotes for the same impression Marzullo.

[27] About 100 on Homer; a small choice on other authors from the first to see a round pattern Müller G., *De Aeschyli Supplicum tempore atque indole*, Halle 1908, 56 ("nam saepe orationes Supplicum ita sunt compositae ut ei qui loquuntur eo redeant, unde inceperant, et sententia in initio proposita in fine iteretur" ... "ita ut quasi orbe circumducat") to Wilamowitz U.v., *Aeschylus-Interpretationen*, Berlin 1914, 35, Ziegler K., "Lykphron" 8, *RE* 13(2), Stuttgart 1927, 2325ff., or Herter H., "Kallimachos", *RE* Suppl. 5, 1931, 446, Katicic R., "Die Ringkomposition im ersten Buche des thukydideischen Geschichtswerkes", *WS* 70 1957, 184ff., Schmied N., *Kleine ringförmige Komposition in den vier Evangelien und der Apostelgeschichte*, Tübingen 1961, Hurst A., *Apollonios de Rhodes, manière et cohérence, contribution à l'étude de l'esthétique alexandrine*, Institut Suisse de Rome 1967, 41ff., Beck I., *Die Ringkomposition bei Herodot und ihre Bedeutung für die Beweistechnik*, Spudasmata 25, Hildesheim New York 1971 against ring composition in Homer Hainsworth J.B., Rec. Lohmann,. *JHS* 92 1972, 187f. ("That certain regularities of structure exist is clear, as it is clear that structural rules of this degree of

rigidity do not exist,...However, it is not to be disputed that a tendency to certain arrangements exists").

[28] A lot of ancient and modern texts such as Pindar's, Herodotus', the New Testament, Gotthelf's novels or films such as *Pulp Fiction* show the same principle but cannot be analyzed in terms of *Homeric* ring composition. Other texts are simply reluctant to this approach.

[29] Arguments for this and the following descriptions in Steinrück 1997.

[30] Bertman S., "Structural Symmetry at the End of the Odyssey", *GRBS* 9 1968, 115-123.

[31] Aristoteles *Rhet.* 1418b23 says, that Archilochus represents the ἦθος, the character expressed by the style, "of a father speaking about his daughter". Archenaktides must be the father (so Burnett A. P., *Three Archaic Poets: Archilochus, Alcaeus, Sappho,* Cambridge, Mass.1983.), and not Lycambes (so Treu M. ed., *Archilochos*, München 1959), since "*the* father" has an article and because he is mentioned in the first line after the direct discourse. Neither can the father mean Archilochus' father (so Lasserre F. Bonnard A. edd., *Archiloque, fragments*, Paris 1958, with Archenaktides as bridegroom), if our hypothesis is right. Line 12 according to Peek.

[32] Cf. Men. *Sam.* 727f.:
προῖκα τἀμὰ πάνθ' ὅταν ἀποθάνω γ' ὃ μὴ γένοιτ' ἀλλ' <εἰς> ἀεὶ ζώην.

[33] The linguist Herodianus in fr. 115 W stresses a similar figure of Archilochus, the declension of names.

[34] Fränkel H., *Dichtung und Philosophie, Eine Geschichte der griechischen Epik, Lyrik und Prosa bis zur Mitte des 5. Jh.*, München 1962, 154, takes Charon seriously and thinks that in the continuation another person will be attacked (also cf. p. 153 n. 12). But Aristotle (*Rhet.* 1418b23) makes clear that Charon's ἦθος is aimed. Furthermore, also in the imitation in Horace's *ep.* 2.67 is the speaking "I" (Alfius) a third person and he is mocked.

[35] Radermacher L. ed., *Der homerische Hermeshymnus*, Wien 1931, thought that the *hMerc* could be dated of the 5th c. BC. The type of puns we find in this text could corroborate such a hypothesis.

[36] Cf. fr. 25 W. on the seer Batusiades who seems to come to public events like games to preach the future without seeing that his own house is meanwhile burning.

[37] "ἀφραίνει ξεῖνος νέον ἄλλοθεν εἰληλουθώς.   360
ἀλλά μιν αἶψα, νέοι, δόμου ἐκπέμψασθε θύραζε
εἰς ἀγορὴν ἔρχεσθαι, ἐπεὶ τάδε νυκτὶ ἔίσκει."

[38] Gerber D. E. (ed. vert.), *Greek Iambic Poetry*, Cambridge Mass. London 1999.

[39] Cf. Ps.-Long., *De subl.* 9.10.

[40] *Il.* 4.339-355, in the epipolesis. The trick works, even the tricky Odysseus gets angry and Agamemnon smiles (ἐπιμειδήσας ... ὡς γνῶ χωομένοιο *Il.* 4. 356f.).

[41] *HVen* 22ff.

[42] Fr. 7, 22f. Pellizer-Tedeschi (Ὀλύμπιοι / ἔδωκαν ἀνδρί)

[43] Hes. *Op.* 59ff.

[44] In fr. 25 W., Archilochus might mock his own procedure of introducing in the first lines of an iambus a speech without indication of the speaker. Everybody might think that once again, Archilochus lets speak another, but this time it is "Archilochus" speaking. In this perhaps self-ironic text Archilochus recommends himself with *father Zeus*.

[45] Cf. T 14.5 Davies

[46] Cf. Schol. Il. 1.5 = F 1 Davies

5 "Calves"

5.1 Oxen

The first time we hear of young men in the *Odyssey*, they are related to cows. According to the proem, Odysseus' fellows must die because they slaughtered the cows of Sun. The first impression we get of their brothers, the *Suitors*, is that of slaughterers of cows, too. When Athena, disguised as a captain of pirates and ancient host of Odysseus, arrives at the court of the Ithacan palace, the first thing she sees, and following her eyes, we see, are Suitors sitting on the furs of cows they slaughtered themselves (*Od.* 1.108):

ἥμενοι ἐν ῥινοῖσι βοῶν οὓς ἔκτανον αὐτοί
sitting on the hides of oxen they themselves had slaughtered (Rieu)

The Scholiae read the description as expression of violence. However, a comparison with the very imperfect way the fellows try to sacrifice Helios' cows (they have no sacrificial barley and use leaves[1]) gives us a hint how to read those carpets with the eyes of a Homeric audience. Furs of sacrificed animals often belong to the priest or if it is a "private" sacrifice maybe to the owner—but it is the owner who sacrifices. The Suitors, however, did not wait for an offer of Penelope or someone else. They killed the animals themselves and used the furs as carpets; maybe they even did not sacrifice at all. This might be an allusion to their status: the sacrifice of blood is reserved to men. Even in men-excluding female festivities, the only man is a sacrificer. But on the male side of the gender-system there is a similar opposition (if not structurally the same) between non-adult and adult. The non-initiated, non-married ephebes can stem the oxen to be sacrificed, but normally they do not cut the animal's throat. The Suitors as young men show an ambiguous behavior: There are passages where the sacrificial rite is mentioned in their context, but usually absence or imperfection of the sacrificial rite marks them (whereas "the unmarried good slave" Eumaeus seems to be almost an expert of it).

Except for the allusion to sacrifice, what might strike a goddess like Athena first? What is actually wrong with the killing of cows or oxen? For sure it is not simply the enormous value of these animals. When the hero of young men, Herakles, attempts to defy the tyran Syleus, the father of a possible bride, he starts with devouring his oxen[2]. This can be read as an attack at Syleus' goods. But then, Herakles kills Syleus himself. The association of young men and ox killing repeats and is worth a broader look into the ancient Greek "syntax" of images.

If man-killer and ox-killer go together, the ox might be an image not so much of the father as of the husband. Oxen work with the husbands on the ground. Archilochus associates once a "proud ox" with "the house"[3]. The first stage of the Athenian wedding-rite evokes this marriage-image: During the *eggúe*, the bride-father says to the bridegroom: "I give you my daughter, ground to sow"[4]. But this is not the only acceptation of the image. When Homeric Clytaemestra slaughters her husband "like an ox" with the sacrificial tool, the double-axe, the connotation is mainly sacrificial[5]. But Cassandra in Aeschylus' *Agamemnon* goes further. She designates Agamemnon as a bull and Clytaemestra as a cow[6]. When in the beginning of the play the spy has held his prologue and hears the chorus of old men entering the orchestra, he introduces his silence by a superposition of the old men's and an ox' steps: "an ox stood on my tongue"[7].

Young men are not oxen, but when one half of Odysseus fellows are transformed into swine, Odysseus goes for freeing them and leaves the other half "alone". When he comes back they are waiting for him, desperately, and receive him like calves are longing for their mother-cow (*Od.* 10.410):

ὡς ὅτ'ἂν ἄγραυλοι πόριες περὶ βοῦς ἀγελαίας

"when cows come home full-fed from the pastures and are welcomed by their frisking calves" (Rieu)

The Scholiae explain the word πόριες by νέαι βόες, young cows or calves, an image which would fit the Italian gender-system, where young men, in another situation but with similar imagery are called "vitelloni", big calves. Cows or oxen are thus an image of adult, married people, male or female. Odysseus is described as an ox like Agamemnon, a father or husband when facing young men. We now understand, what the connotation might be the first impression Athena gets of the Suitors: sitting *on* the skins of cows they slaughtered themselves. They are against established husbands and are able to kill them. It is noteworthy, that Medon, the only Suitor-near servant Odysseus does not want to kill after he slaughtered the young men, signalizes his obedience by hiding *under* an oxen's skin[8].

Even when Callimachus 300 years later tries to re-invent the iambus by substituting the aggressive iambic style of the battle (μάχη) for a rather "fair" struggle among scholars and poets, for a καλή μάχη this pun on "Calli-machus'" name is iterated by a pun of what seemed to him representative of the iambic style: Hipponax himself comes back from the

Underworld to speak. But he does not say "underworld", he says: "I am coming from that place where a 'bous' is worth nothing (in hell, prices fall), so I shall no more fight in a bou-paleian battle". Not only is the ox representative of iambic aggressive style (without "bous", iambus is tamed), even the iambic husband Boupalos is associated with an ox[9].

5.2 Young men

These are the images. We have already observed that the concept of young unmarried men fits very well the two sons of Aigyptios which did not inherit the father's ground but went, one to the war with the king, the other to the group of the Suitors. But how are they called[10]? The word we take from Archilochus fr. 196a W, the νέοι ἄνδρες, this very fragile colloquial expression sometimes replaced by νέοι, sometimes by ἄνδρες, appears in the *Odyssey* and determines the Suitors[11]. Aigyptios himself asks a question, at the beginning of the 2nd book-assembly, involving the division of the Ithacan male state into the young men and the "older" men (*Od.* 2.28f.):

Νῦν δὲ τίς ὧδ' ἤγειρε; τίνα χρειὼ τόσον ἵκει
ἠὲ **νέων ἀνδρῶν** ἢ οἳ προγενέστεροί εἰσιν;

"Who is it that has summoned us now, one of the old men or one
of the young men? And what emergency has made him take this step?"

We could think, that Aigyptios asks whether young men or older men assembled the people. But according to the accent and the commentary of the Scholiae, this is not the pattern of the question[12]. Therefore Aigyptios does not ask a double question, he simply asks "who" and distinguishes the two groups from which the "assembler" might come. One of them is called the νέοι ἄνδρες.

One might also object that νέος could simply mean the opposite of προγενέστερος, of "first-born or older" and that the distinction is one of age of mostly married men and not of social status between married and unmarried. But we have seen that in this case all young men present really are unmarried, they are μνηστῆρες.

Furthermore there is a difference in power each group has. The νέοι ἄνδρες, are strong by number, they impose their rules to the other group. In order to abolish their rules, Odysseus would have to disperse them. The Narrator expresses this in *Od.* 1.116f.:

μνηστήρων τῶν μὲν σκέδασιν κατὰ δώματα θείη,
τιμὴν δ'αὐτὸς ἔχοι καὶ κτήμασιν οἷσιν ἀνάσσοι.

drive all these Suitors pell-mell from the house,
and so regain his royal honors and reign over his own (after Rieu)

"King" Odysseus would have a gathered power himself by the τιμή the δῆμος gives him without arrogation. The two types of power, the two groups reappear in other texts as an almost accepted reality and show the same conflict between young men and old. This cannot be simply the opposition between two "classes d'âge", young and old, but rather between the husbands and the elder non-married, which would have some power by age, but not by their social position. The rich and first-born ephebes bound to marry might hesitate between the two groups, but the ideology of the *Odyssey* or of the iambi seems to link them rather to the husbands. Nevertheless, there is an ambiguity, well perceptible in the linguistic use. When Aigyptios asks who assembled people Telemachus answers him as an epheb bound to get married (Nestor will tell him) and as a boy who has been told he is no longer one and who has presented himself already twice as an ἀνήρ (*Od.* 2. 40):

οὐχ ἑκὰς οὗτος **ἀνήρ**, τάχα δ' εἴσεαι αὐτός
ὅς λαὸν ἤγειρα.

"The man who summoned that gathering is not far to seek
It was I –" (Rieu)

Already in *Od.* 1.358, Telemachus has strengthened this specific gender-status by opposing himself to the women, represented, then, by the queen. The confrontation with his mother is told as one important stage of a whole proxemic evolution. Firstly, Athena has waked Telemachus from boyish fears. She had to deliver him from his encapsulation, the uncertainty of being his father's son. After this initial impulse, Telemachus reaches wider and wider spaces to act within: first the inner realm of the house, the female one, then the outer realm, of men, then the politics of the demos (the assembly), and finally, the world of Pylos and Sparta. Within this development (in the etymological sense of the word), the encounter with his mother is the first occasion to affirm himself as a man. There is maybe a touch of irony on the lips of the Narrator. For when Athena leaves the boy alone with the Suitors, the singer Phemius still performs what the Suitors like: disastrous returns of the fathers such as the killing of Agamemnon. This provokes Penelope behind her curtain to an intrusion into male territory: In a maybe too maternalistic tone as if she spoke to children, she forbids the theme she cannot stand. And Telemachus, though politically on her side, takes advantage of the scene in order to affirm himself as a member of men: he defends their right to hear what they want and, offended that she spoke directly to the singer and not to him, he underscores his new position (*Od.* 1.358):

> Μῦθος δ' ἄνδρεσσι μελήσει.
> μάλιστα δ'ἐμοὶ· τοῦ γὰρ κράτος ἐστ' ἐνὶ οἴκῳ.
>
> "The story must be the men's concern
> and mine in particular; for I am a master in this house."

And yet this does not mean that Telemachus would count himself among the adult, it simply means, that ἀνήρ has another meaning in a sheer male context than in a mixed one. Telemachus invokes his solidarity with the ἄνδρε as an opposition to the γυναῖκες. The order he implies is very different when Penelope has him left alone with the Suitors. He announces the assembly for the other day and explains its function: to get rid of the Suitors. Their reaction is rather amused then furious: they mock at him by asking whether he has the intention to become a king (or however we translate the word βασιλεύς). It has been shown that Telemachus reacts for the first time as a real son of Odysseus. He puts on the mask of what he is no more, the mask of a naive little boy: "what is wrong with becoming a king, it's a good thing to be a king" (*Od.* 1.392). He not only makes the Suitors forget their suspicions he might have become a serious rival, but also releases their natural fear he might attend to the father's place. For the boy seems to allude not to "the one King" of Ithaca, but to the "kings", the princes, the chiefs (*Od.* 1.394f.):

> ἀλλ' ἤτοι βασιλῆες Ἀχαιῶν εἰσι καὶ ἄλλοι
> πολλοὶ ἐν ἀμφιάλῳ Ἰθάκῃ, νέοι ἠδὲ παλαιοί.
>
> "However the Achaeans are not short of kings;
> young and old they swarm in sea girt Ithaca." (Rieu)

There are young and old "kings". This could of course make think of something like a "ancien" and "nouveau régime", something like the old king Odysseus and the new king chosen by the Suitors, but Telemachus underlines the plural (πολλοί). There are not only two of them but several on both sides, the young and the old. Thus Telemachus, alone among the men, invokes the bipartition of young and old kings, which cannot mean either of adults and children.

In the same line, we can find an allusion to a normal double male institution when at the end of the assembly Telemachus tries to ask for a ship. In *Od.* 2.293 Mentor reminds both the fathers and the Suitors, that there are many ships at disposition "νέαι ἠδὲ παλαιαί". It is a little bit absurd to think that there are a lot of new made ships. It makes more sense to think that this is a hypallage and refers to the two parts of the audience: ships belonging to the institution of the old, and others that are at the disposition of the young warriors.

As in Canadian native tribes the bipartition of the young and the old chiefs is doubled by two councils[13], the Suitors Antinous and Eurymachus bear the title of a "king", a *basileus*. However, even if we can find the same opposition in the Iliadic world of warriors, this system's words, like in the gender-system, are by no means objective, but depend on the gendered viewpoint. On the linguistic level, at least, the specification of young men and old men, as well as the initiation opposition between ephebes and men has its importance within the male society only. Ephebes differ from young men by their expectancy of being husbands; they are potentially "men" and seem to be on their side at least from the viewpoint of young men. But all this differentiation is fading from a female viewpoint: all these groups can be called either νέοι or ἄνδρες (*Od.* 17.502). Similarly, the differentiation between παρθένοι and γυναῖκες can disappear to a male eye. Thus, when young men are described in relation to women, they can be called ἄνδρες[14]. But from a critic male eye the same group is called νέοι ἄνδρες. When Odysseus asks who did fail to care about his hunting dog Argos, the answer comes from Eumaeus, the "good" slave whose ideology is even more correct than Odysseus'. From his point of view only one group of the men can be as careless: the νέοι ἄνδρες (*Od.* 17.294). They used Argos for hunting, but did not preserve its ἀρετή as the Suitors do not preserve the goods of Odysseus' palace. Opposed to a beggar, Irus, the Suitors are called νέοι only (*Od.* 18.6).

Another point of view is the opposition between gods and humans. Rather puzzling, for instance, might be the mask that Athena wears in the center of the *Odyssey*, when Odysseus woke up on the beach of Ithaca without acknowledging his own island. The goddess approaches the human in the body of a νέος ἀνήρ (*Od.* 13.222). The expression, however, is ambivalent: ἀνδρὶ δέμας εἰκυῖα νέῳ. On one hand ἀνήρ might be used as "male human" in opposition to a goddess, on the other hand the clothes of Athena get an erotic appeal to express the beauty of a young man or epheb. This second aspect would be justified by its opposition to the bald γέρων into which Odysseus will be turned at the end of this scene[15].

5.3 A bipartition

One use of the word νέος is left to be discussed, the comparative νεώτερος. Sometimes, this comparative could be interpreted as the expression of the (supposed) archaic shame (or politeness) of saying things in a direct or absolute way. Thus one might understand νεώτερος (with respect to the older) as a polite way of saying "young". But there are passages using νεώτερος in the precise meaning of "younger than". When, on Circe's island, Odysseus' fellows are freed from their pig's shape, they have become νεώτεροι in the meaning of "younger than they were before". A similar passage is to be found in the assembly scene of the second book where the youngsters meet one of their genuine enemies, the seer Halitherses. Halitherses is caught between the camps. A member of Odysseus' court, he defends the king and reads the signs in his favor. But he takes part in the feasts of the Suitors and will pay his lacking of loyalty with his life (the name can be translated as the one whose courage is in vain). In the assembly Halitherses' reading of the eagle sign gives them the impression that he works for the establishment, a seer paid for telling lies and fairy tales to young men as if they were children. The young men's enlightenment-ideology can be felt in their threatening. They declare their own threatening as prophecy (*Od.* 2.188f.):

> αἴ κε νεώτερον ἄνδρα παλαιά τε πολλά τε εἰδώς
> παρφάμενος ἐπέεσσιν ἐποτρύνῃς χαλεπαίνειν
>
> If you, his senior, with the ideology of the old
> misuse your eloquence to incite this younger man to reluctance. ...

This is a curious inversion of the accusation against Socrates. The Suitors warn the representative of the old not to set people younger than the Suitors against the Suitors. Halitherses' ideology is well expressed by εἰδέναι + *an adjective neuter plural*. This expression usually means "to have the temper of". Thus, παλαιὰ εἰδώς probably means exactly that the seer not only knows a lot, but also that he has a "conservative attitude", that he is a representative of the fathers, who could easily persuade the epheb to defend their cause. Otherwise νεώτεροι is frequent but precise and does never occur in opposition to the old, whereas νέος, νέος ἀνήρ or the formula νέων ὑπερηνορεόντων do.

A similar bipartition is to be found in wartime. In Euripides' *Hecuba*, the last daughter of Hekabe is to be sacrificed. The mother thinks of the groups of youngsters and their leader Neoptolemus when she expresses her fear the Greeks could abuse her Polyxena's body. Later the messenger tells her how they killed Polyxena and confirms that the sacrifice was exclusively performed by the νέοι[16]. Polyxena, he says, tried to save her chastity by claiming help from the γέροντες, from Agamemnon. She claimed to be ready to die but in another way and Agamemnon changed the rite of the young people[17]. Eteocles, at the beginning of Aeschylus' *Seven against Thebes* speaks as well to two parts of the army, the young and the old[18].

We also can see this bipartition in Callinus' and Tyrtaeus' elegies. Even the form of the composition corresponds[19]: two halves (in each text), each shaped as a ring composition of equal length, try to induce the husbands and the νέοι to fight. The husbands are reminded of their wives and children and threatened by expulsion in case they refuse. Raising the independent νέοι, which might be expulsed at any rate, is a more difficult matter. In order to push them to die in the first rank, an erotic rhetoric is used: Rather than to be alive and to provoke the desire of women and men, death, so claim the poets, would be beautiful and can offer them the love or the acknowledgment they are longing for. The change of the tune is important: reasons for the husbands, a rather rude tone for the youngsters.

Another event of the Spartan "history" of the 8th (or 7th) c. shows very well the link between the young and the older warrior class. The first Messenian war becomes that long that the Spartans fear a lack of progeny. They decide to send the young warriors (as one source explains, the one, who did not swear the oath) to sleep with the girls (or the wives). Yet the descendants of these youngsters are called the "Partheniai", the sons of girls or the girlish and shall not be acknowledged by the Spartans[20]. As they claim their civil rights, the Spartans send them away to found a colony.

The legend, true or not, reflects at least, that the second part of the army exists in Sparta too, that their civil rights are not without doubt, and that therefore they are not necessarily held to take part in war. And this could be the scenario to which the Iliad-plot alludes. In the *Iliad* there is a council of the old that consists of Odysseus, Agamemnon, Aias, and of course Nestor. Sometimes, a young but married warrior, Diomedes joins the group. Even if the elder members mock at him his case shows that not age but social status enables him to take part in it[21]. There is no official council of the youngsters in the *Iliad*, but in the beginning of the text, an unmarried youngster gathers an assembly. A sex and honor-quarrel results from it, which—in addition to the narrative function—could presuppose tensions between the young and the old in the army[22]. The young warrior Achilles who assembled the Greeks has not only his own troops, the Myrmidons. He also represents the young unmarried in Agamemnon's eyes. For Achilles refuses to continue to fight and after some defeats Agamemnon has to acknowledge that he cannot win the war without Achilles who (at least in some of the versions) is not held by oath to take part in. In the 9th book of the *Iliad*, Agamemnon tries to make up his failure without losing his face. He does not go himself for negotiations but sends two heralds and two members of the council, Odysseus and Aias, a delegation joined by the unmarried Phoenix[23]. During this assembly of the old, Agamemnon tries to impress the other by his list of reparations, rather a demonstration of power than an expression of how sorry he is.

Latacz's reading of this passage is interesting in this context[24]. Agamemnon promises that he had no sexual intercourse with Briseis, the girl he took from Achilles although—and here is the strange expression—"this would be normal between husbands and wives" (ἣ θέμις ἐστ' ἀνδρῶν τε γυναικῶν). Agamemnon's remarks on another girl, Chryseis, make sure that by *husband* he refers to himself, by *wives* to Briseis. This, Latacz said, could be a sarcastic allusion to the different social status of Achilles. The Roman dramatist Seneca seems to have read this passage in the same way. He defines Achilles as *nondum vir*, not yet a husband or a man[25]. But to go back to the *Iliad*, Agamemnon promises to help Achilles for reaching the upper status and to accept him as bridegroom in his own family. This would be a marriage by which Achilles would not bring home a girl that would give him paternal rights on her, but the type of wedding where the girl remains under the control of her father. Even if Achilles has other motives for refusing, only poor Heroes would accept this bargain. All the more, husband Agamemnon implies that bachelor's Achilles' relationship with Briseis is nothing serious and socially misfit. Neither the king nor the members of the council of the old can seriously expect Achilles to accept this part of the reparations. The opposition between Agamemnon and Achilles remains that of *married-unmarried*.

It is true, the *Iliad* pays less attention to the exact distinction between νέοι and γέροντες, perhaps because its story is entirely heroic whereas the *Odyssey* is more precise with regard to the bipartition between the heroic time (of the νέοι) and the adult époque. But the difference of the two groups is very well reflected by what happens in the *Iliad*, when Achilles refuses to take part in the war with his Myrmidons. The γέροντες have to reorganize the whole battle order. Nestor sends the ἄνδρες in their original political organizations (φρατρίαι and φῦλα), which are all summoned to affront the enemy and not to stay behind. This time, he says they will fight by themselves (κατὰ σφέας γὰρ μαχέονται *Il.* 2.266). Commentators wondered what could be new in this reorganization[26]. However, this can imply one thing: Achilles and the Myrmidons formed the first rank. They took the risk the νέοι took in Homer's time: to fight as kamikazes who bite like ants even if they are to be killed—this is an old meaning of the metaphor *Ants* or *Myrmidons*—and to die before the old[27]. This order fits exactly the epithet associated with Achilles during the quarrel (*Il.* 1.505): ἕρκος' Ἀχαιῶν, the "protection-wall of the Greeks"[28]. With Tyrtaeus we can read this as "the first rank". Without this wall, Nestor must dissolve the broad phalanges that were behind the Myrmidons and place several contingents in front in order to distribute the risk of death among all the contingents. As this does not work, they replace the wall of young men by a real wall, a metaphoric transfer the Spartans made inversely by affirming that the city of Sparta does not need a wall, because it has already a wall of men.

If thus Achilles and his "Ants" are associated with the Tyrtaean νέοι in battle whereas Agamemnon represents the husbands[29] we should find as well an argument for associating the Suitors of the *Odyssey* with the wall and with Achilles. In fact there is a metaphor Odysseus uses himself to designate the Suitors in *Od.* 23.121f.

ἡμεῖς δ' ἕρμα πόληος ἀπέκταμεν, οἳ μέγ' ἄριστοι
κοῦροι εἰν Ἰθάκῃ, τὰ δέ σε φράζεσθαι ἄνωγα·

"But we have killed the wall of the city, the pick
of the Ithacan young nobility. There is a problem for you."

Odysseus knows that he not only killed the children in the eyes of very important families, but also from the point of view of the rest of the δῆμος: by slaughtering the Suitors he destroyed the "wall of the city" in case of war. Another link between Achilles and the Suitors is established at the end of the *Odyssey*, by the representation of their death: guided by Hermes they arrive directly at Achilles' place, be it the isle of Blessed or in general the realm where the heroes of the Trojan war dwell after their death.

To conclude this investigation of the term νέος: there is a special use of νέος within the male area during peace. The bipartition between married and unmarried men reappears in war. This opposition will survive some time to the end of the *genre* iambus (and to some extent of the epos) at the end of the 6th century, with Socrates and his νέοι of the 5th, with the new comedies on the νέοι and the corporations of νέοι in the 4th century. In Hellenistic age the political power of the νεανίσκαρχος in Hellenistic Egypt seems to reflect that the opposition we found between the epos and the iambus has disappeared together with the redefinition of the *genre*s iambus and Epos and of the gender.

The aim of this book is to perceive the role of the νέοι from the intertextual polemic between the Epos, with special regard to the polemic character of the Epos. Its attack can explain the strange tendency of the Narrator to apologize as in the beginning of the *Odyssey* (*Od.* 1.6):

ἀλλ' οὐδ' ὣς ἐτάρους ἐρρύσατο ἱέμενός περ.
αὐτῶν γὰρ σφετέρῃσιν ἀτασθαλίῃσιν ὄλοντο
"But he failed to save those comrades, in spite of all his efforts.
It was their own fault that brought them to their doom."

"Qui s'excuse s'accuse". Weren't there the attacks of the fathers, we would not understand why a proem has to say that the young men are responsible for their death themselves. Although the *Odyssey* explains that the death of the fellows and that of the Suitors is necessary for the re-marriage of Odysseus, this expresses as well a strange bad conscience for killing sons of fathers. The same pattern of an excuse with regard to an implicit blame can be found some verses later, at the beginning of the divine assembly (*Od.* 1.32).

ὢ πόποι οἷον δή νυ θεοὺς βροτοὶ αἰτόωνται·
ἐξ ἡμέων γάρ φασι κάκ' ἔμμεναι· οἱ δὲ καὶ **αὐτοί**
σφῇσιν ἀτασθαλίῃσιν ὑπὲρ μόρον ἄλγε' ἔχουσιν.
What a lamentable thing is that men should blame the gods
and regard us as the source of their troubles, when it's as well their own
wickedness that brings them sufferings worse than any which Destiny allots them.

It is the father Zeus whom we sketched in the first half of this chapter, this father-god who defends himself against human accusations. He thinks about a young man killed by his own fault. An intertextual answer to his speech might be the lament of an unidentified son of Zeus at the end of the *Catalogue of women*[30]. He is disappointed of the father's βουλή: the decision to kill all the heroes in a war (or to send them on an island). Zeus' attitude can be described as typical of the father of young men and might explain his bad feelings. He does not apologize by denying his responsibility for the βουλή and the death of young men; he only says that Aegisthus is *also* responsible. But this is only one of the many iambic stories the *Odyssey* alludes to.

Notes

[1] *Od.* 12.357ff. For the rules of sacrifice Durand J.-L., *Sacrifice et labour en Grèce ancienne, essai d'anthropologie religieuse*, Paris Roma 1986, and Vernant J.-P., "À la table des hommes. Mythe de fondation du sacrifice chez Hésiode", in M. Detienne J.-P. Vernant edd., *La cuisine du sacrifice en pays grec*, Paris 1979, 60.
[2] Diod. 4.31.7.

[3] Cf. Archilochus fr. 35 Gerber where a proud ox is associated to the house.
[4] Cf. for instance Menandrus, *Samia*, 741f.
[5] On this subject Viret-Bernal F., *Au fil de la lame*, Paris 2007.
[6] Cassandra in Aeschylus, *Ag*. 1125f. ἆ ἆ, ἰδοῦ ἰδοῦ· ἄπεχε τᾶς βοὸς τὸν ταῦρον·
[7] This proverbial expression is used in Aesch. *Ag*. 36f.
[8] *Od.* 22.362-364: The theme of the oxen's skin is highlighted by a parallelistic repetition.
[9] Call. *Iamb.* 1.1-4 Pf.
[10] On the young also Lateiner D., *Sardonic Smile, Nonverbal Behavior in Homeric Epic*, Ann Arbor 1995, and Yamagata N., "Young and Old in Homer and in Heike Monogatari", *G&R* 40 1993, 1-10.
[11] Clearly unmarried "young men" in Aristoph. *Eccl.* 1015, Archil. fr. 196a.14 W. On the oscillation between κοῦρος and νέος ἀνήρ Ulf Ch., *Die homerische Gesellschaft*, München 1990, 59.
[12] According to the scholia the particles ἠὲ .. ἤ are not part of the question (like in attic πότερον ... ἤ), but are disjunctive conjunctions : οὗτοι μὲν ἐγκλίνονται διαζευκτικοὶ ὄντες.
[13] Cf. Bonanni M., *Il cerchio e la piramide, l'epica omerica e le origini del politico*, Bologna 1992.
[14] On the relation between male and female cf. Steinrück M., "*Gender* ou initiation", forthcoming in *actes du VIIIe Congrès des Historiennes* (Genève 27-28. 9.1996).
[15] In this scene all possible gender-roles are presented before they become crucial in the second part of the *Odyssey*: Odysseus is first opposed as an ἀνήρ to a νέος ἀνήρ, then, when Athena changes herself into a γυνή, Odysseus is transmogrified into a γέρων.
[16] Eur. *Hec.* 547ff.
[17] Polyxena had the right to die without being lashed, like Iphigeneia. The young protest against the order of the old. Within the army of the Euripidean theatre, neither Neoptolemus nor Agamemnon seem to have an absolute power of decision. Polyxena reacts by leaving it up to the king of the young: she bids him throat and naked breasts, offering herself to both, sexual abuse and sacrifice. Neoptolemus goes - but unwilling as the text ads more precisely - for sacrifice and cuts her throat. Loraux underlined the sexual metaphors of the passage and read it as a rape. Mossman J., *Wild Justice, A Study of Euripides' Hecuba*, Oxford 1995, 143 ff., saw the death of a warrior rather. But to these aims, both of them have to change or to put under suspicion the text. Those problems could be solved by accepting the bipartition of the army as one of the conditions of the strange scene.
[18] Aesch. *Septem* 10f.
[19] Callinus fr. 1 W, Tyrtaeus fr. 10 W.
[20] The story in Strabo, 6.3.2, on the word Ogden D., *Greek Bastardy in the Classical and Hellenistic Period*, Oxford 1996, 18.
[21] We have thus not to wonder why according to the *Nostoi* (Sévryns A., *Le cycle épique dans l'école d'Aristarque*, Paris 1928, 276) Diomedes shares the husbands' (Odysseus', Agamemnon's, Idomeneus') destiny of being challenged by a νέος after his return.
[22] The order of Plato's ideal state goes so far to claim only unmarried men and women to be warriors. It is noteworthy that those unmarried policemen and –women are associated with the people of the Heroes which, according to Hesiod, lived before the Iron people representing the lowest platonic position, the working class, but after the δίκαιοι whose correspondents in Plato's state, the philosophers, take the role of rulers.
[23] I see enough arguments in the narrative structure of this passage to follow Segal's solution of the "Dual problem" (the duals are the two heralds). Segal Ch., "The Embassy and the Duals of Iliad 9.182-89", *GRBS* 9 1968, 101ff.
[24] Latacz 1996.

[25] In Sen. *Tro.* 343. Agamemnon still says, he is "nondum vir".
[26] Cf. Kirk G.S., *The Iliad, A Commentary I: books 1-4*, Cambridge London 1985, 154f. on *Il.* 2.362-366.
[27] For the meaning of *ants* cf. West 1997, 500; Archilochus (fr. 23.16 West) uses the same metaphor for a probably unworthily married man and thus, maybe, a "still" young man in the eyes of his wife.
[28] Latacz J., Kampfparänese, *Kampfdarstellung und Kampfwirklichkeit in der Ilias, bei Kallinos und Tyrtaios*, München, 1977, has shown that the first fighters, the πρόμαχοι of the *Iliad* are to be understood as single fighters, teasing the enemy by jumping into the field between the armies. But Van Wees H., "The Homeric Way of War: The 'Iliad' and the Hoplite Phalanx I + II", *G&R* 41 1994, 1-18, 131-155, has also shown that several times the contemporary (of Homer) conception of a phalanx is present as well.
[29] ...A strange reflection of the pragmatic relationship between the Heroic-young-Age of the text and the Iron adult Age of the audience.
[30] Fr. 204.120ff. M-W.

6 Stories

There are several equivalents to the Suitors. Cook has already demonstrated that the Suitors have the same relation to Odysseus and his son as Aegisthus towards Agamemnon and his son[1]. However, the Suitors and Aegistus fall into the group of the young men who stayed at home. The one sent to found a colony is represented by the Phaeacians, the group of spear-fodder by Odysseus' young fellows. Odysseus loses/kills the latter two groups without consciousness, asleep in both cases, while the fellows sacrifice in an odd way the Sun's cows and during the journey to Ithaca that will cost the young ferrymen's lives. By doing so he also kills or loses another member of the young men, the one Odysseus used to be himself.

6.1 The pattern of erotic adventure

In the *Odyssey*, the Narrator sometimes uses iambic narratives to speak of young men. Since they like to listen to them, those stories characterize the young men. The common theme of these stories is the phantasm of unsuccessful Suitors, of how young men could persuade a girl or a wife to make love to them against the rules (feared even by Zeus and Hera) before or despite of marriage. In Hipponax' texts we find at least twice the story of how the narrating "I" slept with a girl or a wife by night after having entered the door. It appears from the fragments that this theme is sometimes connected to a fight between the youngster and the older father (of the girl) or husband. The young man of course wins. On the narratological level, the girls or wives often play a helper's part, as does Hermes, often called *he who strangulates dogs* (in order to cover burglars at night). Unfortunately, Hipponax' fragments 84 W and 104 W are very mutilated. But the narrative elements are still perceptible. We take fr. 84.10ff. as an example:

    ἐκδύντες α[10
    ἐδάκνομέν τε κἀφ[ιλέομεν
    διὲκ θυρέων βλέ[ποντες
    μὴ ἥμεας λάβ[
    γυμνοὺς ἐρυ [
    ἔσπευδε δ' ἡ μ[ὲν   15

    with our cloths off...
    we were biting and kissing...
    looking through the doors...

in case we be caught...
naked...
she was in a hurry...(Gerber)

What remains is sufficient to understand that a male "I" and a "she" form a couple of lovers who do not want to be discovered. From time to time they glance through the open door. This vigilance allows inferring the presence of a sleeping or possibly entering father/husband. Here and in other stories of Hipponax, the door is almost the only sign that evokes space. On attic vases of the 5th century BC doors indicate the female realm. In Hipponax' text, the male "I" tells his adventure and the male phantasm of female complicity. The fight, after an ambush (a λόχος) is not preserved but perhaps alluded to. In verse 18, the Narrator tells how they made love in order to make the rival cry. The ambush, however, is entirely conserved in fr. 104 of Hipponax. It starts by aorists of the 3rd person sg. Since we know from the following lines that there is a first person Narrator, we can suggest that he is in an observing position:

```
 . ] . . [
 ] . [ . ] . εξεν[
 ]τέγραψ[ε]
 ] . ρου
 ] . [ . ] . αι·                          5
 ]ησε
 ]ρρήσσων
 ήρ]αξε
 ]ιου
```

he (did something)
he scratched/wrote
...
...
he (did something)
he (doing something)
he knocked (Gerber)

Someone comes and presumably knocks on the door (ήρ]αξε). But as soon as the third person enters, a fight begins between the 3rd and the first person.

```
δακ]τύλους μεταστρέψας              10
]ος τε καὶ ῥύδην
] . ων δ'αὐτὸν ἀσκαρίζοντα
]ν ἐν τῆι γαστρὶ λὰξ ἐνώρουσα·
] . ις μὴ δοκῆι με λασθαίνειν
```

... bending back his fingers...
... and abundantly ...

... him as he squirmed...
... I jumped on his stomach...
... So that he might not have a mind to curse me (Gerber)

The third person seems to lose this fight, and we can assume that this was an ambush of the first person. What follows is a series of preparations to a love-scene: the hero gets rid of (his own?) cloths, washes his feet.

<pre>
․]δευν ἐπιβρύκων   15
]ηιον καταπλ[ί]ξας
ε]ξέδυσα τὴν χλαῖναν
πό]δας περιψήσας
τὴν] θύρην ἐπάκτωσα
]․ τὸ πῦρ κατακρύψας   20
βακκάρ]ι δὲ τὰς ῥῖνας
ἤλειφον. ἔστι δ' ο[ἵηνπερ Κροῖσος·
]ν Δασκυλείῳ
</pre>

...gnashing my teeth   15
...with legs apart
... I took off my cloak
... moping my feet clean
... I barred the door
...covering the fire   20
... I anointed my nostrils with perfume
such as Croesus had
... Daskyleion (Gerber)

The door serves once again as space-indicator. This time however, it has to be barred[2]. The bound prisoner (a father, a husband?) cannot disturb anymore, but the violent "I", still cautious, locks the door and covers the fire. But there is also a theme we know from ambushes of the *Odyssey*: he perfumes his nose. The following lines (swinging bottom, mocking prostitute) indicate that the preparing measures were not in vain.

Hipponax enacts his iambs for Greeks and Lydians in or from Ephesus, a city that was already ruled by Greek tyrants in Persian dependence. The Persians were slowly cutting down the widespread commercial links of the Ionian cities, and perhaps Hipponax' texts expressed the nostalgia of the Ephesians towards the culturally and commercially stimulating times of the Lydian Mermnads. A lot of versions circulated of how Gyges, entered the bedroom of the King and by doing so founded the dynasty of the Mermnads. Such stories, dreaming in the sub-text of rebellion against the Persians, must have been told in Hipponax' times as well and they are very close to the fantasies of young man who want to accede to power through marriage or sexuality. The most Ionian version is handed down through Herodotus: Gyges is invited, even persuaded by the King Candaules to judge the naked beauty of the queen. Herodotus explains this narrative element in a rather historical way by the king's pride of his wife. It would be very difficult to exclude that Hipponax knew the story and it is probable that he knew another version. In the first iambus of the ancient edition, apparently on a heterosexual adventure too, a metaphor of the labia is connected to the Maeonian people (fr. 2a West). The fragment 3a West seemingly belonged to the same iambus:

> Ἑρμῆ κυνάγχα μηιονιστὶ Κανδαῦλα.
> φωρῶν ἑταῖρε, δεῦρό μοι σκαπαρδεῦσαι.
>
> Hermes, dog throttler, Candaules in Maeonian,
> companion of thieves, come give me a hand (Gerber)

Whether Candaules is really the Maeonian or Lydian word for dog throttler or Hipponax only alludes to the Hermes-like burglar-helping role of Candaules in the Gyges-story or if there actually were versions putting on the stage Hermes-Candaules who helps Gyges to enter the queen's bedroom cannot be determined. But we can justify by the Hipponactean fragment that, on a structural level, Hermes has the same narrative role as Candaules in such burglar-sex-adventures.

In the Herodotean story, Gyges enters the bedroom through the door, observes the naked queen and tries to escape through the door[3]. Yet the queen, aware of the betrayal, makes the young man her ally and "forces" him to kill and to replace the king. In Plato's version (in the *Republic*) twisting a magical finger-ring allows Gyges to be unseen and to enter the room without Candaules' help, in order to kill him.

To join Hipponax, even if his erotic ambush story is clearly not a Gyges-version, there is not only the narrative structure to recall it to the audience: both motives (whether corresponding to each other or not) are present to be alluded to, the finger-twisting we know of Plato's version (cf. v. 10. δακ]τύλους μεταστρέψας) and the father Daskylos (from Herodotus) in the perfume-scene. The narrating "I" uses a perfume not worse than the one used in the palace built by Daskylos, the Daskyleion (v. 24).

The perfume motive appears not only in other Hipponax-texts, but also in a story told by the Iambographer Semonides (16 West). This apparently typical iambic motive shows that the ambush-story not only bears some parodying-political resemblance to the Gyges-story, but stands in a longer tradition, that it is almost a standard narrative, probably of the iambus. And, it leads us to the first Odyssean use of iambus: In the forth book of the *Odyssey*, Menelaus and Helena engage in gender-polemics. She represents herself as an ally of the Greeks in Troy, he shows that she is lying and her guest, Telemachus, finally, is tired of them and goes to bed. But in the morning Menelaus tells him a story that should parallel Odysseus' situation: a tale without Helen, with Menelaus as a desired young man, who fights with the father of a nymph, who seems to be in love with him[4]. Like Calypso helps Odysseus, she helps him to leave her island. In order to do so he has to grasp her father by an ambush. Her father being a "sealherd", Menelaus and his fellows wait for him under strong smelling sealskins. As they cannot stand the smell, the nymph brings a balm to apply into the nose. But the nymph's advances, the handing over of perfume are not the only indication of the fact that the *Odyssey* re-uses a rather erotic, iambic story-pattern. In *Od.* 4.443 Menelaus explains the trick by a surprising formulation:

τίς γάρ κ'εἰναλίῳ παρὰ κήτεϊ κοιμηθείη;
who would choose a monster of the deep for bed-mate?

Not waiting under the skins, but sleeping with seals is the expression that reminds the formula normally used for the sexual act. Finally, not on the narrative level, but in a Greek lexicon of associations, seals would be connected to girls[5]. The nymph's father Proteus could, thus, be an epic transposition of the iambic father of many daughters who does not want to give them in marriage.

Why should Menelaus tell Telemachus an iambus? Yet this is not what he does. It is still an epic narrative, using though elements and the pattern appropriate to iambus, in order to reject iambus or to allude to it in a polemic way. We have to consider that Menelaus pretends at least to refuse the seals and the nymph. Within the argument he develops for Telemachus looking for his father, such an inverted iambus-pattern makes sense. Menelaus says that he was in the same situation as Odysseus: he was prisoner of an island, loved by a nymph and yet he could manage to escape. Why should resourceful Odysseus not? As we shall see, Odysseus' situation is initially that of a young man, and then he starts to reject it. No wonder, Menelaus' argues with (inverted) iambic patterns.

Menelaus' story attests the presence of the erotic ambush-story in the 7th century only by an intertextual reflex and this is maybe why the door motive for instance is lacking. From a realistic point of view, we could of course say that it is difficult to find doors on the beach. However, another epic text of the 7th century uses a similar narrative pattern and manages to introduce doors in a similarly uncivilized context. A young man, aristocrat but second of birth, Anchises is the object of an inverted sex-story. He does not fight with fathers, the father of gods and men himself leads him and Aphrodite in the trap of love. Both Anchises and Aphrodite will be the losers of this game. But as Aphrodite tries to make believe the object of her desire that he is the master of the adventure, iambic patterns are reflected. Aphrodite tells him that she has been stolen out of a dance of young girls, against the will of her father. Of course Hermes has taken the helper's part. Though pumping up the young man's soul with desire, she says what a girl in iambic stories has to ask for: to wait for sex until marriage. Anchises cannot resist the goddess's spell and brings her into the hut through the door.

Archilochus' version of this story (fr. 196a West) does not seem to contain the door- motive, but the "I"-protagonist and -Narrator is speaking to a young girl who was in a dancing group (ἐν ἡμετέρου), the spatial context seems to be a meadow, Hera's precinct where the young man met or ambushed the girl who, like Pseudo-Aphrodite, wants marriage before love. In Greek sexual hierarchy, penetration is a forbidden practice before or outside marriage even for Zeus and Hera, and the young man respects this rule by choosing another way for rape. In a material sense, the door is absent from the Archilochus-iambus, but on a metaphorical level, the young man describes his sexual practice as going beneath the door[6].

Now, we have gathered enough stories from iambus or from inverted reflections in epos to construct the criterion for judging to what extent Odysseus' adventures are an allusion to iambus. Let us recapitulate the typical motives of such a rather iambic story.

	helper	subject	anti-subj.	doors	means	secret	her complicity
Hipp. 1	?	y. man	fath./husb.	yes	?	yes	yes
Hipp. 2	?	y. man	fath./husb.	yes	balm	ambush	yes
Herod.	"Hermes"	y. man	husband	yes	(ring)	ambush	yes
Arch.	?	y. man	father	"yes"	"rhet"	yes	no
Menel.	daughter	"y. man"	father	no	balm	ambush	yes
hVen.	Hermes	y. man	father	yes	?	yes	yes

When Odysseus meets Circe, the first of the three nymphai, Hermes is his helper bearing the epithet, Homeric audience understood as *Killer of the dog Argos*. A magical plant serves as his means, but taking a closer look, the text offers the possibility to consider it an equivalent of the perfume in the narrative parallels. Odysseus enters a door that is highlighted as one of Circe's means of power, and he develops a complicity with her, wins her love against not really a father, but this will become understandable later. Let us begin the reading by considering the whole Circe-story a sort of contest of young men entering a nymph's room.

6.2 First example: Circe and better a young man

Odysseus discovers the smoke of Circe's hearth and sends first a group of young men led by one of the fellows bearing the significant and often iambic name of Eury-lochos, "the one experimented in ambushes"[7]. Observing her house, they see strange lions and wolves that behave too gently for beasts. Fooled by the beautiful voice they come closer[8]. The entering through the door is too easy (*Od.* 10.230f.)

> ἡ δ'αἶψ' ἐξελθοῦσα θύρας ὤιξε φαεινάς
> καὶ κάλει, οἱ δ' ἅμα πάντες ἀιδρείησιν ἕποντο.

And the next moment Circe came out, opened the polished doors, and invited them to enter. In their innocence, the whole party followed her in.

This is one of the passages the audience of husbands and wives must have enjoyed: outcasts, who claim the same level by birth as the audience has got, are just too dull to reach the audience's own social position. They brought themselves in that bad situation by their own fault, just as the first lines of the *Odyssey* have underscored. They cannot even make it in their own stories. The young men enter and eat the κυκεών the sorceress offers and—after a touch with the magic stick—turn into swine with human consciousness. Suddenly, the handsome lions and wolves do not only remind us the image of a mistress of beasts (like an Artemis or Aphrodite for instance), but they could very well be other male victims. Lions are often the image of heroic warriors, but the later Homeric *hymn to Dionysus* also offers a pun between the lion, λέων and simple people, λεώς. Wolves, as has been stressed, are often associated with outcasts, especially with iambic poets[9].

But there is more intertextual potential in this motive. If gender-polemics as the *Margites* accuse a young husband of inability because he is still a young man, Semonides attacks in the same way young wives by telling the audience that they remain girls. The wives of his catalogue "come from" beasts. In the "imaginary" of the archaic period this must raise the image of girls organized in dancing groups during their initiation-time. They were called—and often disguised as bears, horses, doves, maybe a deer according to what is attested.

When married Mestra decides not to be a mother or wife, she goes back to her girlhood by turning into a fox. Having escaped her husband in this shape and reached her father's house, she becomes a girl again[10]. Turning members of the opposite gender into animals means to denounce them as non-adult, as still being in the dancing groups. Archilochus attacks one girl, Neoboule, because she still goes to the dances instead of being married. This might explain that, when Odysseus forces Circe to give them back their human shape, the sorceress applies a balm (*Od.* 10.392):

ἐρχομένη προσήλειψε ἑκάστῳ φάρμακον ἄλλο.
She went in and smeared them each in turn with some new salve she had.

The fellows become νεώτεροι, younger than they were before. It is, therefore, Odysseus who succeeds in the (male) iambic story, while his fellows are typical victims of a (female) iambic story. Odysseus, who will be the *anér* par excellence, is, at this moment, a better young man than his fellows. This is probably why he can (morally and esthetically) live with Circe like Achilles with Briseis, like Herakles with Iole, like Jason with Medea—without marriage.

6.3 Another intertext: oar breaking and stag hunting

We have seen that the *Odyssey* normally uses inverted iambic features. Why then, does Odysseus start as a positive iambic hero? To answer this and the already raised question about the absence of the father, we have to enter another intertext. The *Odyssey* itself gives a hint where to look: with Circe's, Medea's aunt's, island the young men enter the path of song and the route of the Argonauts, of the Ἀργὼ πᾶσι μέλουσα (*Od.* 12.70). This becomes already apparent in the first lines of that comparison. Odysseus kills a stag on the way back from his first excursion into the island (*Od.* 10.156-184). As Birge has seen, the narrative motivation—food for the fellows—is a little bit weak compared to the importance this motive assumes in the following tradition down to the stag Aeneas kills for his fellows[11]. Birge suggested, probably correctly, an interpretation as gender-symbol[12]. But if we try to reconstruct the narrative of the *Argonautica* version Homer alludes to, the stag gets a more polemic significance[13].

How to reconstruct this lost context? Maybe the very late *Orphic Argonautica* can give us a hint[14]. This text of the forth century AD, though borrowing the narrative pattern almost entirely from Apollonius Rhodius, conforms to the esthetics of its time. As Quintus of Smyrna or the author of the *Blemyomachia*[15], it rejects the allusive Hellenistic aesthetics and becomes a very tight "imitator Homeri"[16]. It has no Herakles breaking an oar and leaving the crew in order to carve another one, the Apollonian version also taken into account by Valerius Flaccus[17]. Instead, he often alludes to Odyssean formulations and replaces the broken oar by the need of meat, by a stag-hunter Herakles. We perceive, thus, a kind of intertextual polemic and of equivalence. For, perhaps, the author of the *Orphic Argonautics* did not invent this equivalence of motives. If he was not a Roman himself, he knew very precisely the Roman epic tradition[18]. For when Vergil makes Aeneas a stag-hunter, he is not in the part of the *Aeneid* inspired by the *Odyssey*, but in the love-story that alludes to Apollonius Rhodius' *Argonautica*. We cannot say whether stag hunting or oar breaking was the motive of the pre- or co-Odyssean *Argonautica*. But the later intertext, that probably still reflected a reading of those old *Argonautica*, furnishes some evidence that the motives were considered equivalents between the *Argonautica* and the *Odyssey*[19].

This firstly means that Odysseus acts as a polemic figure against Herakles, the hero and god of young men, and we will see that this polemic is maintained during the whole of the *Odyssey*[20]. We can only make a guess about Herakles' role in that lost epic. The fact that all existent versions first make him the equal of Jason and exclude him, then, from the journey shows an ideology that acknowledges the overriding Dorian value of this hero, but does not want to link this young man too closely to the *heroes*, the young men.

In the *Odyssey* Herakles represents the Suitors and is even more a young man. If Odysseus is introduced as a better young man than the other – unmarried - fellows, he is, from the very beginning, the man who wants to help them, but loses them not really through his, but through their own fault. Within this context the stag-hunter who thinks of his hungry fellows becomes significant as a polemic against the act of breaking an oar and leaving the crew. Odysseus might be an even better young man than the real young men, but shows solidarity, unlike Herakles who breaks this sign of solidarity by sheer force. In order to maintain such a reading, we should be able to show that the *Argonautica* Odysseus had in mind really knew oar braking. This cannot be properly proved, but there are some strange coincidences regarding this assumption.

When the fellows are tired of waiting for Odysseus, they drag him from Circe away and she sends them all to the dead, in order to interview the seer Tiresias, she says. At least one of the fellows does not return. The typical young man Elp-enor ("the Optimist to be once a husband"?) breaks his neck and meets Odysseus at the gate of the "Underworld". He asks for a burial and has a special wish: they should plant an oar on his tomb. Did the suppressed motive come back? After all, there is an oar and Odysseus cannot but use it. Tiresias provides him the rite that should enable him to avoid Poseidon's anger. He has to wander with an oar on his shoulder until someone asks him why he is carrying a wheat-shovel. As Segal has shown, Homer used a very widespread narrative pattern to say that Odysseus must find a place where

Poseidon is not known. Within this narrative tradition, the object is not fixed; it can be a snow-shovel at the Yukon[21]. If therefore the oar can be a substitute, the repeated use of it is by no means inspired by the realia-context and poetically fortuitous. Especially not if the motive occurs twice in the first half, marked by the "catalogue of women", of book 11 and has a "rhythmical" counterpart in the second half, a sort of catalogue of men, where the corresponding echo is held by an encounter between Odysseus and Herakles[22]. Going into details would mean a lot of guess-work, but the concentration of motives linked to the construction of book 11 is enough to say that there is an argument of coherence in favor of an allusion to a version of the *Argonautica* having an oar-breaking Herakles.

6.4 Hermes and Athena: plain and inverted iambic stories

The function of Odysseus' first, iambic encounter with a first νύμφη (of the three: Circe, Calypso, Nausicaa) gets more plasticity when compared with his second encounter, this time with Calypso. As we have seen, the conditions have changed, because the fellows are dead. While they had to remove Odysseus from Circe, no young man will remind him of returning in Calypso's case. So Odysseus' decision to leave the nymph is even stronger than on Circe's island.

But there is another motive: the role of Hermes. When the gods send him to warn Aegisthus, the god is "ἀγαθὰ φρονέων (*Od*.1.42f.)": He is on the side of this unmarried, song and dance-loving young man, who entered the bedchamber of another's wife. But Hermes has to follow Zeus' orders and cannot preserve his proselyte from the anger of the father of gods and men. He does not conceal his sympathy for the iambic unmarried couple Calypso represents[23]. He obeys Zeus' orders (οὐκ ἀπίθησε), but unwillingly. Like the messengers of the *Iliad* sent by Agamemnon to Achilles who do not like to transmit with what they do not agree, Hermes waits until Calypso summons him to speak (κέλεαι γάρ). Only then does he tell her Zeus' plan to let Odysseus go; Hermes does not like his duty (*Od*. 5.99):

> Ζεὺς ἐμέ γ' ἠνώγει δεῦρ' ἐλθέμεν οὐκ ἐθέλοντα·
>
> It was Zeus who sent me. Otherwise I should not have come. (Rieu)

Of course, he does not say he is against Zeus and being polite he assumes the mask of the civilized god not accustomed to the savage realm Calypso prefers, deprived of sanctuaries and sacrifices. But when he goes on, we understand that this is not the real reason for his unease. The plan is, in fact, Athena's work, the child who is even more γνήσιος than any child from Hera ever could be. The νόθος (bastard) Hermes, who - according to the *Homeric Hymn to Hermes*- had to fight for being acknowledged by his father, must obey to her orders and cannot restrain from attacking her covertly: it was Athena's wrath which misled the Greek warriors and brought Odysseus to the island of Calypso, she has her share of reponsibility for the fellows' deaths[24]. Calypso must obey and so must Hermes. Although called "killer of the dog Argos" and a helper rather of intruders, he helps for once to leave a closed space as Proteus' daughter did in Menelaus' story.

In the third encounter between a νύμφη and Odysseus, Hermes assumes again the role of the helper of burglars, but he is even more under the influence of Athena: When Odysseus enters unseen the palace of Alcinoos to clasp the knees of the queen for supplication, the Phaeacian evening party is bringing out the last toast to Hermes. Hermes has thus to assure the entrance but it is Athena who sent Odysseus through the doors[25]. From now on Hermes will re-appear twice but every time against Odysseus and for the young men.

Odysseus has left the realm of young men marked by Hermes and entered the realm of Athena. The divine intervention superposes therefore the relationship between the life of the fellows and the love of the nymphs. Both relationships are landmarks in Odysseus' way from a quasi-young man to a quasi husband and explain why Odysseus is a young man in the Circe-story: It caracterizes the state he leaves. As Hermes' independent helper role in the Circe episode (nr 2 below) marks the iambic status of Odysseus, the hero's ambivalent behavior corresponds to both the change of his feelings and Athena's increasing influence. From this point on, the iambic stories cannot be used but with an inversion of the winning and losing roles. The transition from plain iambic to inverted iambic stories is marked by Hermes role in the story, which Demodocus tells a plainly iambic audience.

		Chronological Order			
1 (*Od.* 1)	2 (*Od.*10)	3 (*Od.* 5)	4 (*Od.* 7)	5 (*Od.*8)	6 (*Od.* 24)
Hermes	Hermes	Hermes	Hermes	Hermes	Hermes
(for Aeg)	(for Od.)	(duty)	(duty)	(ag Od.)	(for Suitors)
Athena	Athena	Athena	Athena	Athena	Athena
(and Od.)		(hidden)	(hidden)	Absent	(and Od.)
	1st nymph	2nd nymph	3rd		Wife
	(love)	(love-refusal)	nymph (refusal)		(love)
	Young men Alive	Young men Dead	Young men Dead		Young men killed

The Phaeacians are young men too, but good ones who left their country and went far from the *andres*[26]. However, they like Demodocus' burglar story with adultery in it and interpret it as a kind of contest between young men and husbands. It recalls the female λόγοι ἀφροδίσιοι Semonides talks about when he asks a good wife not to attend them[27]. Neither can Demodocus sing this sort of story for a mixed audience. This is only possible when the feast has been dislocated, far from the house of Alcinoos and far from the women. And within the story, the *lectrices in fabula* are excluded too. Let us recall the story.

> Ugly Hephaestus has married beautiful Aphrodite and had, therefore, to give a lot of gifts to the bride-father Zeus. But when Hephaestus goes out, Aphrodite's lover enters the house. Helios, not only here on the side of the husbands[28], observes it and betrays them. Hephaestus builds a trap, which immobilizes the lovers *in actu*. The betrayed husband invites the other gods and goddesses to be his witnesses. But only the gods come to judge.

Braswell has shown that Demodocus' song is a reading of the altercations between the young men and Odysseus, the one side arguing for the importance of strength and beauty, the other for the importance of wits[29]. Witty Odysseus wins in Demodocus' song, the divine *lectores in fabula* are clear about it: the lame outnumbered the fastest god by his wits. But Odysseus unmistakably loses because he is compared to an ugly husband. And, all the more, under the threat of the other gods Hephaestus must release his prisoners. But Odysseus can take it and laugh with the Phaeacians, even if Hermes takes Ares' side in the tale, not Hephaestus-Odysseus': he would not mind, the god says, to be captured if only he could sleep with Aphrodite. Odysseus' laughter, then, might be rather polite, because it is the first iambic laughter against him.

6.5 Knocked-out teeth

One of the themes iambus prefers seems to be box-fighting between young men and old. We have already seen a similar scene in the ambush-story of Hipponax. Another example is fr. 79 West:

```
           . ] ][
        ἀ]λοιᾶσθα[ι
     τῆς] ἀνοίης ταύτη[ς
     τὴ]ν γνάθον παρα [
     ]ι κηρίνους ἐποι[                5
     ]κἀνετίλησε[
     ]χρυσολαμπέτωι ῥάβδωι
```

]αν ἐγγὺς ἑρμῖνος·
Ἑρμῆς δ' ἐς Ἱππών]ακτος ἀκολουθήσας
... to be cudgeled...
... of his foolishness ...
... his jaw...
... he made them waxen...
... and he shat upon...
...staff gleaming with gold..
... near to the bed post..
And Hermes providing an escort to the house of Hipponax (Gerber)

The beginning provides a recurring element of these stories: one of the enemies hits hard on the other's jaw making the teeth fly out of the mouth. In archaic medicine, it was difficult yet not impossible to reinsert them into their roots: with a patchwork of wax and threads according to Hippocrates[30]. Maybe the passage "he made them waxen" refers to this practice, but commentators as Gerber read it as the sign of paleness (why then the plural "them"?) in connection with another symptom of fear in the following line. Once again there is Hermes and again he seems to be the ally of an "I"-Narrator, the young man who wins against the old. Another fragment shows the husband or father Bupalos fighting and losing against the young man (Hipponax?). This passage reached such popularity that "Bupaleian strike" became proverbial. Attic comedy uses it to design the out-knocked teeth[31]. Fragment 74 W underscores the theme of deprived jaws.

ὤμειξε δ'αἷμα καὶ χολὴν ἐτίλησεν·
ἐγὼ δ'ἐγ[   ]οἱ δ' ἐμέο ὀδόντες
ἐν ταῖς γναθμοῖσι πάντες ‹ἐκ›κεκινέαται.

he pissed blood and shat bile
but I ... and all the teeth
in my jaws have been dislodged (Gerber)

Yet here, it appears to be the "I" who loses his teeth. Though this does not necessarily imply that it is the Narrator (another character could relate what he suffered since he speaks in the present of the perfect). This fragment (P. Oxy. 2174.4) has been found in a papyrus that also offers a story of epic color: the night-ride against the Thracian king Rhesos. In the 10th book of the *Iliad* Diomedes and Odysseus attack him. Another text of the same papyrus bears the title *Odysseus*.

There is a link between parodying aggression against the *Odyssey* and box-fight stories. If we look in the *Odyssey* for such scenes, the beginning of book 18, the Irus story contains iambic features, as Nagy and Sutor have already pointed out. One of these features is pun: *Irus* not only means messenger like the divine messenger Iris, but from the beginning on the name is linked to the word ἴ and understood as strength and the pun is reenacted, when the Suitors realize that the seemingly strong is unstrong: Ἶρος ἄιρος. Irus is a normal heroic name. The father of the Argonaut Eurytion is called Irus, but Eurytion is as well the name of a Centaur, which can be presented as an image of the Suitors.

Iambic names are not innocent. Commentators have stressed that when this young fat beggar Irus calls the old beggar names, he uses a vocabulary we know well from ancient comedy. The word *bougaios* for instance has the affix *bou-*, meaning something like "ox-" or "huge". The second occurrence of this prefix is found again in a typical, iambic or Suitor-story. The Suitors like to tell the story of Echetos, whose name means "husband" and whose father, according to the Scholiae, bears the name *Bou(e)chetos*, thus a Super-Echetos or Super-possessor (Super-husband, perhaps Super-father). And Hipponax using the name or nickname of a possibly real person for a fictional (if not fictive) father/husband in his stories recurs to the same tradition: Bou-palos (some suggested "Super-penis" but one could think as well of "Super-wrestler").

Not only the vocabulary points to the iambus but also the themes such as teeth knocked out of the jaws of an old man by a young man. The young beggar Irus tries to chase the older one away. He threats to knock his teeth out of his jaws (*Od.* 18.27ff.):

> ὃν ἂν κακὰ μητισαίμην
> κόπτων ἀμφοτέρῃσι, χαμαὶ δ'ἐκ πάντας ὀδόντας
> γναθμῶν ἐξελάσαιμι συὸς ὡς ληιβοτείρης.
>
> But I have nasty trick in store for him,
> a right and left that'll dash all the teeth from his jaws
> to the ground like the tasks of a marauding swine. (Rieu)

From the beginning of the scene on it is implied that this fight is not simply an objective event, but an event for an audience, a text destined for a certain audience, the Suitors. The young beggar explicitly reminds us that this is a struggle between young and old (*Od.*18.30f.)[32]:

> ζῶσαι νῦν ἵνα πάντες ἐπιγνώωσι καὶ οἵδε
> μαρναμένους· πῶς δ'ἂν σὺ νεωτέρῳ ἀνδρὶ μάχοιο·
>
> Tuck in your clothes, and let them see too that we fight,
> if you really dare to mach yourself against a younger man!

If Irus thinks that this struggle is for the Suitors, the Suitors too think it is for them and the word they use for the event is the same Archilochus applies to the parties of the audience he entertains by his iambs: τερπωλή (and not κληθμός as for epic illusion). The noun implies laughter (ἐκγελάσας) and Antinous the little king of the Suitors puts it into the larger context of other entertainment (πάρος). Box-fighting is therefore a theme the Suitors would expect to figure in their texts (*Od.* 18.34):

τοῖιν δὲ ξυνέηχ' ἱερὸν μένος Ἀντινόοιο.
ἡδὺ δ'ἄρ' **ἐκγελάσας** μετεφώνει μνηστήρεσσι·
ὦ φίλοι οὐ μέν πώ τι **πάρος** τοιοῦτον ἐτύχθη,
οἵην **τερπωλὴν** θεὸς ἤγαγεν ἐς τόδε δῶμα.

Antinous understood what they did.
He laughed delightedly and called out the rest of the Suitors:
"My friends, this beats everything. Here is a treat for us
blown straight in from heaven."

6.6 Bellies

All this is intertwined with another highly typical theme of the iambus: the attack against the belly of husbands. In 4th-century lists of the corporations we can find a distinction between the young and old. But the words used to indicate this biologically not very clear difference might explain an aspect of the role bellies play in iambus and in the Odyssey. There is not only the often blurred opposition between νέοι and ἄνδρες or νέοι and γέροντες but frequently we read instead the distinction between νέοι and ἀνάλειπτοι, the ones who do not anoint themselves because they do not take part actively in the exercises. The husbands have no more time to join their fellows in the gymnasium, to participate in the physical exercise. They prefer the assembly and the symposium and probably get a little belly. When a former fellow who left the group of hetairoi joined the establishment or the family that detains the power, Alcaeus could attack him with an allusion to his belly[33]. He calls the traitor Pittacus a φύσκων, a "fat guy" and extends the metonymy to a metaphor: Pittacus eats the city, and maybe the δῆμος (people) too[34]. However the iambic belly-theme is to be found thrice in the Irus passage of the *Odyssey*:

Firstly, the Suitors do not think of a weapon, a cloth, or a big piece of meat as prize for the victor in the box-contest, but of a goat's stomach filled with blood and fat. The Greek word is the same as for belly: γαστήρ. Whatever the Suitors imply, it also has to do with the iambic scene. Odysseus (this is the second occurrence of the theme) does not reject their image-code but confirms it. Yet the Narrator unambiguously states that this is an attempt at maintaining (δολοφρονέων) the beggar-mask, which becomes frail by the contest (*Od.* 18.51ff.):

τοῖς δὲ δολοφρονέων μετέφη πολύμητις Ὀδυσσεύς·
ὦ φίλοι, οὔ πως ἔστι νεωτέρῳ ἀνδρὶ μάχεσθαι
ἄνδρα γέροντα δύῃ ἀρημένον· ἀλλά με γαστὴρ
ὀτρύνει κακοεργὸς ἵνα πληγῇσι δαμείω.

... and the wily Odysseus played up to his part and said:
Friends, there is no sense at all in a match between a younger man
and an old fellow worn out by trouble. Yet this mischievous belly
of mine eggs me on to take my thrashing. (Rieu)

Pucci has shown that this use of the word γαστήρ is polemic towards the Iliadic use of θυμός, the instance that pushes heroes to act[35]. We can understand the nature of Odysseus' mask in the light of these words. Odysseus does not want to appear as an aristocrat the more so because he will win the contest. But maybe in the eyes of the singer's audience the mask is risky too. It is probably not ubiquitous that the long scenes staging a disguised aristocrat are introduced by several general considerations on identity, on the relation between external look and inner nature. The swineherd adopts what is probably the audience's ideology and reads an old dog's bad state as a sign of lost aristocracy. Odysseus holds against this a "reading" of the dog Argos, according to which aristocracy can last under a bad exterior appearance. However, Odysseus must maintain the beggar-mask in front of the Suitors.

The question is whether or not he can afford it towards the aristocratic audience. This might be the point of view or the function of Telemachus, when he intervenes in order to answer his father's, the beggar's request for fairness, not to help Irus in case the older beggar won the contest. Telemachus grants this right by answering point by point as Homeric dialogue-esthetics demand. When coming to the belly theme, he translates the beggar-discourse (decision-instance belly) into an Iliadic, aristocratic, and epic discourse (decision-instance θυμός) as if he were not aware of the danger he exposes his father to (*Od.* 18.61):

ξεῖν' εἴ σ' ὀτρύνει κραδίη καὶ θυμὸς ἀγήνωρ
"Stranger, if you have the heart and pluck to match this man... "

The ideological gap between the iambic audience Odysseus has to correspond to and the epic audience the aoidos must satisfy appears very clearly in this "belly-crisis". Yet how does this situation fit the polemic intertext between the *Iliad* and the *Odyssey*? The *Iliad* is, like the *Odyssey*, an epos and by no means an iambic text. But between the two epic texts there is a difference that shows the same proportion we can find between iambus and epos. The *Odyssey* presents itself as a post-war-(hi)story, as the beginnings of the audience's time, as the starting Iron Age of adults, whereas, from this point of view the Trojan war *was* rather the time of unmarried young men[36]. And yet, those young men inasmuch as they are dead grant the aristocracy of the Iron-Age-adults. It is this double-marked quality of the *Iliad* that allows Odysseus to fight against both being unmasked by the Suitors and rejected by the epic audience[37]. As Pucci has shown, the *Odyssey* and, maybe in reaction to it, the *Iliad* too, reuse the iambic polemic belly—theme, usually a negative sign of fathers and husbands, but invert it and turn it into a positive sign of adulthood. We have seen a similar process in the chapter on the eagle-theme, or maybe in the use of the fox-theme between female iambus and male iambus. In the *Iliad* Achilles once wants the Greek army to attack immediately the Trojans, but he is intercepted by Odysseus, the member of the γέροντες, who draws his attention to the fact that the soldiers are hungry and that empty bellies do not like to fight[38]. One of the many Odyssean returns is thus to present the belly as sign of adult realism in a time of malnutrition, of food-shortage[39].

The third occurrence of the belly-theme comes to support the reading of the Irus-scene as an inverted iambus. Unlike the metaphor in Odysseus' case, the metonymy attributes the physical belly not (as it is in iambic texts) to the old adversary in the box-fight, but to the younger (*Od.* 18.1ff.):

ἦλθε δ' ἐπὶ πτωχὸς πανδήμιος ὃς κατὰ ἄστυ
πτωχεύεσκ' Ἰθάκης μετὰ δ' ἔπρεπε γαστέρι μάργῃ
ἀζηχὲς φαγέμεν καὶ πιέμεν· οὐδέ οἱ ἦν ἴς

There entered now upon the scene a common vagabond who used to beg
for his living in the streets of Ithaca and was notorious for his insatiable belly
and his ability to eat and drink all day. Yet he had no strength.

And of course, not the young man beats the old, but inversely, the old beggar crashes the skull of the younger. The belly characterizes all this: A metonymical belly (Irus) fights with a metaphorical belly (Odysseus) for the synonym belly (the sausage).

6.7 Punishment

When the Suitors begin to realize that Irus will lose the contest, they threaten him with a story, which, at first sight, does not seem to be indebted to the iambic tradition. They promise to send Irus to the King Ekhetos, a specialist of akroteriasmos. This means, the king will cut off his senses namely nose, ears or penis. This type of punishment appears once again in a story that is explicitly defined as typical for "the Suitors".

When the old beggar, in book 21, wants to participate in the bow contest, the economy of honor, well described by Thalmann, forbids the Suitors to admit him[40]. The little Suitor-king Antinous explains that the beggar has drunk too much and goes too far. He already has the right to share the meal with the young men and *their* stories (*Od.* 21.289ff.):

οὐκ ἀγαπᾷς ὃ ἕκηλος ὑπερφιάλοισι μεθ'ἡμῖν
δαίνυσαι οὐδέ τι δαιτὸς ἀμέρδεαι, αὐτὰρ ἀκούεις
μύθων ἡμετέρων καὶ ῥήσιος οὐδέ τις ἄλλος
ἡμετέρων μύθων ξεῖνος καὶ πτωχὸς ἀκούει.

Aren't you content to dine in peace with your betters!
To get your share of every dish and to listen
to **our stories** and our talk, which no other
visitor or tramp is privileged to hear!

Antinous tells him the aetiology for why the ἄνδρες, not simply "men", but "husbands" are in war with the Centaurs. The Centaur Eurytion was invited to a human, Lapithean, wedding, he drinks a lot and falls in love with the bride. When he tries to approach her, the Lapiths draw him outside and cut off his nose and ears. Hence there is a polemic between ἄνδρες and centaurs (*Od.* 21. 295ff.).

οἶνος καὶ Κένταυρον, ἀγάκλυτον Εὐρυτίωνα
ἄασ' ἐν μεγάρῳ μεγαθύμου Πειριθόοιο
ἐς Λαπίθας ἐλθόνθ'· ὃ δ' ἐπεὶ φρένας ἄασεν οἴνῳ
μαινόμενος κάκ' ἔρεξε δόμων κάτα Πειριθόοιο.
ἥρωας δ'ἄχος εἷλε, διὲκ προθύρου δὲ θύραζε
ἕλκον ἀναΐξαντες, ἀπ' οὔατα νηλέι χαλκῷ
ῥῖνας τ' ἀμήσαντες· ὃ δὲ φρεσὶν ᾗσιν ἀασθεὶς
ἤιεν ἣν ἄτην ὀχέων ἀεσίφρονι θυμῷ.
ἐξ οὗ Κενταύροισι καὶ **ἀνδράσι** νεῖκος ἐτύχθη,

Remember Eurytion the Centaur! It was the wine
that got at his wits, in king Peirithous' house,
when he was visiting the Lapithae. Fuddled with drink,
what must he do but run amuck in the palace?
His hosts leapt up in anger, dragged him to the porch,
and threw him out of doors; but not before they had sliced
his ears and nose off with a knife. Away went the maddened brute,
with his damage and punishment for his silly soul;
and so the feud started between Centaurs and men.

Neither the beggar nor the audience is as dumb as not to understand the innuendo of the story. Antinous compares the drunken beggar to the centaur and threatens him as he did in Irus' case by *akroteriasmos*.

But the audience knows more than Antinous[41]. Not the beggar is invited to the Suitors' wedding, but the inverse is the case: The Suitors are the guests at Odysseus' own wedding with his wife. Although having slaughtered the Suitors, Odysseus does not dare to mutilate the bodies, the *akroteriasmos* is applied to the slave who worked for the young men: as it is often done, slaves are punished instead of their masters, Telemachus will deprive Suitor-loyal Melanthius of ears, penis and nose. In the audience's eyes Antinous ignores that the Centaur, in fact, represents the Suitors.

Furthermore, the audience of the *Odyssey* might have known iambs such as Archilochus' "rhapsody" on the Centaur Nessus trying to rape Deianira[42], maybe with a pun on her name as Bacchylides does in a rather suggestive way: "she who kills men"[43]. This bundle of indices points into the direction of gender-polemics. Still Pindar, when he attacks Archilochus, tells the story of how the Centaurs are born out of a rape (*Pyth*. 2.44). And when Xenophanes defines the rules of the husbands' symposium in the husbands' elegiac discourse, he excludes violent stories such as the Centauromachy, maybe as rather suitable for the iambus[44]. In general, Centaurs have the same difficulties with marriage, the same heterosexual phantasms as the young men. To be sure, it would be too hazardous saying that Centaurs such as foxes are an image of young men, but the association was easy: they were grown up (they have beards on vase paintings), but not entire ἄνδρες (they are half horses). So that there is not only the argument that Centaur stories as a variety of the burglar-stories might be a standard-element of the iambic repertoire but also the fact that Antinous says twice that Centaur-stories are often told among the Suitors. We can, thus, consider this story a probable iambus, once again inverted by the *Odyssey*.

However what does this mean for the Ekhetos-story they tell Irus? If the Suitors and the audience of the iambus like stories ending with the punishment of the protagonists that have a certain resemblance to themselves, this could express their fear to be punished for desire or pleasure. If one of the Scholia is right, this was exactly the context the Odyssean audience and the Suitors added to the simple narrative nucleus of the cruel king Ekhetos[45]. According to the Scholia Ekhetos castrated the young men who slept with his daughter. This king, or tyrannos, is, thus a perfect enemy image of young men. He not only incarnates the unwilling bride-father, but also the husband who can, in fifth century Athens, punish himself the adulterer (cf. Lysias *or*. 1). His name as we have already seen sounds like a paronym of the verb ἔχειν, "to have", and joins thus the wordplays of the *Iliad* (*Hektor*, "he who has"), of Semonides (ὁ ἔχων having a destiny = having a wife[46]) and other uses of the verb for being married. Even if the *Odyssey* inverts this story too, here the Suitors show their fears and desires in the clearest way and come very close to Archilochean father-iambus such as fr. 122 W and 172ff. W.

6.8 Baldness

At the end of the same book, the conjunction of a typical iambus-scene and the epic inversion occurs once more: Not young men enter the bedchamber of women or girls, but girls enter the male-marked hall during the night. And Odysseus succeeds in hindering the girl Melantho, who loves Eurymachus, from being close to him. This is not the mere epic inversion of an iambic narrative pattern; we also find here the situation and the themes of iambus.

It is interesting that the Suitors are described as a group without much cultual coherence. They do not seem to be an ἔρανος, a cultic group of men, to Athena-Mentes (*Od.* 1.226). They do not sacrifice as requested at meals. There is no libation mentioned and even in the structure of their group there is not one basileus, ceremonial master of a symposium, but two "kings" or βασιλῆες are prominent.

Furthermore, the Narrator cares to distinguish their characters, a rather choleric Antinous and a phlegmatic Eurymachus. One of the means to distinguish them is the narrative pattern they offer to their fellows: Antinous likes more violent stories of box fights and struggles, whereas Eurymachus both preferes erotic adventures and jibes. Both presentations are introduced as entertainment for the group.

When Eurymachus decides to take his revenge for his girlfriend, he uses more rhetoric than Antinous did; he is a tougher enemy for the beggar. This time Odysseus will not succeed in isolating the basileus from the group as in Antinous' case. The group will remain on Eurymachus' side. The discourse and the pragmatic situation is, as usually, mentioned in the speech introduction of a direct speech (*Od.* 18.349f.):

> τοῖσιν δ'Εὐρύμαχος Πολύβου παῖς ἦρχ' ἀγορεύειν
> κερτομέων Ὀδυσῆα. γέλων δ'ἑτάροισιν ἔτευχε·
>
> It was Eurymachus' turn to contribute a jibe
> at the stranger and raise a laugh among his friends.

The verb κερτομέω indicates a discourse of critique, γέλων δ'ἑτάροισιν ἔτευχε circumscribes the situation of a leading member of a group of hetairoi: he has to assure his position by stories. Sappho for instance seems to be concerned by this preoccupation (τάδε νῦν ἑταίραις ταῖς ἔμαις τέρπνα κάλως ἀείσω fr. 160) but the closest parallel comes from Archilochus' iambs (fr. 168 W):

Ἐρασμονίδη Χαρίλαε,　　　χρῆμά τοι γέλοιον
ἐρέω πολὺ φίλταθ' ἑταίρων,　　τέρψεαι δ' ἀκούων.

Charilaus son of Erasmon　　by far the dearest of my companions
I shall tell you something funny and you will be delighted to hear it. (Gerber)

Eurymachus chooses a typically iambic code, a mixture of anti-superstition and default mocking: some of the Suitors imagined that there might be hidden a god in disguise of a beggar. Now the moment has come to use this joke. Since the beggar Odysseus is bald and he wants to stay with the Suitors as a lamp-keeper, his head reflects the light and it looks like a divine aura. Eurymachus is keen enough to connect both elements to a joke (*Od.* 18.351ff.):

κέκλυτέ μευ μνηστῆρες ἀγακλείτης βασιλείης,
ὄφρ' εἴπω, τά με θυμὸς ἐνὶ στήθεσσι κελεύει.
οὐκ ἀθεεὶ ὅδ' ἀνὴρ Ὀδυσήιον ἐς δόμον ἵκει·
ἔμπης μοι δοκέει δαΐδων σέλας ἔμμεναι αὐτοῦ
κὰκ κεφαλῆς, ἐπεὶ οὔ οἱ ἐνὶ τρίχες οὐδ' ἠβαιαί.

"Listen! It has occurred to me- and I really must share
this idea with the Suitors of the queen
that some divine being must have guided this fellow to Odysseus' palace.
At any rate it seems to me that the torch-light emanates from the man himself, in
fact from that pate of his, innocent of the slightest vestige of hair."

Baldness is a sign of male old age and we find this theme in iambic attacks of Semonides (fr. 40 West). This would not be enough evidence for declaring baldness as an iambic theme, but the text connects it to the theme of the belly. Eurymachus waits until the laughter has ebbed and starts again with a typical refusal-story, the refusal normally bride-fathers impose on the young man (cf. Archilochus fr. 122 W). He hires the beggar as land-worker but fires him at the last moment because of his belly. The beggar has already proved to be only metaphorically a belly so that the attack is not really understandable if not considered an allusion to iambic discourse (young men as victims of the fathers) by Odyssean inversion (a father as victim of the young men).

There is as well an allusion to the door-theme in *Od.* 18.385. In answer to the provocation, the beggar threatens the young men with the husband's return. They would, he says, prefer to flee and this description focuses on a door too narrow to escape:

αἶψά κέ τοι τὰ θύρετρα καὶ εὐρέα περ μάλ' ἐόντα
φεύγοντι στείνοιτο διὲκ προθύροιο θύραζε.

you would soon find that wide doorway there
too narrow in your hurry to get safely out!

Door, refusal-discourse and belly, i.e. iambic features, join the baldness-theme. Yet there is also the typical mockery of a superstition bound to intimidate people, a theme we have already met in the analysis of the seer-discourse. We have seen that, as usual in archaic intertext, the metaphors and the vocabulary of ideologically opposite texts are the same. What changes is the point of view of the stories. Never do the Suitors have any chance to catch the perspective, even when they are described as audience, their stories are always re-used, but with a figurative inversion that allows the audience of γέροντες, as Plato says the typical audience of epics, to look at them[47].

6.9 Allysis: a possibility

There is one story the Suitors tell time and again, an inversion of their victory too, but that seemed until now a sheer epic text. Yet, the Suitors' lament about Penelope's indeterminacy could contain a genuinely iambic theme. Telemachus confirms their version. Penelope cannot or does not want to decide neither for nor against the Suitors (*Od.* 1.249). When they tell the story of the wife's trick for the last time, they tell it the married man Agamemnon (*Od.* 24.125ff.):

μνώμεθ' Ὀδυσσῆος δὴν οἰχομένοιο δάμαρτα·
ἣ δ'οὔτ'ἠρνεῖτο στυγερὸν γάμον οὔτε τελεύτα
ἡμῖν φραζομένη θάνατον καὶ κῆρα μέλαιναν.

In the prolonged absence of Odysseus we began to pay our addresses to his wife.
These proved distasteful to her, but instead of refusing us outright or taking
the final step, she schemed to bring about our downfall and our death.

She pretends to have still to weave the shroud for her father-in-law Laertes but does not refuse being courted (and this is what the Suitors blame, *Od.* 24.131ff.):

Κοῦροι ἐμοὶ μνηστῆρες, ἐπεὶ θάνε δῖος Ὀδυσσεύς,
μίμνετ' **ἐπειγόμενοι** τὸν ἐμὸν γάμον, εἰς ὅ κε φᾶρος
ἐκτελέσω, μή μοι μεταμώνια νήματ' ὄληται.

I should be grateful to you young men, who are courting me now that
bright Odysseus is dead, if you could restrain your ardor for my hand till I have
done this work, so that all the threads I have spun may not be utterly wasted.

What points into the direction of a maybe inverted iambic discourse is firstly the vocabulary: in Archilochus' fr. 196a.3 a girl uses the same probably pejorative verb for the desire of young men to get married: ἐπείγεσθαι (Horace's *ardor* in *epod*. 11). The address κοῦροι is interesting, because it underlines the Suitors' unmarried status and because we will also find this term in an iambic text. Penelope, however, does not keep her promise. During the day, she is weaving, by night she undoes the textile's knots (*Od*. 24.139f.)

> ἔνθα καὶ ἡματίη μὲν ὑφαίνεσκεν μέγαν ἱστόν,
> νύκτας δ'ἀλλύεσκεν ἐπὴν δαίδας παραθεῖτο.
>
> by day she wove at the great web, but every
> night had torches set beside it and undid the work.

Even if this is an epic text implying maybe the epic metaphor of weaving as composition of text, there are iambic elements such as male intrusion into female space. The maidservants betray teir mistress and so the young men enter by night Penelope's domain (*Od*. 24.145):

> Καὶ τήν γ'ἀλλύουσαν ἐφεύρομεν ἀγλαὸν ἱστόν.
>
> we caught her unraveling her beautiful work.

Again the repetition of the same syncopated form "allu-" instead of a metrically possible "analu-" is interesting, because it seems to remind the audience, maybe less of an iambic feature than of an epic one that has been answered by the iambus. There is one Archilochean fragment that could be (this is a mere hypothesis) the occurrence of a similar vocabulary and of similar themes. In fr. 148 W we find remains of the word δέννος, used especially to blame male hubris, there is maybe νητή, the word that designates spun wool (cf. νήματα), there is probably the word κοῦρος, and καλλυ-, mostly completed as καλλυ[νῶν, or something like that, but in this context and from its metrical position, another solution might be possible. The upper strokes of the word ΥΒΡΙΝ are missing in fr. 148 W, but reappear in the lower part of fr. 158 W. Joining the two fragments results in the following text:

>]οσ[.]επαρθηναι[ι
> δ]έννος ὕβριν αρ[
>]νήτην καλλύ[
> κου]ρους ἀλκίμους[
>
> ...to be proud...
> ... abuse insolence...
> ... resolve (?)...
> stout-hearted (youths?) (after Gerber)

This is the center of a trochaic tetrameter, with the dihairesis before the omikron in the first line, before ΥΒΡΙΝ in the second, before καλλυ in the third. If really the future tense of the verb καλλύνειν, the only form that would metrically fit, are to be read, then the dihairesis probably cuts the immediate link between object and verb, which at least for Archilochus would be harsh. We would rather expect a connector like δέ or καί after the dihairesis. This makes less absurd a blend (or crasis) between a καί and the verb ἀλλύω that is attested by Byzantine dictionaries very eager to explain archaic poetry. The form κἀλλύουσα for instance would have the advantage to fit in an easier way both the metrical scheme (with the epic short ypsilon of λύω in the present stem) and the syntactical possibilities in this metrical position. We cannot exclude the possibility, that the iambographers felt concerned about the Suitor-Penelope story, even if it has an epic character originally. This guess holds all the more if we compare the fr. 146 West coming from the same papyrus and evoking a situation of attacks that are ironically called "gifts" or even of "hosts" who seem to fear an attack, but are ready to defend themselves, once they have assembled. Then they would be able to encircle the enemy (ἀμφικουρίη). This could fit the Suitors' situation and lead us to the last story of a betrayal of hosts[48].

    [ ] .σα[
    [ ]μη[
    [ ]μφα[
    [ ]ιδερεισ[
    [ ]προσβαλόντε[ς .]σ[5
    [] ν ξεινίων φειδοίατ[ο
    [ ]ων ἀθρόοι γενοίμεθ[α
    [ ]σης τεύχεσιν πεφρ[
    [ ]σφας ἀμφικουρίη λάβ[

... striking against...   5
... were sparing of guest-gifts...
... we were all together ...
... fortified by arms...
... capture by encirclement...

6.10 Herakles

The last story is neither an inversion nor a pure iambic story; it is an epic story, the killing of the Suitors. But it is connected by many links to the intertext with the iambus, making up the justifying myth of revenge. It is a story about Herakles, beside Hermes, the only god all three iambographers, Archilochus, Semonides and Hipponax, speak about and, what is more, in a positive way[49]. Not only is he the typical young man deprived of his heritage, forced to work for surviving and gaining a wife, but also he recalls the ideological link between young men and heroes in his name. Still the 4th century BC-corporations of νέοι reserve their reverence for two gods: Hermes and Herakles. And we have seen that Herakles plays a very little role in the *Odyssey* so that the few occurrences are significant. They show him as a representative of young men. In the intertext with the *Argonautica* he is replaced by an Odysseus as a young man. In his last occurrence he plays the role of an enemy of Odysseus, but of an Odysseus as a "man". Although this iambic story is not explicit in the 21st book, it has been prepared in the former books by allusions, in the 8th and the 15th book, and we read the composite fabula in Apollodorus' mythological *bibliotheke*[50].

Eurytus like Ekhetos, Lycambes or Oinomaus is a father who does not want to give in marriage his daughter, Iole. He provokes her Suitors to a bow-contest. They always lose because Eurytus shoots best. But when Herakles, the iambic hero, faces him, it is the father's turn to lose. Nevertheless, Eurytus refuses the marriage to Herakles. Who takes both, the city and Iole.

This is the hidden story. When Penelope prepares the contest and goes for Odysseus' bow and the arrows, the Narrator offers the following part by a description of the weapon (*Od.* 21.13f.):

δῶρα τά οἱ ξεῖνος Λακεδαίμονι δῶκε τυχήσας
Ἴφιτος Εὐρυτίδης ἐπιείκελος ἀθανάτοισι.

gifts that had been given to him by his friend
godlike Iphitus when they met in Lakedaimon.

This second story runs like this: The dead Eurytus left his bow to his son Iphitus. He has to bring back 12 female horses stolen by a hitherto unknown thief. In archaic poetry, female horses are a very superficial and widespread image of girls (Alcman, Anacreon, Semonides) and since the thief is Herakles, the audience could easily recognize in this story the subsequent part of the first story: Iphitus tries to bring back the lost treasure of his father. At the same time, young Odysseus has a similar quest, but for sheep. They meet in the house of Ortilochus and conclude ξενία, a mutual contract a reciprocal relationship between guest and host. To have a sign, a σύμβολον ξενίας, they exchange their weapons as δῶρα: This is the way Odysseus got Eurytus' bow.

But never will the contract enter in effect, because Iphitus will not reach Odysseus' house. Actually Herakles invites him. When Iphitus discovers that he is the thief of the horses, Herakles kills him. The Narrator took care to underline the criminal situation: not so much to kill is criminal, but to kill a host (*Od.* 21.27).

ὅς μιν ξεῖνον ἐόντα κατέκτανεν ᾧ ἐνὶ οἴκῳ,
σχέτλιος, οὐδὲ θεῶν ὄπιν ᾐδέσατ'οὐδὲ τράπεζαν,
τὴν ἥν οἱ παρέθηκεν· ἔπειτα δὲ πέφνε καὶ αὐτόν,
ἵππους δ'αὐτὸς ἔχε κρατερώνυχας ἐν μεγάροισι.

He killed him in his own house, though he was Ipithus' host,
caring no more in that cruel heart of his for the vengeful eye of god than
for the hospitality he had given him—feasted the man first, then killed him,
took the mares himself, and put them in his own stables.

This establishes the second equivalence between Herakles and the Suitors: not only to be the heroic representative and god of the Suitors, but to act like them: The Suitors have planned to kill their hosts, Telemachus and Odysseus, too. The fact that Odysseus will use Iphitus' bow to kill the Suitors is justified by the contract of ξενία: Odysseus takes revenge for Iphitus by killing the people Herakles stands for.

The thematic analysis of the iambic stories used in the *Odyssey* firstly has shown that there is a strong polemic of the epos against the iambus. Secondly there is a difference to later (and our) rhetoric. Our representatives of the power say "flexible" or "cooperative" for what the powerless say "obedient", and similar oppositions are to be found in classical rhetorical treatises. If thus after the archaic period, the vocabulary can indicate the origin of a voice or the perspective of the audience, the polemic intertext of archaic epos and iambus (as well as that between women and young men) use the same words, the same themes, but mark the perspective by the narrative figure of inversion. The Suitors or an audience consisting of young men would have no chance to identify themselves with the Odyssean use of their stories.

Notes

[1] Cook 1995, 21f.
[2] The verb Hipponax uses is the same Archilochus has already chosen (fr. 279 W), perhaps in a similar situation.
[3] Hdt. 1.8.3-1.12.2, for other versions Pichler R., *Die Gygesgeschichte in der griechischen Literatur und ihrer neuzeitlichen Rezeption*, München 1986.
[4] The full interpretation of Menelaus' speech in Steinrück M., "Der Bericht des Proteus", *QUCC* 71, 1992, 47-60.
[5] Whenever Greek literature deals with seals there are girls to be mentioned: the nymph who transformed herself in a seal in order to escape Aeacus, seals eating sexual active girls (*Od.* 15.480), love stories between a sponge diver and a seal (Ael. *N.A.* 4.56) . On Helena and

the "sealherd" Call. *Aitia* 3.5. Holy Thekla escapes the horrible seals because of her refusal of sexuality *(Acta Theclae* 34.8 Lipsius).

[6] When Horace alludes to Archilochus frr. 196 and 196a one of the elements he transforms but keeps nevertheless is the door-motive. Horace makes them real doors in a traditional παρακλαυσίθυρον, transmogrifying the aggressive style of archaic iambus in a gentle and seemingly innocent entertainment of the Augustan audience. And yet, it does not remain innocent, but this change is emphasized: for in a παρακλαυσίθυρον people traditionally brake their foot tips, even their heart, but not, as in Horace's epode, their limbs. So maybe Horace not only adapts the discourse of Archilochus' iambus to severe Augustan readers, but he underlines that he adapted it or had to adapt it.

[7] Think of Archi-lochus, Orsi-lochus, and the Achilles-like young man Anti-lochus in the *Iliad*.

[8] True, they wonder whether she is a guné or a goddess. But this use of *guné* does not exclude the sense of "girl" for νύμφη. Guné means in opposition to goddess simply what anér would mean in opposition to god: human. Male domination of female is very perceptible in Greek society but this should not force us to infer that this domination is enacted by the very double-sided system of marked (female) and unmarked (male and female = men). Greek gendered power goes through the opposition of adult and non-adult. Therefore guné means both non-girl and non-goddess.

[9] Cf. Miralles Pòrtulas 1983.

[10] Hes. fr. 43a.41-43 M.-W.

[11] Verg. *Aen* 1.184ff.: tris litore **ceruos** /prospicit errantis; hos tota armenta sequuntur / a tergo et longum per uallis pascitur agmen. / constitit hic arcumque manu celerisque sagittas / corripuit fidus quae tela gerebat Achates, / ductoresque ipsos primum capita **alta** ferentis / **cornibus** arboreis sternit.

[12] Birge D., "Ambiguity and the Stag Hunt in 'Odyssey' 10", *Helios* 20 1993, 17-28. with a critique of Schmoll and Roessel.

[13] Meuli K., *Odyssee und Argonautika: Untersuchungen zur griechischen Sagengeschichte und zum Epos*, Berlin 1921, and Dräger P., Argo Pasimelousa. *Der Argonautenmythos in der griechischen und römischen Literatur*, I, Stuttgart 1993.

[14] *AO* 639ff. Ἡρακλέης δ' ἠπείγετ' ἂν' ὑλήεντας ἐναύλους,/τόξον ἔχων παλάμαις ἰδὲ τριγλώχινας ὀιστούς,/ὄφρα κε θηρήσαιτο, πόροι δ' ἐπὶ **δόρπον ἐταίροις**,/ἢ σύας, ἢ **πόρτιν κεραὴν** ἢ ἄγριον αἶγα.

[15] Maybe Olympiodorus according to Livrea H., *Anonymi fortasse Olympiodori Thebani Blemyomachia (P.Berol. 5003)*, Meisenheim am Glan 1978, but see Steinrück M., "Neues zur Blemyomachie", *ZPE* 126 1999, 99–114.

[16] As do the *Lithika* transmitted together with the *AO* in the manuscripts and associated by Tzetzes with Orpheus (cf. Schamp J. Halleux R., *Les Lapidaires Grecs*, Paris 1985). Both texts imitate achaic features and try to correct Hellenistic variants of the same theme (Nicandrus, Apollonius of Rhodes).

[17] A.R. 1.1187ff..: Αὐτὰρ ὁ, **εὖ δαίνυσθαι ἑοῖς ἑτάροις ἐπιτείλας**, /βῆ ῥ' ἴμεν εἰς ὕλην υἱὸς Διός, ὥς κεν **ἐρετμόν**/ ͵οἷ αὐτῷ φθαίη καταχείριον ἐντύνασθαι, and Valerius Flaccus 3.545: sic ait et celerem frondosa per avia **cervum**/ suscitat ac iuveni **sublimem cornibus** offert.

[18] Vian, F. ed. vert., *Les Argonautiques orphiques*, Paris 1987, 45 : "Sa langue, par ses vulgarismes et ses étrangetés, suggère qu'il n'est qu'à demi hellénisé. " I.e. the author's Greek cannot be that of a native speaker. Furthermore his use of the caesura in the hexameters does not recall anything in Greek hexametric epos, but Roman epic and especially Ovid's use of it (cf. Steinrück 2007, 30f.).

[19] When Dio of Prusa tells an inversion of social evolution during the reign of Domitianus (the emperor who expelled Dio) in his Euboean speech, he represents himself as an

Odysseus. This Odysseus comes on the island without his fellows (they are fishermen and decide to continue without him like the Argonauts do with Hercules) after shipwrecking. There is no reason for a stag-hunt, but it figures in the text: a stag has been chased by hunters and has made a fall from the rocks near the coast. In Dio's reading of the *Odyssey*, therefore, the dead stag is linked to Odysseus and maybe to the argonautic Herakles too.

[20] Cf. Hunter R., *The Argonautica of Apollonius, Literary Studies*, Cambridge 1993, 26, et Knight V., *The Renewal of Epic, Responses to Homer in the Argonautica of Apollonius*, Leiden New York Köln 1995, 131. Spaltenstein F., "Continuité imaginative et structure des Argonautiques", in H.J. Tschiedel ed., *Ratis omnia vincit, Untersuchungen zu den Argonautica des Valerius Flaccus*, Hildesheim Zürich New York 1991, 89-100, esp. 99.

[21] Segal Ch., "Teiresias in the Yukon: A Note on Folktale and Epic ('Odyssey' 11, 100-144 and 23, 248-287) ", in R. Pretagostini ed., *Tradizione e innovazione nella cultura greca da Omero all'età ellenistica, scritti in onore di Bruno Gentili* I, Roma 1993, 61-68.

[22] *Od.* 11.601ff.

[23] Peradotto J., "The Social Control of Sexuality: Odyssean Dialogics", *Arethusa* 26 1993, 173-182, interprets this in Bachtinian terms as polyphonic voice.

[24] Cf. Clay J. S., *The Wrath of Athena, Gods and men in the Odyssey*, Lanham 1997 (1983).

[25] On Hermes as the one who enters doors Kahn L., *Hermès passe ou les ambiguïtés de la communication*, Paris 1978.

[26] Already Solon reads the *Pheacians* as legend of colonization: In fr. 19 W he represents them as a model of the colonial enterprise of king Philocyprus.

[27] Semonides fr. 7.90 W or Pellizer-Tedeschi.

[28] In *hCer* 82ff. he tries to convince Demeter to leave her daughter to the γαμβρός Hades.

[29] Braswell B.K., "The Song of Ares and Aphrodite: Theme and Relevance to Odyssey 8", *Hermes* 110 1982, 129-137.

[30] Hipp. *De articulis*, 32.11.

[31] Ar. *Lys.* 360f.

[32] The intertextual play of later epic often associates this passage with iambic themes such as contests between Centaur and man.

[33] Fr. 129 LP. Alcaeus is considered an iambographer by Julian (in the beginning of the *Misopogon*) or by Horace and certainly shares some of this tradition. But his audience, hiding like mafiosi in the mountains of Lesbos, seems to be mixed of both husbands and young men. This is perhaps why we can find in his fragments as well formal elements of Theognis' elegy as of Archilochus' iambus.

[34] Since the pun on *dêmos*, people, and *demós*, fat, runs down to Aristophanes, this also might be an allusion to the image of fat-eating kings. Cf. Ceccarelli P. Létoublon F. Steinrück M., "L'individu, le territoire, la graisse: du public et du privé chez Homère", in F. de Polignac P. Schmitt Pantel edd., *Public et privé en Grèce ancienne: lieux, conduites, pratiques, Ktema* 23 1998, 47-58, and Steinrück M., *La pierre et la graisse, Lecture dans l'intertexte grec antique*, avec une préface de P. Pucci, Amsterdam 2001.

[35] Pucci 1987.

[36] For this interpretation Pucci P., *The Song of the Sirens. Essays on Homer*, Lanham, 1997.

[37] On this double marked quality cf. *infra* chapter 7.

[38] *Il.* 19.215, esp. 19.225.

[39] On shortages not only during the 7th century Garnsey P., *Food and Society in Classical Antiquity*, Cambridge 1999.

[40] Thalmann 1998.

[41] So Rutherford R.B., *Homer, Odyssey, Books XIX and XX*, Cambridge 1992, 64f.

[42] Arch. fr. 34 W, which Schneidewin joined with the reference to this rhapsody by Dion Chrysostomus (60.1). We could add fr. 276 W as a reference to the story Dianira sings

about Achelous deprived of his horn by Herakles (cf. *LIMC* s.v. Acheloos, 261 a and 261 b).
[43] Bacchyl. 5.173 S-M.
[44] Xenoph. fr. 1.21-24 W.
[45] Schol. Od. Hypoth. 85.16 H.Œ.
"Εχετος βασιλεὺς ἦν τῆς Ἠπείρου, Εὐχήνορος παῖς, ὠμὸς καὶ ἀπότομος, ὃς καὶ τὴν θυγατέρα Μετώπην ἢ Ἄμφισσαν ὑπὸ Αἰχμοδίκου φθαρεῖσαν πηρώσας ἠνάγκαζε σιδηρᾶς ἀλεῖν κριθάς, λέγων τότε ἀποδώσειν τὰς ὄψεις, ὅτε ἀλέσει τὰς κριθάς. τὸν δὲ Αἰχμόδικον ἐπὶ ἑστίασιν καλέσας ἠκρωτηρίασε καὶ τὰ αἰδοῖα αὐτοῦ ἀπέκοψεν. ὕστερον μέντοι μανεὶς καὶ τῶν ἰδίων ἐμφορηθεὶς σαρκῶν ἀπέσβη.
[46] Semon. fr. 7.68 W and fr. 7. 114 W.
[47] Plat. *Legg.* 658d7.
[48] A new commentary to this fragment in Da Cunha Corrêa P., *Armas e varões, a guerra na lírica de Arquíloco*, São Paolo 1998, 258.
[49] Cf. Poland F., *Geschichte des griechischen Vereinswesens*, Leipzig 1909, 193. About Herakles and Hermes in the Gymnasium cf. Graf F., *Nordionische Kulte*, Roma 1985, 98, on ephebs 105, on Hermes Hippios 271.
[50] Marcozzi D., "Connotazioni messeniche nella leggenda di Eurito, l'epica e la tradizione", in *Scritti in memoria di Carlo Gallavotti, Rivista di Cultura Classica e Medioevale* 36 1994, 79-86, (the link with *Od.* 8.224ff.); Pralon D., "L'invention des cadets: la faute exemplaire", in M. Segalen G. Ravis-Giordani edd., *Les cadets*, Paris 1994, 59-65, shows that Herakles also exemplifies in *Il.* 19.86-138 the relationship between (the husband) Agamemnon and (the youngster) Achilles.

7 Point of view in the *Odyssey*

7.1 Objectivity versus identification-readers

Winners are in no need of epics. The *Nibelungenlied*, the *Geste* of Roland, the *Song of Hildebrandt*, the tales around Marko Kraljevic, *Sir Taddeusz* or the *Last Ride into Lithuania* (Mickiewicz), the *Song of Igor* (Karamzin?), the *Digenis Akritas*, the *Blemyomachia* (Olympiodorus?), or the *Olympic Spring* (Spitteler), most of known heroic (and in their way historical) epics help losers manage the past with humor or change it into victories. For them, as well as for the *Iliad*, the *Odyssey*, the *Cypria*, the *Theogony* or the *Catalogue of Heroines* inventing the past in an ironic-sentimentalist manner means, ideologically, not only constructing the past of the Heroes but also, through it, the time of the audience, that is to say: the present. This has been called (cf. chapt. 1) "the husbands' and wives' ambivalent point of view on the epic past". Exactly like in tragedy and comedy, after the journey into the other realm, there is always a return to 'reality'. What is special in the *Odyssey*: the audience has not to return itself to reality after the singer has ended because that return is the very subject of the tale. To return means preferring the actual own world to the visited one, affirming the actual world as the better one. Since the glorified past must fail, the decadent present turns out to be the better alternative. If, as we argued, the boundary between heroic and human times was imagined as a sort of wedding, as a transition from youth to adult status, then, one element of the Athenian wedding rite fits the image. A boy used to pass among the tables of the wedding dinner repeating the phrase "we are going from the worse to the better".

Thus, the general view of the external audience at the epic tableau has been defined. Segal singled out how internal audiences react to the stories of the past. The Pheacians enjoy it, the Suitors like nothing more than dancing and singing; they are young men and could find themselves glorified in the heroes of the songs[1]. Odysseus, Telemachus, and Penelope are very different: they weep at epic performances and have to learn to moderate their feelings—be it by self-therapy, by drugs or by social rules—and never to give themselves away to the past, but to be there *and* here at all times[2]. What distinguishes, thus, the mere joyful nostalgia of a non-married audience from the husbands and wives is a viewpoint directed by both nostalgia and refusal, joy and grief.

There is grief perhaps because listening to the singer is associated with the feeling of imprisonment in an Age (or age). Twice an Odyssean "mise en abyme" highlights this image of listening to epic songs. In the adventures of the Lotophages and the Sirens, song has the power of a drug that makes the audience forget about return, wives and children or, as in the case of the Pheacians, about the present. The texts call it *kelein* or *thelgein*, verbs which also design the witch's spell, and probably all of Homer's readers feel that this spell must be very close to what we call the epic illusion, "epische Schein" or "illusion épique". We know this feeling from reading novels of the 18th and 19th centuries. We even associate this spell with the 18th century concept of epic genre. And yet, before the creation of modern novel, readers of Homer had another impression. The French "Modernes" and still the 19th century scholars felt a difference between Homer on the one hand, and Tolstoy, Zola, Musil, Sterne or Prus on the other hand[3]. They saw a very objective, simple and naïve Narrator at work. Kleist's text on the puppet-theater compared Homeric space to a rather medieval two-level painting without any Renaissance perspective and Zielinski showed that no explicit representation of simultaneous events is possible in Homer. But with the analysis of works such as *Tristram Shandy*, the discipline of narratology evolved and was concerned with the strange feeling that readers have, of being transferred to another place, into another time. Criteria were found to explain epic illusion: the metaphor of the point of view, deixis, direct speech, character-discourse in the Narrator-discourse, elements of the text that allow us to look through the character's eyes at his world. There where sufficient witnesses of late antiquity (Minucius Felix, Pseudo-Longinus, Hermogenes, Heliodorus) to extend this explanation to antiquity if not to whole mankind[4].

In the area of Homeric scholarship, Irene de Jong broke through against the older description of the Iliadic Narrator as objective and simple: she applied the concept of focalization and showed that we can read Homer by identifying ourselves with the characters, by looking through their eyes. And this is, according to her conclusion, what the Homeric Narrator called *kelein*[5].

Perhaps because he was more sensitive to the mechanics of (Stalinist) domination, Mikhail Bachtin offered a slightly different, maybe better-defined concept of the *voices* that occur in a narrative[6]. He considered the history of literature a constant rising and falling of both narratives with voices that are controlled by other voices (for instance the voice of the character controlled by that of the Narrator) and "carnavalistic" texts such as Dostoevsky's in which different voices are involved in an unhierarchisized dialogue. In order to show how to find those voices he used the concept of the "foreign discourse" (chuzhoe slovo), borrowed from the Russian formalists. But the easiest way to enter the problem ist a more specific type of foreign discourse described first in 1912 by Saussure's pupil Charles Bally : the "discours indirect libre"[7]. An example of free indirect speech will explain this concept more clearly. It is taken from Virginia Woolf:

> "Of course, he was invited tonight."

The Narrator's voice can say, "he was invited" using the past and the third person (from the point of view of his performance). A character, from his point of view, would have to change person and time of the verb (I am invited). The Narrator, on the contrary, cannot utter *tonight*, because the word refers to the present (he would have to say *that evening*). This word belongs to the character's point of view, to the time he is invited and which is a present time to him, his "hic et nunc". For, in a direct speech, the character would say: "I am invited tonight". Thirdly, *of course* can be used from both the Narrator's (a judgment) and the character's point of view (interjection in a direct speech). Therefore only *tonight* is a foreign discourse regarding to the Narrator.

Why would this word help the audience to identify itself with the character? The answer is: because the Narrator's point of view prevails in the narrative discourse and the intrusion of the character's point of view into that of the Narrator compels the audience to look with the character's eyes at his world. Conversely, the character's point of view prevails in direct speech. Plato and Aristotle already believed that this discourse creates the mimesis, a concept very close to that of epic or dramatic illusion[8]. The more the Narrator's point of view controls the domain of the character, the less we can speak of a Bachtinian dialogue of voices, and the more we are dealing with a Narrator-controlled text. Accordingly, such a phenomenon would go with the absence of foreign discourse in the Narrator's speech. This would be Bachtin's definition of what Page, Wilamowitz and Welcker or the French *modernes* called an objective Narrator, whereas the presence of strong foreign discourse or what Irene de Jong calls an "embedded focalization" in the Narrator-speech and a strong (very different from the Narrator/Locutor's) point of view in the direct speeches, a free indirect speech, would force us to categorize Homer's text as appropriate to identification-readers, or as a subjective Narrator (Irene de Jong) or as a carnavalistic text full of voices in non-hierarchical dialogue (Bachtin)[9].

However, in order to define what could be called "the Suitor's viewpoint" in the *Odyssey,* we shall start with an attempt to define the type of text in general. Then, we should be able to say to what extent Homer's audience could or could not follow the Suitors' point of view.

7.2 *tomorrow*

In order to inquire into the type of epic illusion we are dealing with in Homer, let us start with the intrusion of character discourse into the Narrator's speech. Since *tonight* has no equivalent in other languages (*heute abend* is too strong, ἑσπέρας or *ce soir* is too weak), a very strong marker of foreign discourse that would be common to several languages and traditions shall be adopted as a criterion: *tomorrow*. Käte Hamburger made this word famous in her book on literary genres and their discourses[10]. One of her examples was taken from *The suitors of Babette Bomberling* of Alice Berend[11]:

"Aber am Vormittag hatte sie den Baum zu putzen. Morgen war Weihnachten."

"But in the morning she had to set the Christmas-tree up. Tomorrow was Christmas."

Morgen is foreign discourse. The Narrator cannot use it without referring to his own present. He takes it from the character's speech. In a direct speech "she" could say: "*tomorrow* will be Christmas". The Narrator would have to say "*the other day* was Christmas", if he wanted to preserve his point of view. German readers are not shocked by this sentence; their narrative tradition allows such a strong marker as *tomorrow* in the Narrator-speech. However, when Hamburger's book was translated into French, the translators and the readers felt that this sample did not fit the French narrative tradition. Ten years ago most French native speakers corrected the phrase "*demain* était Noël" into "*le lendemain* était Noël"[12]. It seems, therefore, that French readers or readers grown up in the French narrative tradition at least felt or still feel uncomfortable towards this strong identification with the time and the glimpse of the characters and prefer to maintain the temporal distance of the Narrator's point of view. Perhaps, this different attitude to the characters "present" in the narrative is indebted or mirrored in the difference between French and German syntax of indirect character-speech depending of a past tense. In German grammar an indirect speech depending of a past or a present tense are both put into the same modus, the conjunctive of the present.

Er fragte (past), ob er krank *sei*. (present conjunctive)
Er fragt (present), ob er krank *sei*. (present conjunctive)

In the same cases of the French grammar a change is requested:

Il demanda (past) s'ilétait (past) malade.
Il demande (present) s'il est (present) malade.

Whereas the German Narrator of a story written in the past may invite the audience to enter the character's ideas as if it were now, French Narrators are closer to the Locutors. They use a syntax that invites the audience to consider from a certain temporal distance words or ideas thought or spoken in the past. So French and German indirect speech syntax seem to be related to each other in the same way as they accept or not the strong identification marker "tomorrow" and in the same way as they do or do not constrain a reader to take up the characters point of view, to enter "his" present[13].

This introduction is not meant to show that only two types of languages or literary traditions exist, but that they are different in every language and that epic illusion can be constructed in different ways. How does Greek literature behave then? We have to distinguish between the archaic tradition and classical or postclassical Greek. Athenaeus' Narrator can say (148A): "Καὶ ἐς αὔριον παρεκάλει συνδειπνῆσαι" Just like Alice Berend's Narrator in *Die Bräutigame der Babette Bomberling*, he can use *tomorrow* as a foreign discourse in order to make us lose the distant feeling towards the past and, therefore, enter the character's time. And this narrative phenomenon fits the grammar of those centuries. When uttering indirect speech in the past, a Narrator uses the same present tense (in a relation of simultaneity) as when he deals with an indirect speech depending on a present tense. No wonder Pseudo-Longinus 9.10 tells us that readers (of the first century AD) enter the character's point of view (συνεμβαίνειν).

But how does Homer use "tomorrow" and indirect speech? Never does his Narrator use the word αὔριον, he is restrained to the equivalent of *le lendemain, the other day*: ἠῶθεν[14]. The word αὔριον only occurs in direct speech. Can we deduce from it that Homer's audience identifies itself less with the characters and shares more the distant point of view of the Narrator? The *Homeric Grammar* by Pierre Chantraine seems to confirm this conclusion. He says about indirect speech[15]: "lorsque le verbe principal est au passé, ... pour exprimer la concomitance, là où l'attique garde le présent, Homère emploie toujours l'imparfait."

7.3 Control and freedom of character-speech

Homer does not seem to expect his audience to use identification reading, but a rather distant look directed by the Narrator. This conclusion is consistent with what linguists observed. According to Schwyzer II 333, the *optativus obliquus*, the Attic verbal form that distinguishes a character's thought in indirect speech assertions from remarks of the Narrator expressed by indicative forms, does – stricto sensu – not exist in the Homeric tradition. There are optatives instead of conjunctives or taking place even in indirect questions and we could translate them as the character's voice in the Narrator's speech, but in assertions this phenomenon starts around 500 BC.

As we saw in Irene de Jong's work, this does not exclude that Turgenev's, Musil's[16] or even Virginia Woolf's readers could make their accustomed identifications with Penelope or Eumaeus, but it does mean that Homer's audience would have felt unconfortable with Musil's or Turgenev's texts. And this emerges even more clearly from the level of direct speech, the second bias that can construct the point of view of a character and, thus, the focalization of the reader's identification.

As we have seen in the chapter on Odyssean composition, there is a very sharp borderline of knowledge between what the Narrator and what characters may tell the audience. All seems to depend on the temporal start of the story. At the beginning of the *Odyssey*, ten lines are used to define the starting point after which the Narrator, the voice of a divine girl coming out of the mouth of a male singer, can tell "his" story[17].

> Gérard Genette drew some distinctions between different types of flash-backs or "analepses" according to this temporal criterion: A Narrator or a character can recall during the story events that belong to the same story but happened before this starting point. Genette called it an externat analepse. But the same Narrator or character can recall as well things that happened before the recall but after the start of the story. This would be an internal analepse. Of this latter type there are two more specific analepses. One can recall things that have already been mentioned (an internal repetitive analepse) and things that have not been mentioned: An internal completive analepse[18].

The same ten lines of the proem also define the narrative material preceding this starting point and a character will tell this realm. This work-division can be applied to the whole Homeric corpus. Characters are free to tell all the stories that happened before the beginning of the song. To use Genette's terms: they may make external analepses. But they are restricted to one type of analepse or flash-back after the starting point. They can only tell what the Narrator has already told (or make what Genette called an internal repetitive analepse). They may develop a Narrator's remark in their speeches, but never, with a small (and Odyssean) exception[19], will they tell the audience what they saw or heard after the starting point if the Narrator has not yet described it before[20]. That is, character-speech seems to be free to make internal repetitive analepses, but no internal completive analepse. The way Musil's characters can describe the world they see and to invite the reader to look at it with them without any Narrator/Locutor-control, this window to another world, which accustoms the reader to the character's point of view, is almost forbidden for Homeric characters. And a character-speech that opens the narrative and forces the reader to a character's point of view before the Narrator has the chance to say anything, as in the beginning of Turgenev's *Fathers and Sons*, is not possible for Odysseus, Penelope and Telemachus. One might object that I propose a universal system of narrative possibilities associated, as Bachtin suggested, to political thought on power. But as Thalmann has recently shown, narrative point of view is not only a mirror of hierarchical relationships in a given society, it can also be a bias for maintaining these hierarchies. It seems that both the Narrator's control over the knowledge of the characters (or over what they perceive) and the refusal to admit character-intrusion into Narrator-speech are not a simple anthropological archaic rule, but rather an epic tradition. First-person-Narrators of other 7-6th century-traditions (where the voice of the muse is absent) can start their texts with character-speech (cf. Archilochus' fr. 122 West) and can use the present for indirect speech uttered in the past (cf. Sappho's fr. 1 Voigt). Therefore, the very powerful point of view of the Homeric Narrator/Locutor and his strong control of the character's point of view are not necessarily the consequence of a vernacular language, but appear to be a choice against other literary traditions.

One can ask how non-identification-narratives construct the epic illusion, the κηληθμός. I tried to give an answer elsewhere[21]. Only one comparison should satisfy curiosity: Homeric epics show a distribution of imperfect and aorist-forms that do not always coincide with the rules of the handbook. It might be, for instance, that the very high percentage of speech-introductions in the imperfect (75%) has to do with epic illusion. Whereas aorist-tense stresses the temporal distance between tale and teller, imperfect-tense erases this impression of past (by underscoring the—semantic—properties of the action). In other terms, the Narrator/Locutor is more present in his/her function as Locutor (some say: poet), speaking to the audience rather than a mere Narrator who could give free access to the characters' point of view. It could be that a Homeric audience jingled from one imperfect over a gap of aorists to the next sure imperfect or the very frequent speeches (in the present tense). The epic illusion would, then, rather be a Tarzan-flight between high trees seen from the ground than an elevator that transports us to the same height. We will see that the second mean is not completely excluded, but it is not as important as for instance in German, Russian, or maybe to a lesser extent Anglo-Saxon traditions.

7.4 Point of view of individuals: πόσις

These short glimpses at the two principal means of constructing a prevailing or controlled character-point of view, of inviting the audience to identify itself with the characters should prevent us from projecting our identification reading of Turgenev, Musil or Woolf on Homer too easily. We will start our inquiry with the hypothesis that deictic markers that do not force us to assume an identification reading **can** be understood from the rather distant point of view of the Narrator/Locutor. Once we have defined the general conditions of Homeric point of view and the possible forms of identification reading, we will be able to analyze the Suitors' point of view and to set it into its context. For the sake of clarity the viewpoint of the audience will be called *perspective*, whereas the focus, focalizer, or *lector in fabula*, which guides the perspective, will be called *point of view*. Furthermore, we will try to distinguish between two positive points of view and one negative:

1) the individual and exclusive point of view of a character constraining the audience to look through his eyes (assisted only by a Narrator).
2) the point of view of a Narrator/Locutor whose discourse refers not to an individual, but to a group and who narrates as if he were among the characters.
3) the negative point of view of a group, visible only in polemic or in intertext. This is the type we have already described in former chapters.

We will set out to inquire into some passages, where Turgenev's, Musil's and Woolf's readers (and even Flaubert's but not necessarily the readers of Zola) would incline to an identification reading. One of the most interesting passages is found after the slaughter of the Suitors. Eurycleia announces to Penelope that Odysseus is back and that he killed the νέοι. At first Penelope thinks that her maidservant has lost her mind, then she seems overwhelmed by joy, and then, again, she cannot believe the news. She chooses the formula that was used in the 7th century by Stesichorus to introduce his dementi-song, and says clearly that she cannot consider this murderer to be Odysseus[22]. The slaughter must be the work of some god, and this Odysseus must be a ghost just as Stesichorus identified Helena in Troy as a mere phantom in his *Palinode*[23]. Eurycleia tries it again, this time with the argument of the scar: she has recognized Odysseus by the scar left of an injury made by a boar when Odysseus was a boy. But Penelope confirms her interpretation: Gods are perfect in deception. Nevertheless, she wants to see her son and the stranger. Yet, when she goes downstairs, the Narrator gives a puzzling comment (*Od.* 23.85ff.)[24]:

ὣς φαμένη κατέβαιν' ὑπερώϊα· πολλὰ δέ οἱ κῆρ
ὥρμαιν' ἢ ἀπάνευθε φίλον πόσιν ἐξερεείνοι
ἦ παρστᾶσα κύσειε κάρη καὶ χεῖρε λαβοῦσα.

As she spoke she left her room and made her way downstairs,
without decision. Should she remain aloof as she questioned **her** husband, or go
straight up to him and kiss his head and hands?

We argued in the second chapter that the second part of the *Odyssey* is made according to the same pattern as the first half. This part of the recognition between Odysseus and Penelope would correspond to the part where Odysseus meets Nausicaa and where he reacts in the same way as Penelope, doubting whether he should go closer or speak to her from a certain distance (*Od.* 6.142):

ἢ γούνων λίσσοιτο λαβὼν εὐώπιδα κούρην
ἢ αὔτως ἐπέεσσιν ἀποσταδὰ μειλιχίοισι...

whether he should throw his arms round the beautiful girl's knees,
or be content to keep his distance and beg her with all courtesy

Contact or distance is the question that both ask themselves. But the situations are different, and Penelope's case allows a lot of interpretations of the alternative. Penelope hesitates between

1) deceiving the stranger *as if she had* accepted him as her husband and maintaining the distant αἰδώς attitude in case he is a god. This explanation, though hard to accept, is difficult to exclude.
2) deceiving Odysseus, as if she took him for a stranger and adopted the convenient attitude of a wife towards her husband, if she *really knows already that the beggar* is Odysseus.
3) recognizing and *failing to recognize Odysseus*.

What follows our passage seems to speak in favor of the third explanation. Penelope decides to stay within a certain distance of the stranger and is wondering (*Od.* 23.94):

ὄψει δ' ἄλλοτε μέν μιν ἐνωπαδίως ἐσίδεσκεν,
ἄλλοτε δ' ἀγνώσασκε κακὰ χροΐ εἵματ' ἔχοντα.

her eyes were busy, at one moment resting full on his face,
at the next falling on the ragged clothes that made him a stranger again.

An innocent oscillation between knowing and ignoring seems to be the best description of Penelope's feelings, but the Narrator uses words that seem to stand against this interpretation, especially when he says that Penelope doubts whether to question *her husband* or to kiss him. To a Virginia Woolf-reader, the reflexive pronoun φίλον in the expression φίλον πόσιν, "*her* husband", suggests an identification reading: If the Narrator relates Penelope's thoughts, he only transposes an interior monologue like "my husband" into the third person "her husband", and this means that Penelope already knows that the beggar is Odysseus. If we adopt this reading, then the second situation would be the conclusion. But nothing hinders us from understanding *her husband* (and the context even suggests to read it) as the mere knowledge of the Narrator, perhaps used in a slightly ironical way as we see it more clearly in *Od.* 19.209: As the beggar is telling stories about Odysseus, the queen starts to cry because she is longing for her husband who is in fact sitting next to her.

κλαιούσης ἑὸν ἄνδρα παρήμενον
as she wept for the husband who was sitting at her side

Here the Narrator/Locutor calls the audience into Odysseus' and his own vision. Penelope is crying for the man whose presence she does even not expect. Things are different in *Od.* 23.86 (Penelope goes downstairs), and a Virginia-Woolf-reader might feel uncomfortable with the same ironical pathos in this passage (*Od.* 19.209). It is important to discuss the question because very different interpretive theories have been based on the choice between identification reading and Narrator reading, as evidence for Penelope's knowledge of the beggar's identity before the recognition scene and for the playful revenge she takes on Odysseus because he mislead her. Have we to choose the second or the third (or even the first) explanation? Let us have a look at the commentaries and the translations:

Ameis-Hentze takes the identification reading (which we suppose to be normal in the German literary tradition) for granted: "φίλον πόσιν daran glaubt sie im Grunde doch" (deep in her heart she believes that he is her husband)[25]. Dealing with all decision-scenes and though aware of the ambiguity, Ch. Voigt cannot restrain from assuming that these are Penelope's thoughts[26]. Accordingly, Heubeck is confident to read it as "la rappresentazione dello stato d'animo di Penelope"[27]. This point of view seems to be possible in the Anglo-Saxon tradition, too. Katz, putting forward the hypothesis of the resourceful Penelope, understands the passage as the only clear indication of the queen's knowledge: "... in one of the rare episodes in the poem where the inner workings of her mind are described, 'whether standing apart to question her dear husband closely'"[28]. Irene de Jong mentions the passage as embedded focalization[29]. But there are other perspectives in the Anglo-Saxon tradition. Van Leeuwen could not see another speaker of φίλον πόσιν than the Narrator[30], and Stanford hesitates between Ameis-Hentze and Van Leeuwen before choosing, finally, the latter explanation[31]. After what has been said about the elder French narrative tradition, Bérard's[32] translation might be representative: "Quel trouble dans son coeur! Elle se demandait si, de loin elle allait interroger l'époux ou s'approcher de lui..." Not only does Bérard emphasize the character's confusion (Quel trouble dans son coeur! = πολλὰ δέ οἱ κῆρ ὥρμαιν'), but also he obliterates the reflexive possessive pronoun by simply translating "*the* husband". This does not rule out an identification reading, but attenuates its necessity.

The mere fact that identification-reading is not necessary but dependent on the tradition, that the Homeric tradition seems very restrictive in using individual point of view, further the immediate context of the passage and the following analyses lead to the conclusion that in *Od.* 23.86 the expression φίλον πόσιν probably represents the Narrator's knowledge, not Penelope's.

7.5 The point of view of the group: ἄναξ

The relation marker ἄναξ has been one of the favorite evidences for identification reading or for embedded focalization of this type. To be sure, Aristotle developed the relation between master and slave or master and attendant (δεσπότης-δοῦλος) as an opposition between two terms calling each other when one of them is mentioned[33]. Such a relation marker seems to be appropriate, thus, to guide perspective into an individual's point of view, especially when it is linked to a verb of perception or implying perception. When an attendant says "the master", readers of Virginia Woolf will incline to hear "my master" and when the Narrator represents this attendant as seeing the master readers will easily complete: "his master". Sat into the Narrator-speech, ἄναξ might, thus, work like αὔριον (in Athenaeus), only to a lower degree. Let us then examine the most compelling passages:

In *Od.* 14.5 Odysseus arrives at the countryside of Ithaca and finds the swineherd Eumaeus sitting in his hut. We would expect the Narrator to prepare us for Odysseus' point of view, his look at the farm. But our expectation is disappointed. The Narrator, in fact, describes new things, not yet known by Odysseus. Eumaius has built a new hurdle (*Od.* 14.7-9):

> ἦν ῥα συβώτης
> αὐτὸς δείμαθ' ὕεσσιν ἀποιχομένοιο ἄνακτος,
> νόσφιν δεσποίνης καὶ Λαέρταο γέροντος.

> The herdsman
> had made it himself for the swine, the master being absent,
> without help from his mistress or the aged Laertes.

A Turgenev-reader could smooth his disappointment by assuming that this word belongs to the slave's vocabulary and expresses his point of view, a sort of longing for his master during his absence. Entering into Eumaeus' mind through the word ἄνακτος, we would have to translate with an embedded focalization:

> The slave built the hurdle himself, *when* **his** master was absent.

But the absolute genitive also allows another translation, which fits the context even better.

> The slave built the hurdle alone, *though* the master was absent.

The concessive relation would mean that the slave continues to work, *although* the master is not watching him, which is, in the *Odyssey*, one of the great virtues of the slave Eumaeus in comparison to other, bad (Thalmann's definition), slaves ceasing to work immediately, after the master has gone. The concessive translation is further confirmed by the following verses. They tell us that Penelope and Laertes have not left Ithaca. The slave cannot long for those masters, nevertheless the slave worked without any order.

Once the concessive translation accepted, we are constrained to leave the identification reading. For if the temporal translation allows to obliterate the Narrator's voice and to introduce the character's thoughts (*when* **his** master was absent), a concessive translation makes the judgment of the Narrator/Locutor too loud to admit another voice. Even if we translate "*though* **his** master was absent", **his** *master* would answer to the Narrator/Locutor's knowledge, not to that of Eumaeus[34].

Neither has this interpretation to be modified some verses later, in *Od.* 14.450: Once again, the Narrator/Locutor stresses the independent work of Eumaeus. The slave bought a slave named Mesaulius[35], without having been told by the ἄναξ of the house. It is difficult to see in the word ἄναξ an indication of Eumaeus' knowledge all the more, as Eumaeus does not know that the beggar is Odysseus. Like with the mark πόσις, the Narrator creates ironic situations with the word ἄναξ. When, for instance, the slave is greeting the beggar in *Od.* 14.36;

> ὃ δὲ προσέειπεν ἄνακτα
> He said to his master

he does not know the guest's identity. Furthermore, we had expected Odysseus' point of view. Now that we see that our first disappointment is doubled by a second (neither Eumaeus individual point of view is offered), we can put forward an alternative working-hypothesis: ἄναξ appears to be less an individual relation marker than a very weak title. The word ἄναξ is used at the same level as δέσποινα and γέρων, as *mistress* and *the old*. Laertes, Odysseus, and Penelope are all masters who could give orders to the slaves, but only Laertes is called *the old*." Ἀναξ is maybe, as γέρων **just a title used not to give an individual viewpoint but rather a general recall of the social order, of the viewpoint of a group that is addressed and guided by the Locutor/Narrator, not directly by the characters.** Odysseus might be for all characters the master of the house. Just like the sentence "the tourists/the people saw the queen" does not imply the understanding: "they saw their queen" (because in direct speech even monarchist subjects would not say, "she is my queen", but "she is *the* queen").

That ἄναξ does not necessarily mean more than "king" or "house-master" without much relational deixis, also emerges from passages where Penelope would be the grammatical subject and the potential focus of a perspective. In *Od.* 21.9 she is going into the storage-room to fetch the bow of Odysseus:

> ἔνθα δέ οἱ κειμήλια κεῖτο ἄνακτος.
> where the King's treasure was kept.

If we took the character's view we could, of course, deduce from this passage that wives had the same status as slaves. But we have seen that the Narrator calls Penelope δέσποινα. It rather appears that ἄναξ means to Penelope what it means to all members of the οἶκος: the chief, king, master of the house. Even Odysseus himself when handling the bow in *Od.* 21.395 and being the first possible candidate for a point of view must accept this language. He examines the bow, in the fear

> μὴ κέρα ἶπες ἔδοιεν ἀποιχομένοιο ἄνακτος.
> that the worms might have eaten into the horn in the absence of the anax.

Odysseus cannot function as a direct focalizer of the word ἄναξ because he is not a slave but the master himself. Yet a Virginia Woolf-reader could find a convenient focalizer: Some verses before, the cowherd Philoetius has been informed of the beggar's true identity, he even plots together with Odysseus against the Suitors. After having closed the door of the hall he sits down, looking at Odysseus (εἰσορόων ’Οδυσσῆα *Od.* 21.393). We therefore could say that ἄνακτος refers to the slave's point of view who sees "his" master handling the bow. It is true that he fulfills all conditions of a character's point of view: he knows who the stranger is, he looks at him, and he does not speak, a silent member of the plot. An identification reading would, thus, be possible and the only argument against it can be that it is not necessary. But one can make plausible, that it is not necessary by a comparison with Philoetius before recognizing Odysseus: in *Od.* 21.83, he is weeping at the sight of the bow, the τόξον ἄνακτος. This passage only shows that the slave's knowledge has nothing to do with the word ἄναξ, but another similar passage is able to show that Odysseus can handle his bow as the bow of the ἄναξ without any slave looking at him. During the slaughter of the Suitors, Odysseus shoots the arrows, and again the Narrator superposes paradoxically the possible perspective on Odysseus (ἄναξ) with the possible point of view of Odysseus (he is shooting, *Od.* 22.119):

αὐτὰρ ἐπεὶ λίπον ἰοὶ ὀιστεύοντα ἄνακτα,

But when the arrows failed the archer anax,

Since the arrows represent the grammatical subject of the clause, an identification reader could pretend that they hold the place of slaves of their master, but there is nothing in the broader context to support this interpretation.

We have seen that no ἄναξ-marker necessarily implies the point of view of a character; in some passages, it was even impossible. The hypothesis according to which ἄναξ has the function of a title that refers rather to the whole society of the characters than to the relationship of individuals (master-slave) has been corroborated. The fact that even the master of the house, the king, can handle things as belonging to the "master" shows that perhaps ἄναξ is the indication of the order of social groups, the order which would be familiar to the audience rather than an inter-individual relation mark.

To be sure, this does not totally exclude an identification reading, but it shrinks the potential of point of views: if ἄναξ is not the indication of a slave's point of view, the Narrator can still hide his knowledge and use titles as if he spoke not with the voice of a special individual, but of somebody among the characters. This seems to be considered a virtue in the autoreferential passages of the *Odyssey* itself. In *Od.* 8.491, Odysseus praises the Pheacian singer Demodocus for his vivid style, "as if the singer had been attending the event he is telling, or a direct witness had told him" (ὥς τέ που ἢ αὐτὸς παρεὼν ἢ ἄλλου ἀκούσας *Od.* 8.491). We can improve our hypothesis and say that maybe the marker "master" is a mask worn by the Narrator/Locutor, a sort of point of view of a group never specified in the text, because the group is also external, in front of an audience consisting of (fe/male) masters[36]:

The whole 14th and parts of the 15th book are based on the fact that Eumaeus works without having been given order, that he does exactly what his master wants him to do and this without knowing that his master is present. Eumaeus passes this exam very well and gets his grade at the end of the day, in the very last verse of the 15th book (*Od.* 15.557):

ἐσθλὸς ἐὼν ἐνίαυεν, ἀνάκτεσιν ἤπια εἰδώς.

loyal heart, with none but kindly feelings for the masters.

Sensitive to the harshness or the smoothness of the way words are linked in poetry, Dionysius of Halicarnassus would have enjoyed this very subtle form of contempt for mankind. All words begin with a vowel except for εἰδώς, which recalls that once there was a smooth initial Digamma. Otherwise, in pronunciation, every first word-syllable begins with the last consonant of the preceding word[37]. And this syllabic type of word-sandhi is one feature of what Dionysius called the smooth style[38]. Even the hardest-boiled positivist could not exclude that, at least on the ideological level, the audience projected its ideals of the "good slave", very clearly described in the verse, into this sound. The verse and the scene are touching, and this is why the change (the μεταβολή) from the usual singular ἄνακτι to the plural ἀνάκτεσιν is perhaps not innocent. We could, of course, believe the Scholia and think that Eumaeus' kindness towards the *masters* is a tacit foreshadowing to what comes in book 16, the arrival of the young master Telemachus (which would prove once again the power of the Narrator/Locutor's point of view, since Eumaeus cannot know that he is coming). But we have seen that the verse has rather the function of a moral (positive) judgment of Eumaeus' former deeds, his hospitality, and his faith towards Odysseus. The strong rhetoric of this verse also suggests that the audience is supposed to be touched by the scene. The plural is, then, rather a reference to the plural of masters in the audience. And the Narrator-controlled character-language of a whole group seems to be a suitable point of view-mark for this audience, better than a single, individual point of view that would constrain the masters to look through the eyes of a slave, the husbands through the eyes of a wife or a young man.

7.6 A counter-example: ξένος

Until now we investigated passages that are said to be worth identification reading. None of them is convincing. But let us invert the method and ask: "Are there really no passages with a foreign discourse?" As far as I can see, there are in the *Odyssey* only one and some related phenomena. Nevertheless, this counter-example will confirm the tendency found in the πόσις and ἄναξ samples.

In book 17, Telemachus has brought a escaped murderer to Ithaca. Since he fears, that is what he says, the Suitors' cruelty, he sends him first to a friend, Piraeus, but promises to invite his guest later according to the rules of hospitality. After having seen that things are not too dangerous in the palace, he goes to join the stranger in the city, on the market. Waiting there he can see how the stranger arrives with Piraeus (*Od.* 17.71ff.):

> τοῖσι δὲ Πείραιος δορίκλυτος ἐγγύθεν ἦλθε
> ξεῖνον ἄγων ἀγορήνδε διὰ πτόλιν· οὐδ'ἄρ' ἔτι δὴν
> Τηλέμαχος ξείνοιο ἑκὰς τράπετ' ἀλλὰ παρέστη.

The spearman Piraeus came up
with the xénos whom he had conducted through the streets
to the market place. Telemachus rose to meet the xénos.

This is one case where the Narrator renounces to his knowledge. In fact, he told the audience who the stranger is, the seer Theoclymenus, but (according to the transmission of the text) Telemachus does still not know his guest's identity and in calling Theoclymenus a ξένος, the Narrator seems to accept the point of view of the characters in his own speech. And yet, the case is special as are most of the ξένος-passages[39]. For never will Telemachus or the other characters know the seer's name, which is an argument in favor of the translation "stranger" rather than "guest". The Narrator must not necessarily enter the special relationship of Telemachus and Theoclymenus, the relationship of hosts, but ξένος can correspond just as ἄναξ to the point of view of all characters, i.e. the habitants of Ithaca.

In a negative way, therefore, this exception confirms the rule: there is no evidence for the point of view of individuals (Penelope thinking of *her* husband, Eumaeus of *his* master, Telemachus of *his* guest), but a general point of view of the group, less in contradiction to the eager Narrator/Locutor's point of view (Penelope, Eumaeus, Telemachus linked to what people and the audience would call husband, master, guest) which guides in general the audience's perspective.

We can invert the method in another way too, and ask whether or not there are passages, where (according to the rules we tried to establish) we find a character-point of view though no Woolf-reader would expect any. Perhaps one of these samples might be *Od.* 19.62. The maidservants enter the hall of the men to clean the tables.

> Αἱ δ' ἀπὸ μὲν σῖτον πολὺν ᾕρεον ἠδὲ τραπέζας
> καὶ δέπα, ἔνθεν ἄρ' ἄνδρες ὑπερμενέοντες ἔπινον.
>
> They began to clear away the remains of the meal, and the tables
> and cups, which the men folk had used for their debauch.

Nothing would disturb an English or German identification or relation-mark reader, but in the light of the opposition of νέοι and men, ἄνδρες is only one, rare terminus for the Suitors. The Narrator calls them sometimes νέοι ὑπερηνορέοντες. The word ἄνδρες, thus, could be indebted to the opposition ἄνδρες - γυναῖκες and obliterate the opposition νέοι - ἄνδρες[40]. We cannot prove it, but perhaps explain: Here the Narrator takes the point of view not even of the maidservants, but of the female sex in general, once again of a group.

All this is not to say that the characters have no "perspective" of their own at all. In direct speech not only can they modify (but only modify) what the Narrator told before, but also they can tell freely all that happened before the tale began. In general no Narrator dares an intrusion into that domain. Only scarcely, when narrative circumstances urge, he does, and then, sometimes, somewhat like an individual (character) point of view within the Narrator speech can originate. This is the case of Eurycleia's tale about Odysseus' scar.

In *Od.* 19.393ff. Eurycleia is washing the beggar's feet in Penelope's presence. Discovering the scar on the knee, she should now pronounce a direct speech and explain the memories the scar evokes to her. For, according to the rules of Zielinski or the context-rules described in the beginning of the chapter, only a character-speech freely can manage external analepses[41]. But perhaps, the Narrator cannot afford to let the character speak. In this situation Penelope is sitting side by side, the last person who should know who the beggar is. That is the reason, I think, the Narrator breaks into the character's domain and relates everything the character is expected to say[42]. Otherwise, however, the Narrator respects all the rules. As in Odysseus' tale, he makes sure that whatever is told could have been known by the character. Furthermore he frames the whole speech-like ring composition between two similar speech-introductions or termination-like expressions that avoid the sense of sound: twice he says "she recognized"[43]. Character-identification, thus, is possible if the Narrator intrudes into a domain, where characters have from beginning on the right to a perspective of their own.

Another, more disputed passage is *Od.* 18.281. Penelope decides to appear among the Suitors. She makes a last fruitless attempt, not understood by Telemachus and the Suitors, at rendering childish her son, at doubting his newly attained adulthood. Then she tells a story that happened, she says, before the Trojan War. Odysseus told her to marry another man when Telemachus first beard would have grown. The Suitors, overwhelmed by her beauty, accept to send her marriage-gifts. Odysseus assists to the scene, though his presence is only recalled after the Suitors have reacted on Penelope's beauty. We will see in the next chapter that such a late spot on a character is not innocent, but avoids a character's point of view. Modern identification readers, however, focused on what he thinks rather than on that limelight:

ὣς φάτο, γήθησεν δὲ πολύτλας δῖος Ὀδυσσεύς
οὕνεκα τῶν μὲν δῶρα **παρέλκετο θέλγε** δὲ θυμόν
μειλιχίοις ἐπέεσσι, νόος δέ οἱ ἄλλα μενοίνα.

She spoke. Odysseus was delighted, he liked to see her
extorting tribute from her lovers and bewitching them
by her coquetry, while her heart was set on quite a different course.

The question of the ancient readers, "an Penelope ad artes meretricias descenderit", has been (rightly) negatively answered by Büchner[44]. For the effect of her body on the Suitors is not calculated or better, neither does Penelope know nor mean it. This very traditionalistic wife does not even know that Athena eluded her. She had decided to go to the Suitors without any preparation, but the goddess made her fall asleep and put some rouge on her cheeks[45]. As for Penelope, no priest could defend her virtue better than the Narrator does, but Odysseus' thoughts seem to be a problem. Does he think his wife is a resourceful cheater? Do παρέλκετο and θέλγε mean that her story of Odysseus' order 20 years ago is a pure fabrication? In which case Odysseus must think that Penelope knows what she is doing, whereas the narrative context seems to indicate that she ignores her effect and that παρέλκετο means only the effect and not the intention.

Identification readers would underlay Penelope's intention without any hesitation and this interpretation seems to be supported by the third verse: "she bewitched the Suitors' heart by sweet words, yet her mind went in another direction". This could be an evidence for Penelope lying to the Suitors. According to the story told by the Narrator/Locutor and the speeches, the phrase "her mind went in another direction" is the expression of Penelope's refusal of this marriage. Even the Suitors could know, that the marriage is στυγερός to her. Penelope does not want to get married, she must. Some scholars have said that in previous, more traditional versions of the *Odyssey*, Penelope and Odysseus must have plotted together against the Suitors[46]. But would this really be the one traditional version? As we have seen in chapter II, the version of not recognizing a wife is as traditional as the other (both are mentioned in the *Odyssey*) and there is no reason to think that there is another story behind or before this one. Neither can we say that Penelope's intention of cheating is Odysseus' interpretation and independent of Penelope's mind. Because if Odysseus thinks that the story is invented, Penelope is betraying the Suitors too. Is the story a lie? Three arguments can be listed against this understanding based on identification reading:

    a) The context (neither does Penelope understand why she wants to go to the Suitors, nor does she want to prepare herself, and she ignores Athena's effect) excludes frankly that Penelope has any (conscious) intention to betray somebody.

    b) Her desperate maternalistic attack on Telemachus (please, you are still a child aren't you?) would be without narrative function, if she did not try to report the deadline of possible marriage. If Telemachus is still a child, Penelope has not to marry anyone. Her attempt would be absurd if the story were a lie.

    c) An evidence of form also stands against the identification - reading. Lying speeches that are *false internal analepses*, in general are well marked as lies by the discrepancy with the context; sometimes the Narrator prepares the audience to the lie. But *lie-speeches dealing with the time before the beginning of the tale* are marked in all other cases by the Narrator, before the speech. If Penelope's story of Odysseus releasing her were invented, we would expect the Narrator to warn the audience. Accustomed to this convention, the audience would be ready to interpret the absence of any warning as a sign of Penelope telling the truth. Any other interpretation (a non-marked but deceiving external analepse) would be singular and surprising.

The three passages analyzed above demonstrate at first that identification reading originates less in anthropological structures, in Geistesgeschichte or other concepts, than in political or ideological choice. It is rather defined by the audience the *Odyssey* aims at: Rulers can accept the rulers' viewpoint in the text, which are, here, the Narrator or sometimes his substitute *Odysseus*. Yet secondly, they confirm our reticence to take for granted identification reading in the *Odyssey*.

7.7 Hindering perspective: the Suitors

We have seen both the type of point of view we can and the one we cannot expect the Narrator to prepare for the Suitors: It would not be by (compulsory) sneaking into an individual's mind, but a general, ideological point of view of a group seems to be possible. This is exactly what we would expect in the Suitors' case: the point of view of a group. But there is no passage, where the Suitor's viewpoint is found to be on the level of a group's point of view. The following passages should, but do not, involve a (in Homer possible) viewpoint of a group on what is happening. With the purpose to find and to define such narrative situations I propose two criteria.

a) The first criterion is the economy of knowledge or in other words: who knows more than the other characters? In most cases the Narrator knows more than all characters and demands the audience's attention. But a character such as Odysseus, who knows more than the Suitors would have more chances than them to become the accomplice of the audience in an event involving both of them, Odysseus and the Suitors. In that case, Odysseus knows roughly as much as the audience or the Narrator. This is perhaps the reason why indirect speech or "foreign" discourse (that confines the Narrator himself to the character's knowledge) may allow, in rare cases, a switch to the point of view of a character such as Eurycleia, or more often, of a group such as the habitants of Ithaca on Theoclymenus or of the women on men. The audience looks on the events with the instance that is as close as possible to his own knowledge.

2) The second criterion is silence. It is linked to the first. Usually the character who knows more, lets the others speak or act and just observes or deceives. All authors who study how the audience's perspective is canalized within the text, such as the theoreticians of "ich-origo" (Hamburger), of "embedded focalization" (De Jong[47]), or of "deixis" (Bühler, Kerbrat-Orecchioni) stress the role of verbs that express observing, looking, perceiving in general. For identification-readers these would be the most compelling entering into the character's point of view. But silence and perception are linked. He or she, who is condemned to hear, becomes a *lector in fabula*. The Pheacians are described as an attentively listening audience through their silence. We have seen that the Pheacians are akin to the group of the Suitors. But they have acquired another status, which seems to give them the right to be a *lector in fabula*. This is not the Suitors' case. In this chapter we will focus on their viewpoint. The very last chapter will deal with the colonists' perspective.

Both criteria "knowledge and silent perception" are often connected and linked to a Narrator sometimes very close to Odysseus, but sometimes they are separated. For instance when Odysseus becomes "loud" or an acting person and, thus, a potential object of perception, Penelope or the Suitors could obtain the status of observers, and thus of a *lector in fabula*. One of these situations is the already mentioned recognition-scene between Eurycleia and Odysseus. The old slave washes Odysseus' feet, while Penelope sits beside, near to the fire. When Eurycleia discovers that the stranger is her master, she is scared and lets go of the washing-basin. Although Odysseus does everything to force the slave to keep quiet, the noise of the falling basin transforms him into a possible object of Penelope's attention. But Athena hinders her (*Od.* 19.479):

τῇ γὰρ᾽ Ἀθηναίη νόον ἔτραπεν
for Athena distracted her attention

Usually, Penelope adopts another device to pull to her the attention of the audience: her indeterminacy (a possibly higher knowledge). But in this moment she has the possibility to look at Odysseus and to know more. But Athena and, with her, the Narrator steals her point of view. This passage is interesting because the same thing happens when the Suitors become spectators (and thus a potential *lector in fabula*) and Odysseus a spectacle. In the beginning of book 18 the young beggar Irus and the old Odysseus have strife. This is not only, as we have seen, a typical iambus-theme and must attract the Suitors' attention, but also, very soon, Irus sees that the Suitors are watching their altercation. Indeed, Antinous observes them and gives the occasion an institutional outlook, gathering the round of spectators, looking for a suitable prize. Never again will the Suitors have a better chance to invert the roles of observer and observed, never will Odysseus be more afraid of being detected. Antinous' perspective is stressed in *Od.* 18.34:

τοῖιν δὲ ξυνέηχ᾽ ἱερὸν μένος᾽ Ἀντινόοιο.
Antinoos understood what they did.

But his possible perspective is blocked by his mood, which is a group-characterizing property, the laughter of the Suitors (*Od.* 18.35):

ἡδὺ δ᾽ἄρ᾽ ἐκγελάσας μετεφώνεε μνηστήρεσσιν·
He laughed delightedly and called out the rest of the Suitors:

Odysseus' fear increases as Antinous forms a regular audience for the struggle. This marks the Narrator's difficulty, but of course, it also helps avoiding it. By emphasizing the character's fear, the Narrator describes him as a cheating person (*Od.* 18.51 δολοφρονέων). Since he cannot avoid showing the muscles of his breast and thighs, physical signs of aristocracy that do not fit the mask of a beggar during the fight, he decides instead, to strike only lightly (*Od.* 18.94):

> ἦκ'ἐλάσαι, ἵνα μή μιν ἐπιφρασσαίατ'' Ἀχαιοί,
> He decided on the lighter blow, to avoid attracting too much attention.

As Irus crashes under his strike, the Suitors are struck by deafening iambic laughter, and, thus, hindered from a quiet perception (*Od.* 18.100): γέλῳ ἔκθανον. All the same, when Odysseus has carried away his victim and returns into the men's hall, disguised again by his wraps: their laughter (*Od.* 18.111: ἡδὺ γελόωντες) retains the Suitors from rethinking the contrast between beggar and winner.

The laughter is a substitute for Athena's intervention in Penelope's blinding, and yet, the narrative scheme is better fulfilled: in a scene that follows immediately the fight, a dialogue between the "good" Suitor Amphinomus and the beggar, the young man becomes aware of the danger, but Athena hinders him (πέδησε *Od.* 18.155). She wants him as fodder for Telemachus' spear. Laughter also is used for hindering the Suitor's viewpoints on seers (Theoclymenus).

But there is another type of viewpoint the young men are known for and that would—in a text designed for identification-readers very well serve to canalize the audience's perspective through heir eyes. The voyeuristic, erotic peeping of Centaurs, of Hermes in Demodocus' hymn or, in the *Iliad*, of Paris, are enough evidence that Homeric audience expected young men to look at others' wives with desire. And there are enough passages where this viewpoint is enacted—but it never becomes a point of view. This viewpoint is always mentioned after the description of the admired object, never before.

The first occurrence is found in the first book, after Athena's departure: Phemius is still singing the *Returns* from Troy. The Suitors are listening in silence (σιωπῇ *Od.* 1.325) and are good candidates for an internal audience. Penelope cannot stand it anymore and interrupts the feast against the rules of hospitality and, what is more, loudly. She has, thus, every chance of becoming the object of longing eyes, but there is no more mention of the Suitors, no perception verb of which Penelope would be the direct regimen. Instead of a possible conflict between the queen and the young men, as often in the *Odyssey*, a dialogue between mother and son drains the audience's attention. For the first time, Telemachus shows how Athena has changed both his mind and his social status. He does not answer the queen as son and child, but defends the rights of the adult male gender: to control its discourse and to listen to stories they have chosen. According to the dissimulation-code of Odysseus, Telemachus is too honest, too proud of his feelings to really be an adult and would be a suitable target to be focused on for a person summoned to keep silent, a person such as Penelope. Yet Penelope's reactions are told only at the last moment, when she is vanishing behind the veils that shut the female space only: at that moment she wonders why her son has changed (θαμβήσασα *Od.* 1.360). The Suitors are not aware of the child's revolt either, though they should be interested in it. Their blindness is motivated by a twofold trick of the Narrator. The young men have eyes for the queen only (*Od.* 1.365f.):

μνηστῆρες δ' ὁμάδησαν ἀνὰ μέγαρα σκιόεντα·
πάντες δ'ἠρήσαντο παραὶ λεχέεσσι κλιθῆναι.

In the shadowy hall the Suitors burst into uproar
and each man voiced the hope that he might share her bed.

While lust blinds the Suitors for Telemachus in a narrative pattern that we have already seen before, their glances on Penelope have not been mentioned until now that she is already gone. They never have the opportunity to serve as a possible point of view to the audience, Penelope is never seen through their eyes, neither is Telemachus. The Suitors' ignorance even plays a role in what follows. Like Penelope, they are surprised and they bite their lips when Telemachus announces a public assembly and its subject: the expulsion of the Suitors. But before they might become victims and, thus, take a silent and prudent point of view on a loudly boasting Telemachus, Odysseus' son changes his strategy and puts on the mask of a naive little boy. The Suitors, therefore, lose their first chance of becoming a point of view by two devices: either because they are concerned with other subjects, or because the Narrator does mention their view upon some thing, but only after its description. And again, the second time they see Penelope, we cannot look through their eyes (*Od.* 18.212):

τῶν δ'αὐτοῦ λύτο γούνατ', ἔρῳ δ' ἄρα θυμὸν ἔθελχθεν,
πάντες δ'ἠρήσαντο παραὶ λεχέεσσι κλιθῆναι.

Her appearance staggered the Suitors. Their hearts were melted by desire, and every man prayed that she might sleep with him as his wife.

If the enthusiastic sight of the young men were to introduce a description of Penelope's beauty, we would be free to take their point of view. But it seems that the Suitor's point of view underlies the same rules as direct speech: the Narrator always tells first what could be seen, then introduces the character's vision. Penelope's divine make-up has already been illustrated by the Narrator for the audience (since *Od*.18.184) and after he mentions the Suitors' weak knees there is no place for her beauty because a dialogue begins between mother and son.

We can conclude our investigation on the Suitor's viewpoint. We have seen in this chapter that the individual point of view is not what the singer and the muse are expected to offer. Instead the point of view of a group seems to be possible, at least in the case of ἄνακτες like Odysseus or (in spe) Telemachus. Yet this group always fits the Narrator/Locutor's and the audience's ideological group-perspective. The Suitors, as a social group that would not be entirely foreign to Odysseus, are always hindered from offering a point of view to the audience's perspective. This hindrance recalls that the absence of necessary identification reading is probably not indebted to any invariant or to any Geistesgeschichte, but the pattern of a traditional epic style performed for husbands and wives in the position of ἄνακτες and δέσποιναι[48]. We have seen that the Narrator's control of the character's point of view in the Narrator text corresponds to the usual control of what character-speech can and cannot say. The Narrator/Locutor's practice could well reflect the hierarchical social rules approved by the audience of Homer. We have investigated this context of the intertextual viewpoint, the external one, in order to show that an intertextual approach only allows finding the traces of the Suitor's viewpoint.

Notes

[1] The demigods are youngsters or, as the pun ἡί-θεος in Pseudo-Hesiod's *Catalogue of heroines* (Hes. fr.1.12f. M.-W.) says, unmarried youngsters are "like-gods".

[2] For the theatre Henrichs A., "Why should I dance? ", *Arion* 3 1995, 56-111.

[3] For the *Querelle* cf. passim in Létoublon L. Volpilhac C. edd. D. Sangsu coll., *Homère en France après la querelle 1715-1900, actes du colloque de Grenoble 3*, Genève 1999.

[4] A late Antiquity theory of such a link between reader and texts can be found in Hermogenes. The style of *gorgotes* in opposition to a rather Homeric stile, the *hyptiotes* in *De id*. 2.1.57: Ἐξαιρεῖται τοίνυν ὑπτιότητα λόγου σχῆμα τὸ καθ' ὑποστροφὴν καὶ ἔστι σφόδρα χρήσιμον τοῦτο ἐν ταῖς ἀφηγήσεσιν, οἷον ἔστι τοίνυν οὗτος ὁ πρῶτος' Ἀθηναίων αἰσθόμενος Φίλιππον, εἶθ' ὑπέστρεψεν ἐξ ἐπεμβολῆς ὡς τότε δημηγορῶν ἔφη, εἶτα πάλιν ἦλθεν ἐπὶ τὴν ἀφήγησιν ἐπιβουλεύοντα τοῖς Ἕλλησι.

[5] Focalizer: "the person (the narrator or a character) through whose eyes the events and persons of a narrative are 'seen'" (De Jong I., *A Narratological Commentary on the Odyssey*, Cambridge 2001, XIV). Cf. Rabel R.J., *Plot and Point of View in the Iliad*, Ann Arbor 1997, 23, who distinguishes between an implied poet' (what has been called the énonciateur or narrator 1) and a narrator's (the muse or the narrator 2) point of view. I take *narrator* as the voice of the muse through the mouth of a male singer (wedding-situation),

which speaks to the audience in the function of what Calame 2000, for instance 18, calls a Locutor, the pragmatic function directed to the audience. Yet, the analysis of the passages shows that these distinctions, as helpful as they are to name functions, are too normalized. We forget sometimes that they are tools of the analysis and not an (impossible) objective description of narrative discourse. These tools are forged out of a certain literary tradition, which is not the same everywhere and in every genre. Homer's discourse is more marked by its destinateur, the rulers, than, for instance, iambus or even drama are. The Locutor controls the muse, but the muse, the logic of the narrative, phonic, syntactic and metrical rules can constrain the Locutor to give himself away. This polemic between married muse and "married" énonciateur is not always easy to distinguish whithout any petitiones principii. This is why I prefer to analyze the reflexion of this contradictory voice in the relationship between the Narrator- Locutor and the characters. In order to distinguish the two voices I call *narrator* the double voice of Locutor/narrator and highlight sometimes the Locutor function by *Narrator/Locutor*.

[6] Bachtin M., *Problemy poetiki Dostoevskogo*, Moskva (2)1963, 336.

[7] Bally C., "Le discours indirect libre en français moderne", *GRM* 4 1912, 549-556, 597-606.

[8] Plat. *Rep.* 392d, Aristot. *Poet.* 1448a19-28 and 1460a 5-11.

[9] De Jong 2001, XIII: "the representation by the narrator in the narrator-text of a character's focalization. "

[10] Hamburger K., *Die Logik der Dichtung, Stuttgart* (3)1977, 56. On the differences between German, English, and French conceptions and the link with Bakhtin cf. Roy P., *The dual voice: free indirect speech and its functioning in the nineteenth-century European novel*, Manchester 1977, 20 n. 17 and 124 n. 45.

[11] Cf. Roy 1977.

[12] Though Hamburger K., *Logique des genres littéraires*, Paris 1986, 81f., gives "Demain, c'était Noël. " as a litteral translation but the translator notes that it would be too much for a French speaker to translate "Gestern war Weihnachten gewesen".

[13] English, as the titles of "The burglar who thought he was … " proves, seems to be located in between.

[14] Mader B., s.v., *LfgrE* , 1562f.

[15] Chantraine P., *Grammaire homérique* II, Paris 1953, 291f. Cf. D. Muchnova, "Temporalité relative et temporalité absolue en grec ancien", *SLG* 2 1997, 161-174.

[16] Cf. the beginning of Musil's novel *Die Vollendung der Liebe*.

[17] On the nuptial association of this situation Plut. *Coniug. praec.* 142d 32.

[18] Cf. Genette 1972, 92.

[19] Noemon tells in *Od.* 4.655 that he saw Mentor the day before. Which is an obvious possibility, but could be an internal analepsis and has not been explicitly told by the narrator.

[20] If they do, the narrator will denounce it afterwards as a self-deception.

[21] Steinrück M., "Wie entsteht der epische Schein bei Homer (eine Alternative)?", *Poetica* 31 1999, 324-338.

[22] *Od.* 23.62: οὐκ ἔσθ' ὅδε μῦθος ἐτήτυμος, and Plat. *Phaedr.* 243a = Stesichorus fr. 192 Davies.

[23] Penelope's refusal to be deceived perhaps recalls her attitude in the 19th book where she refuses to be determined by men, which give the wives in the audience a possibility to have an internal audience, a possible focalization of their ideological point of view.

[24] Going downstairs to the admiring men could be one of the triplets of the Odyssey (*Od.* 1. 328-366, and 19. 53-604), though there are other scenes of *Penelope leaving her room* (cf. De Jong 2001, ad 1. 328-66) without the "stairs".

[25] Ameis K.F. Hentze C. Cauer P., *Homers Odyssee für den Schulgebrauch erklärt*, Leipzig 1894-1920, ad *Od.* 23. 86.

[26] Voigt Ch., *Überlegung und Entscheidung*, Meisenheim/Glan 1972, 79.
[27] In the Italian edition Heubeck A. Fernández-Galiano M., *Odissea* VI, Lorenzo Valla 1986, 292 ad loc.
[28] Katz M. A., *Penelope's Renown: Meaning and Indeterminacy in the 'Odyssey'*, Princeton N.J. 1991, 162 cf. 175, similarly Clay J.C., "Homeric ἀχρεῖον", *AJPh* 105 1984, 73-76.
[29] De Jong 2001, ad 23.85-95.
[30] Van Leeuwen J. Mendes de Costa M.B., *Homeri carmina cum prolegomenis et annotatione critica*, Leyden 1887, ad loc.
[31] Stanford W.B., *The Odyssey of Homer*, London (2)1965, ad loc.
[32] Bérard V., *Odyssée* III, Paris 1927, 153.
[33] The modern master-servant opposition is in Aristotelian terms a sheer relation (a πρός τι) as "δεσπότης - δοῦλος" (*Cat.* 6B30), but not ἄναξ (Clytaemnestra speaks in Aesch. *Ag.* 599 of an ἄναξ and does not mean anything other than "the king"). But the Scholia are able to see a relation marker in the word (Schol in Il. 1.36b).
[34] One passage goes into this direction. The same formula ἀποιχομένοιο ἄνακτος is found as well in a character-speech (20.216): The slave Philoetius speaks about the Suitors sharing already the possessions of the absent master. Does Philoetius project his own relationship with Odysseus into the Suitors? We would rather assume that "master" means the master of the house, a function, not a relation-marker.
[35] The scene is repeated in a ring composition. Maybe the scene has not only a certain thematic and formulaic resemblance, but the name of the slave repeats also what Eumaeus acquired in the first occurrence, an αὐλή. Mes*aul*ius is just what Eumaeus has to put (midst) into the αὐλή.
[36] A similar passage would be *Od.* 20.11: Odysseus hears a maidservant praying Zeus for the death of the Suitors, a σῆμα ἄνακτι. Once again Odysseus would have to take her point of view to understand and suppose his knowledge in her mind (because she does not know that he is hearing her). An identification reading is not excluded, but would be very complicated; it would be easier to assume that the term ἄνα as title makes clear the identity of one person, the king or the master of the house.
[37] Esth- lo- s/e- o- n/e- ni- au- e- n/a- nak- te- si- n/e- pi- a- wei- dos: Word-boundary coincides only once with syllabic or metric boundary. There are no harsh synkrouseis between consonants (vowel-consonant-/consonant-vowel).
[38] For instance Dionysius of Halicarnassus *De comp.* 23.151ff. et passim.
[39] Cf. De Jong 2001, 21 ad. 1.120, even if not all passages necessarily are embedded focalizations.
[40] For instance *Od.* 20.375, cf. *supra* chapter 5.2.
[41] Cf. *supra* chapter 3.3.
[42] Cf. Steinrück 1992.
[43] *Od.* 19.392 and *Od.* 19.468.
[44] Büchner W., "Die Penelopeszenen in der Odyssee", *Hermes* 75 1940, 141ff.
[45] *Od.* 18.193, cf. *Od.* 18. 178.
[46] Cf. Schwartz E., *Die Odyssee,* München 1924, 180, and Woodhouse W.J., *The Composition of Homer's Odyssey*, Oxford 1930, 70.
[47] I.J.F. De Jong, "Studies in Homeric Denomination", *Mnemosyne* 46 1993, 289-306, the same, *Narrators and Focalizers*, Amsterdam 1987, 228f., and Rabel 1997, 23 (opposition of poet and narrator).
[48] That it is not simply a normal way of telling can be shown by the *Iliad*, where the characters still have less freedom, but the narrator can adopt the Trojan point of view. He does not in the case of the Suitors.

8 Results and remarks

8.1 Summary

We have seen to what extent it is impossible to speak about the viewpoint of the Suitors in the *Odyssey* without, I hope, recurring to an *argumentum ex silentio*. A frame has been constructed that enables us to attribute a measurable quality to this silence. Three types of perspective, three degrees of intensity have been used.

1) A perspective we know from the identification reading of the 19-century novel audience: epic illusion is built when the reader sneaks into the viewpoint of characters. This makes the audience forget about both temporal distance between telling and reading and between telling and the past that is told. Our analysis of one element of this type of reading provides **evidence that strong (Narrator-independent) identification reading was neither intended nor expected within the Greek epic tradition**—even if we tend to use this type out of our epic tradition and even if it were not excluded from an anthropological point of view or from that of the "Geistesgeschichte". However very strong markers of our identification tradition, such as the word *tomorrow* are not to be found in Homer's Narrator speech, but in the character speech only. The deixis of relations such as *master and servant* or *wife and husband* that our traditions use to create identification and some interpreters considered an evidence for the appropriateness of this reading in Homer, reveal at a closer look as Narrator–discourse rather than character-discourse.

2) If, normally, the Homeric Narrator/Locutor controls his characters' perspective, one possible perspective he applies sometimes is the identity of groups, a confirmation of ideological issues rather than a way to create the identification of the audience with a particular character of the story. Often the Narrator reflects the ideological discourse of the social group of characters. Odysseus, for instance, sees his own bow as "bow of the master" just like Penelope takes in her hands "the bow of the master". The Narrator can hide or lose his knowledge about the characters: since the other characters ignore his name, Theoclymenus is called a "stranger" in the Narrator-speech, just like, not a single character, but the society would call him. Therefore, where we would incline to use personal identification reading, the Homeric audience rather perceived titles of oikos-people (such as the doyen, the king, the stranger) able to avoid ideological mistakes.

However we could call these titles a restricted form of identification reading. But the Suitors are excluded even from this weak possibility of social perspective every time there would be an appropriated occasion.

3) In order to perceive, nevertheless, the viewpoint of the Suitors we have entered the polemic intertext, i.e. the inversions the epic texts makes of a discourse that attacks the fathers. This discourse has its mere expression in the iambus, but its stories can be found in the epic as well. Iambic stories in epic are a strange mixture of polemic "quotation" and ideological inversion. Not young men, as in iambus, win against fathers and husbands, but the victory is of fathers and husbands (or the one to become them[1]) against young men. **In this negative allusion we can read the Suitors' viewpoint** inasmuch the audience of the iambus consists in often illegitimate or younger sons who cannot get married and are doomed to die in war or to leave for colonization. Such an audience not only fits very well the social (they are eager to get married, are third and fourth sons) but also the poetic definition of the νέοι which are called the Suitors (μνηστῆρες), as a generic title rather than as indication of their relationship towards Penelope. As the iambic audience, they are superfluous and are called "a burden of the arable land" (ἄχθος ἀρούρης). Like them, they adore dance, song and loud aggressive laughter. They laugh just as the iambographers, at the ceremonious but excessive style of seers, at the slowly growing bellies and at the baldness of husbands. At the opposite of husbands they prefer heterosexuality, a practice the society denies them.

It might be surprising how scarcely Aphrodite, the goddess of sexuality, occurs in the *Odyssey* if we compare this little number to the lot of erotic scenes. Furthermore, whenever she is mentioned, it always has a negative ring. In the Phaeacian hymn, she seems connected to Hermes and Ares (and opposed to the husbands Hephaestus and Odysseus), or then as the divinity the maidservants and girlfriends of the Suitors cherished too much, finally in the metonymy of Penelope's geese. The geese are Aphrodite's animals and mean at the same time, in Penelope's dream, the Suitors she longs for, in a way: The connection between this goddess and the Suitors is frequent.

The absence of *homophily* in Homeric epic has been explained by the historical thesis, that this later very strong social link has not been introduced before the 7th century, from Crete[2]. But there could be a reason as well in the sort of text, or in its audience. At the difference of elegy or iambus it seems that epic texts had a mixed audience where matrimonial subjects (among the gods in the *Iliad*, among humans in the *Odyssey*) are preferred to "Aphrodite's works". In texts with a more homogeneous audience like elegy for husbands or in Sappho's texts for girls and women homophily occurs as one of the main themes, in the iambus of young men almost exclusively heterosexuality.

The Suitors' viewpoint, thus, can be defined at first as suppressed and (in a similar way as the slaves' viewpoint) shaped into the good/bad-young-men pattern, but second, we can read the inversion of the iambic stories as intertextual reflex of their viewpoint.

8.2 A colonial viewpoint

Yet one viewpoint of young men can be positively grasped in the *Odyssey*. The Phaeacians are an internal audience. Their perspective is not obliterated and less stigmatized when they enjoy the Aphrodite-hymn together with Odysseus, or when Odysseus tells the episode of their ancient enemies, the Cyclops, for Phaeacian ears. Twice we even are to superpose our fondness to the *stupor* of the Phaeacians, when Odysseus suddenly stops his narration. But the Phaeacians are not only young men; they are the good ones who went out to found a colony. Nevertheless some of the properties of young men are still to be found in their character and in their society. They like dance and music, they have politically powerful wives, but there also are some institutions of the old: the division in youngsters and oldsters for instance. Some of Alcinous' sons are married, some go to the dancing every night—but they have this right in Scheria, in Ithaca the same thing is not well seen.

This image of colonial structures reflects an ideologically correct matrimonial society which however preserved some elements of its origin, a youth-friendly behavior. A certain consciousness of this two-class civilization can be perceived in the careful way Pindar tells the foundation legend of the colony Cyrene which has documented the humiliating conditions of the colonization (interdiction of return) in its (maybe later written) oath of colonists[3]. Carefully, the ignominious image of a young man coming to the house of the bride is many times transformed until the motive is no more recognizable.

Instead of the founder Battus, a god plays the bridegroom's part in Pindar's *Pyth.* 9, and he is the oracular god Apollo, who in the colonial legends tells the young men where to go and how to recognize the place to be settled. Apollo falls in love with the nymph Cyrene and wants to bring her to the bed Aphrodite prepared for them in Africa. But there is a narrative problem. If the enemy of young men plays their role, who will take the narrative part of the oracle (the *destinateur*)? His is precisely the figure that normally is associated with the young man, a Centaur. All the more Centaur

Chiron was the educator of a young man par excellence, the hero Achilles. Chiron, this half animal and "not yet" ἀνήρ changes narrative roles with the god of ἄνδρες Apollo. Neither him nor the audience can restrain from laughing, when Apollo plays the other role and asks the Centaur origin and name of the nymph (and with that the name of the colony). Chiron answers with a pun that (whether consciously or not) continues the inversion-pattern. Instead of indicating the name "kur-ana" he says "ανα–κυρ" with a rather difficult linguistic twist for obtaining the syllable "kur". This is all he indicates about he girl. Never will he say her name in this ode. When Chiron smiles about the all-knowing god's afterthoughts, his almost human receptiveness for desire and the resulting foibles, he is looking with the eyes of the Phaeacian colonial audience.

In the other song about Cyrene's foundation (Pi. *Pyth.* 4), we can detect the same gesture. One element of the wedding rite serves to shape a long, very sinuous journey across time and space. It is the so-called ἐγγύη, the speech-act of the father of the bride giving his daughter to the future son-in-law. Pindar goes very far in applying the image of a colony as a wedding. The Libyan god Triton predicts the future colonization to one of the Argonauts by handing over to him (ἐγγυαλίξαι) a piece of the ground (ἄρουρα) as the father of the bride hands his daughter over to the bridegroom with the words "this is my daughter, ground to sow". It lasts generations until this initial rite may continue (on the metaphorical level) by the wedding, the foundation itself, but the ignominious structure of a woman-located marriage is obfuscated by the many turns of this long story.

The broader sense of the word ἐγγύη is *security* or *pledge given for another* that one of the seven wise feared (which said ἐγγύα πάρα δ'ἄτα, give a security or hand over as a pledge and damage comes). And even in this sense it seems to be an iambic theme. Be it a father angry with bad sons-in-law or νέοι criticizing the bad promises of fathers, in the Phaeacian comic tradition, the word is used for puns on husbands. In Demodocus' hymn about Aphrodite (*Od.* 8.266ff.) they laugh of Odysseus represented as the husband Hephaestus who can catch a young man (Ares) and accuse him of adultery. But Poseidon gives an ἐγγύη to free the young man. Hephaestus does not want but must accept because Poseidon is mightier than he is. So the husband laments that the ἐγγύη of δειλοί is δειλή, i.e. not very valuable—in two senses[4]. First because he is δειλός, he is weak, ugly, and lame. He cannot claim his wedding-gifts (the thunderbolts) back from the father-in-law Zeus. Neither has he any chances in this ἐγγύη, he must let go Ares, the young man who slept with his wife. The reason why the other gods and his wife prefer Ares, Hephaestus thinks, is to be found in the second sense of the δειλία, in his malformed members, the γυῖα. The pledge and Hephaestus crooked legs are thus put in relation on the semantic level. There is not only a phonic similarity, but an etymological link too. As the smith of gods complains about the ἐγγύη δειλῶν, the Narrator uses, for the first time a traditional epithet that contains the word: ἀμφιγυήεις. How Homer's audience and the Phaeacians exactly interpreted this word, is hard to say. Perhaps the paronomasia does not say more than that the lame/weak is weak even in contracts.

Nor would the ideology of Homer's audience and of the Phaeacians be the same. The Phaeacians and the colonial audience of Cyrene in Pindar's odes have with an iambic audience at least in common the theme of the ἐγγύη of δειλοί, even if they are no more young men in a strict sense. When Pindar composed his ode, Cyrene was already an established city, but 100 years before, the foundation (about 640-631 or even 566[5]) was in a fresh memory. About this time Eugammon of Cyrene composed an after-Odyssey that could be called an Anti-Odyssey. Just like Kazantzakis, Eugammon begins his *Telegony* with the end of the Homeric *Odyssey*, with the burial of the Suitors[6]. A funeral is the occasion of representing the glory of the death and of taking their perspective. As in some other legends, where Odysseus is condemned in a trial for murder and to exile, in Eugammon's version Odysseus leaves soon the island in order to inspect the oxen and cows (!) on the continent. There are, in the first book, some adventures in Thesprotia. The second and last book tells the story of Telegonus, of Odysseus' illegitimate son from Circe. He kills Odysseus during a razzia of oxen. This typical (and Hermes-recalling) young man, the illegitimate son, is opposed to the legitimate son Telemachus (which reminds rather of Apollo). But Telegonus is stronger than Telemachus, as he is stronger than his father. He marries Penelope and brings them altogether on another island. Telemachus thus must become a νέος and leave his country to go to a colony. On Aiaia, he can marry Circe. Eugammon avoids the image of the homecoming mother-marrying tyrannos (in Cyrene they strictly use the word *basileus*), but both, Telemachus and Telegonus, take their father's women as wives, a motive we find elsewhere in iambus-related texts too[7].

One could say that maybe there is a strange (ring compositional) opposition between the burial of young men by the fathers at the beginning of the song and the burial of the father by young men at the end and that there is maybe an allusion to the victory of young men. But why should Telegonus' status as illegitimate son be so important? In a very central passage of his abstract of the *Telegony*, Proclus points, however, into this direction. In the text, there were two journeys of Odysseus between the two funerals, one to Polyxenus, king of Elis, and another to Thesprotia.

Odysseus had promised already in the *Odyssey* that he will steel the missing cattle from other people, and this dangerous old man appears at the court of Polyxenus. The king is very kind, but he gives him, as a sign of hospitality a strange crater. Proclus says that on this crater was depicted the story of Trophonius (τὰ περὶ Τροφώνιον καὶ Ἀγαμήδην καὶ Αὐγίαν). The text had, thus, an ecphrasis, which Proclus would not have mentioned if it were a simple descriptive embellishment. It could have been a mise en abyme. A Scholion tells us this story, which is very similar to the narrative structure of the *Telegony* as a whole[8].

> Agamedes king of Stymphalus marries Epikaste, which brings an illegitimate son (a σκότιος) into the marriage: Trophonius. The stepfather and Trophonius are better in εὐτεχνία than other people. This means that they are cunning thieves, but also famous architects. They build king Augias' treasure house with some special effects the owner does not know. Every night, without being detected, Cercyon, the legitimate son of Epikaste and Agamedes, Agamedes himself and Trophonius carry away some of the king's gold. Augias has Deadalus to build a trap that one night catches and kills Agamedes, the father. The two sons cannot deliver the body and have to fear that they will be detected by means of the father's identity. It is the illegitimate son who knows how to make up to this difficulty: He cuts Agamedes' head off and carries it far away to Orchomenus.

We do not know how far the ecphrasis went, but Proclus' mention in his small account and the parallel structure of the story show that it was functional for the *Telegony*. In this way the king of Elis warns the potential thief Odysseus and ironically the warning includes the future. As Agamedes' head is taken away by his νόθος, Telegonus will carry away Odysseus' corpse from Ithaca. The opposition between the cunning νόθος and the simpler γνήσιος questions the Odyssean opposition of the good young boy Telemachus and the bad young men, the Suitors. Telegonus is, in the *Telegony*, the better son of Odysseus. Therefore his social status *is* important.

Finally we find in the *Telegony* the well-known themes that the iambus and the Suitors use for attacking the husbands and fathers: Odysseus' belly, his enormous appetite in his old age. At least, this is the impression we get from the only hexameter we have (through Athenaeus 10.412d). Odysseus mostly eats:

ἤσθιεν ἁρπαλέως κρέα τ' ἄσπετα καὶ μέθυ ἡδύ

he ate without manners a lot of meat, and sweet wine he ...

This might remind us of the bald fat old men we can see on the vases of the italic colonies[9]. Another iambic element could be what says the Scholion Q (ad *Od.* 11.128): the younger epic poets (the νεώτεροι) substituted the shovel Odysseus is meant to carry on his shoulder in order to get oblivion from Poseidon by a soupspoon. And the journey he undertakes on the advice of the seer Tiresias, does not bring him farther than the Ithacan coast, a last attack against the oracular discourse. Odysseus is ridiculed in the *Telegony* for an audience of colonists which has not forgotten who sent them away.

In the eyes of the fathers of course, this text of ancient Suitors is puerile: Eustathius represents their discourse when he says about Telegonus' marriage: περιττὰ ταῦτα καὶ κενὴ μοχθηρία· "don't even pay attention to it"[10].

Notes

[1] This is a possible reason for the excessive way the text justifies Telemachus' status as legitimate and only son of Odysseus: he will be on the side of the fathers and husbands.
[2] William Armstrong Percy III, *Pederasty and Pedagogy in Archaic Greece*, Urbana Chicago 1996.
[3] Cf. text and commentary in Létoublon 1995, 166f., and Calame 1996, 109ff.
[4] In the archaic iambic adespota 14 W which could be of Archilochus according to West the word δειλοί occurs twice and on a very near scrap fr. 15 εγγυ could even be read.
[5] According to Eusebius cf. Telegonia T 2A Davies.
[6] Cf. Proclus' summary of the *Telegony* l. 3 Davies.
[7] It is perhaps not innocent, that in the 9th book of the *Iliad* Phoenix tells such a story Achilles at a moment Achilles is more than ever furious against fathers like Agamemnon.
[8] Ad Ar., Nub. 508a 114.7 Holwerda
[9] Cf. the grotesque vase-painting opposing the νέος par excellence, Herakles, to a bald old man (Pelike of the Villa Giulia 48238, ARV(2) 287, 27).
[10] Eust. In Od. 2.117.20.

Bibliography

Ahl F. Roisman H. M., *The 'Odyssey' Re-Formed*, Ithaca New York 1996.
Ameis K.F. Hentze C. Cauer P., *Homers Odyssee für den Schulgebrauch erklärt*, Leipzig 1894-1920.
Andrewes A., *The Greek Tyrants*, London 1980.
Arend W., *Die typischen Scenen bei Homer*, Berlin 1933.
Assunçâo T. R., "Nota critica à la 'bela morte' vernantiana", *Classica São Paulo*, 7-8 1994-1995, 53-62.
Bachtin M., *Problemy poetiki Dostoevskogo*, Moskva (2)1963.
Baldick J., *Homer and the Indo-Europeans. Comparing Mythologies*, London New York 1994.
Bally C., "Le discours indirect libre en français moderne", *GRM* 4 1912, 549-556, 597-606.
Beck I., *Die Ringkomposition bei Herodot und ihre Bedeutung für die Beweistechnik*, Spudasmata 25, Hildesheim New York 1971.
Bérard V., *Odyssée* III, Paris 1927.
Bertman S., "Structural Symmetry at the End of the Odyssey", *GRBS* 9 1968, 115-123.
Berve H., *Die Tyrannis bei den Griechen*, München 1967.
Bodson L., "Le renard et le hérisson (Archiloque, fr. 201 West)", in *Stemmata, Mélanges de philologie, d'histoire et d'archéologie grecques offerts à Jukes Labarbe*, Liège Louvain-la-Neuve 1987, 55-66.
Bona G., *Il νόος e i νόοι nell'Odissea*, Torino 1966.
Bonanni M., *Il cerchio e la piramide, l'epica omerica e le origini del politico*, Bologna 1992.
Bowra C.M., *On Greek Margins*, Oxford 1970, 59-60.
Braswell B.K., "The Song of Ares and Aphrodite: Theme and Relevance to Odyssey 8", *Hermes* 110 1982, 129-137.
Brelich A., *Paides e Parthenoi* 1, Roma 1969.
Brown Ch.G., "Iambus", in D.E. Gerber ed., *A Companion to the Greek Lyric Poets*, Leiden New York Köln 1997, 16-25.
Büchner W., "Die Penelopeszenen in der Odyssee", *Hermes* 75 1940, 129-167.
Burkert W., *Greek Religion*, Cambridge Mass. 1985.
Burnett A. P., *Three Archaic Poets: Archilochus, Alcaeus, Sappho*, Cambridge, Mass.1983.
Calame C., *Mythe et histoire dans l'Antiquité grecque, la création symbolique d'une colonie*, Lausanne 1996.
───── "L'hymne homérique à Déméter comme offrande: regard rétrospectif sur quelques catégories de l'anthropologie de la religion grecque", *Kernos* 10 1997, 11-33.
───── "La poésie lyrique grecque, un genre inexistant?", *Littérature* 111 1998, 87-110.
───── Lloyd J. vert., *The Poetics of Eros in Ancient Greece*, Princeton NJ 1999 (Roma Bari 1992).
───── *Le récit en Grèce ancienne*, Paris (2) 2000.
Carlier P., *La royauté en Grèce avant Alexandre*, Strasbourg 1984.
Casevitz, M., *Le vocabulaire de colonisation en grec ancien*, Paris 1985.
Ceccarelli P. Létoublon F. Steinrück M., "L'individu, le territoire, la graisse: du public et du privé chez Homère", in F. de Polignac P. Schmitt Pantel edd., *Public et privé en Grèce ancienne: lieux, conduites, pratiques*, Ktema 23 1998, 47-58.
Chadwick N. K. Zirmunskij V., *Oral Epics of Central Asia*, Cambridge 1969.
Chantraine P., *Grammaire homérique* II, Paris 1953.

Clay J. S., *The Wrath of Athena, Gods and men in the Odyssey*, Lanham 1997 (1983).
Clay J.C., "Homeric ἀχρεῖον", *AJPh* 105 1984, 73-76.
Contiades-Tsitsoni E., *Hymenaios und Epithalamion, das Hochzeitslied in der frühgriechischen Lyrik*, Stuttgart 1990.
Cook E.F., *The Odyssey in Athens, Mythes of Cultural Origins*, Ithaca London 1995.
Da Cunha Corrêa P., *Armas e varões, a guerra na lírica de Arquíloco*, São Paolo 1998.
Danek G. "Die Apologoi der Odyssee und 'Apologoi' im serbokroatischen Heimkehrerlied", *WS* 109 1996, 5-30.
────── "Darstellung verdeckter Handlung bei Homer und in der südslawischen Heldenlied-Tradition", *WS* 111 1998, 67-88.
De Jong I.J.F.., *A Narratological Commentary on the Odyssey*, Cambridge 2001.
────── "Studies in Homeric Denomination", *Mnemosyne* 46 1993, 289-306.
────── *Narrators and Focalizers*, Amsterdam 1987.
Deger S., *Herrschaftsformen bei Homer*, Wien 1970.
Detienne M., *Apollon le couteau à la main*, Paris 1998.
────── Vernant J.-P., *Les ruses de l'intelligence, la Métis des Grecs*, Paris 1974.
Doherty L. E., "Gender and Internal Audiences in the 'Odyssey'", *AJPh* 113 1992, 161-178.
Dougherty C., *The Poetics of Colonisation: From City to Text in Archaic Greece*, Oxford 1993.
Dover K. J., "The Poetry of Archilochos", *Entretiens Hardt* 10 1963, 181-212.
Dräger P., *Argo Pasimelousa. Der Argonautenmythos in der griechischen und römischen Literatur*, I, Stuttgart 1993.
Drews R., *Basileus, the Evidence for Kingship in geometric Greece*, New Haven London 1983.
Durand J.-L., *Sacrifice et labour en Grèce ancienne, essai d'anthropologie religieuse*, Paris Roma 1986.
Erbse H., *Beiträge zum Verständnis der Odyssee*, Berlin New York 1972.
Finkelberg M., "How Could Achilles' Fame Have Been Lost?", *SCI* 11 1991-1992, 22-37.
Forbes C. A., *Neoi, A Contribution to the Study of Greek Associations*, Middletown 1933.
Foucault M., *Histoire de la sexualité* II, *L'usage des plaisirs*, Paris 1984.
Fränkel H., *Dichtung und Philosophie, Eine Geschichte der griechischen Epik, Lyrik und Prosa bis zur Mitte des 5. Jh.*, München 1962.
Gallant Th., *Risk and Survival in Ancient Greece*, Stanford Cal. 1991.
Garnsey P., *Food and Society in Classical Antiquity*, Cambridge 1999.
Genette G., *Figures* III, Paris 1972, 82-105 (Engl. *Narrative Disourse*, Ithaca New York 1980).
Gerber D. E. ed. vert., *Greek Iambic Poetry*, Cambridge Mass. London 1999.
Germain G., *Genèse de l'Odyssée, le fantastique e le sacré*, Paris 1954.
Giangrande I. ed., *Eunapii Vitae Sophistarum*, Romae 1956.
Graf F., *Nordionische Kulte,* Roma 1985.
Graham A.J., "The 'Odyssey', History, and Women", in B. Cohen ed., *The Distaff Side, Representing the Female in Homer's 'Odyssey'*, New York Oxford 1995, 3-16.
Greimas A. Courtés J., *Sémiotique, Dictionnaire raisonné de la théorie du langage II*, Paris 1986.
Haase M., "Hochzeitsbräuche und -ritual", in *Der Neue Pauly, Enzyklopädie der Antike* 5, 652-654.
Hainsworth J.B., *A Commentary on Homer's Odyssey vol.* I, *Books* V-VIII, Oxford 1988.
────── Rec. Lohmann, *JHS* 92 1972.
Halperin D.M. Winkler J.J. Zeitlin F. edd., *Before Sexuality. The Construction of Erotic Experience in the Ancient Greek World*, Princeton 1990.
Hamburger K., *Die Logik der Dichtung*, Stuttgart (3)1977.
────── *Logique des genres littéraires*, Paris 1986.

Henrichs A., "Why should I dance?", *Arion* 3 1995, 56-111.
Heubeck A. Fernández-Galiano M., *Odissea* VI, Lorenzo Valla 1986.
Hunter R., *The* Argonautica *of Apollonius, Literary Studies*, Cambridge 1993.
Hurst A., *Apollonios de Rhodes, manière et cohérence, contribution à l'étude de l'esthétique alexandrine*, Institut Suisse de Rome 1967.
Jakob D., "Die Stellung des Margites in der Entwicklung der Komödie", *Hellenica* 43 1993, 275-279.
Kahil L., "L'Artémis de Brauron, Rites et mystère", *AK* 20 1977, 86-98.
Kahn L., *Hermès passe ou les ambiguïtés de la communication*, Paris 1978.
Kantzis I., *The Trajectory of Archaic Greek Trimeters*, Boston Leiden 2005.
Katicic R., "Die Ringkomposition im ersten Buche des thukydideischen Geschichtswerkes", *WS* 70 1957, 179-196.
Katz M. A., *Penelope's Renown: Meaning and Indeterminacy in the 'Odyssey'*, Princeton N.J. 1991.
Kirk G.S., *The Iliad, A Commentary I: books 1-4*, Cambridge London 1985.
Knight V., *The Renewal of Epic, Responses to Homer in the Argonautica of Apollonius*, Leiden New York Köln 1995.
Krischer T., "Die Bogenprobe", *Hermes* 120 1992, 19-25.
Lacombrade Ch. ed., *L'Empereur Julien, oeuvres complètes* II 2, *Discours de Julien l'Empereur*, Paris 1964.
Lambin G., "Le cheval de Troie", *Gaia* 3 1998, 97-108.
Lang F., *Archaische Siedlungen in Griechenland, Struktur und Entwicklung*, Berlin 1996.
Lasserre F. Bonnard A. edd., *Archiloque, fragments*, Paris 1958.
Latacz J., *Kampfparänese, Kampfdarstellung und Kampfwirklichkeit in der Ilias, bei Kallinos und Tyrtaios*, München, 1977.
―――― Holoka J.P. vert., *Homer, his Art and his World*, Ann Arbor 1996.
Lateiner D., *Sardonic Smile, Nonverbal Behavior in Homeric Epic*, Ann Arbor 1995.
Leduc C., "Comment la donner en mariage? La mariée en pays grec (IXe-Ve siècle av. J.C.)", in P. Schmitt-Pantel ed., *Histoire des femmes* I, *L'Antiquité*, Paris 1991, 259-316.
Lehrs K., *De Aristarchi studiis homericis*, Leipzig (3)1883 (1833).
Lennartz K., "Zum erweiterten Jambusbegriff", *RhM* 143, 2000, 225-250.
Lerner G., *The Creation of Patriarchy*, New York Oxford 1986.
Létoublon F. Volpilhac C. edd. Sangsu D. coll., *Homère en France après la querelle 1715-1900, actes du colloque de Grenoble 3*, Genève 1999.
―――― *La ruche grecque et l'empire de Rome*, Grenoble 1995.
Livrea H., *Anonymi fortasse Olympiodori Thebani Blemyomachia (P.Berol. 5003)*, Meisenheim am Glan 1978.
Lloyd-Jones H., *Females of the Species: Semonides on Women*, London 1975.
Lohmann D., *Die Komposition der Reden in der Ilias*, Berlin 1970.
Loraux N., "Sur la race des femmes et quelques-unes de ses tribus", *Arethusa* 11 1978, 43-87.
Louden B., "An Extended Narrative Pattern in the 'Odyssey'", *GRBS* 34 1993, 5-33.
―――― "Pivotal Contrafactuals in Homeric Epic", *CA* 12 1993, 181-198.
Malkin I., *The Returns of Odysseus, Colonisation and Ethnicity*, Berkeley 1998.
Marcozzi D., "Connotazioni messeniche nella leggenda di Eurito, l'epica e la tradizione", in *Scritti in memoria di Carlo Gallavotti, Rivista di Cultura Classica e Medioevale* 36 1994, 79-86.
Marzullo B., "Archil. fr. 42 W (Reversa Neobule?)", *MCr* 30-31 1995-6, 37-66.
Meuli K., *Odyssee und Argonautika: Untersuchungen zur griechischen Sagengeschichte und zum Epos*, Berlin 1921.
Minchin E., "The Performance of Lists and Catalogues in the Homeric Epics", in: *Voice into Text, Orality and Literacy in Ancient Greece*, I.Worthington ed., Leiden New York Köln 1996, 3-20.

Mösch-Klingele R., *Die loutrophoros im Hochzeits- und Begräbnisritual des 5. Jahrhunderts v. Chr. in Athen*, Bern 2006.
Mossman J., *Wild Justice, A Study of Euripides' Hecuba*, Oxford 1995.
Muchnova D., "Temporalité relative et temporalité absolue en grec ancien", *SLG* 2 1997, 161-174.
Müller G., *De Aeschyli Supplicum tempore atque indole*, Halle 1908.
Nagy G., *The Best of Acheans, Concepts of the Hero in Archaic Greek Poetry*, Baltimore 1979.
Nünlist R., "Der Homerische Erzähler und das sogenannte Sukzessionsgesetz", *MH* 55 1998, 2-8.
Ogden D., *Greek Bastardy in the Classical and Hellenistic Period*, Oxford 1996.
―――― *The Crooked Kings of Ancient Greece*, London 1997.
Page D.L., *Sappho and Alcaeus*, Oxford 1955.
Papadopoulou-Belmehdi I. (N. Loraux praef.), *Le chant de Pénélope. Poétique du tissage dans l'"Odyssée"*, Paris 1994.
Pazdernik Ch. F., "Odysseus and His Audience: 'Odyssey' 9.39-40 and its Formulaic Resonances", *AJPh* 116 1995, 347-369.
Pellizer E., "Per una morfologia della poesia giambica arcaica", in K. Fabian E. Pellizer G. Tedeschi edd., *OINHPA TEUXH*, Alessandria 1991, 15-29.
Peradotto J., "The Social Control of Sexuality: Odyssean Dialogics", *Arethusa* 26 1993, 173-182.
Pichler R., *Die Gygesgeschichte in der griechischen Literatur und ihrer neuzeitlichen Rezeption*, München 1986.
Poland F., *Geschichte des griechischen Vereinswesens*, Leipzig 1909.
Pomeroy S. B., *Families in Classical and Hellenistic Greece, Representations and Realities*, Oxford 1997.
Pòrtulas J. Miralles C., *Archilochus and the Iambic Poetry*, Roma 1983.
―――― *The Poetry of Hipponax*, Roma 1988.
Powell B., *Composition by Theme in the Odyssey*, Meisenheim/Glan 1977.
Pralon D., "L'invention des cadets: la faute exemplaire", in M. Segalen G. Ravis-Giordani edd., *Les cadets*, Paris 1994, 59-65.
Pratt L. H., "'Odyssey' 19.535-50 : On the Interpretation of Dreams and Signs in Homer", *CPh* 89 1994, 147-152.
Pucci P., *Odysseus Polytropos, Intertextual Readings in the Odyssey and the Iliad*, Ithaca London 1987.
―――― *The Song of the Sirens. Essays on Homer*, Lanham, 1997.
Rabel R.J., *Plot and Point of View in the Iliad*, Ann Arbor 1997.
Radermacher L. ed., *Der homerische Hermeshymnus*, Wien 1931.
Rankin H. D., *Archilochus of Paros*, Park Ridge NJ 1977.
Reece S., "The Cretan 'Odyssey': A Lie Truer Than Truth", *AJP* 115 1994, 157-173.
Rengakos A., "Zeit und Gleichzeitigkeit in den homerischen Epen", *AA* 41 1995, 1-33.
Rieu E.V. vert., *Homer, The Odyssey*, Baltimore 1946.
Rosen M.R., "Hipponax and the Homeric Odysseus", *Eikasmos* 1 1990, 11-25.
Roy P., *The dual voice: free indirect speech and its functioning in the nineteenth-century European novel*, Manchester 1977.
Ruschenbusch E., "Überbevölkerung in archaischer Zeit", *Historia* 40 1991, 375-378.
Russo J., *Commentary on Homer's Odyssey* III, Oxford 1992.
Rutherford R.B., *Homer, Odyssey, Books XIX and XX*, Cambridge 1992.
Schamp J. Halleux R. edd., *Les Lapidaires Grecs*, Paris 1985.
Schear L., "Semonides Fr. 7: Wives and their Husbands", *EMC* 28 1984, 1984, 22-46.
Scheid-Tissinier E., "Télémaque et les prétendants, les νέοι d'Ithaque", *AC* 62 1993, 1-22.

Schindler N., *Widerspenstige Leute, Studien zur Volkskultur in der frühen Neuzeit*, Frankfurt/Main 1992.
Schmidt M., *Die Erklärungen zum Weltbild Homers und zur Kultur der Heroenzeit in den bT-Scholien zur Ilias*, München 1976.
Schmied N., *Kleine ringförmige Komposition in den vier Evangelien und der Apostelgeschichte*, Tübingen 1961.
Schubert P., *Noms d'agent et invective: entre phénomène linguistique et interprétation du récit dans les poèmes homériques*, Göttingen 2000.
——— "Le palais d'Alcinoos et les Panathénées", *REG* 109 1996, 255-263.
Schwartz E., *Die Odyssee*, München 1924.
Seeck G. A., "Homerisches Erzählen und das Problem der Gleichzeitigkeit", *Hermes* 126 1998, 131-144.
Segal Ch., "The Embassy and the Duals od Iliad 9.182-89", *GRBS* 9 1968, 101-114.
——— "Teiresias in the Yukon: A Note on Folktale and Epic ('Odyssey' 11, 100-144 and 23, 248-287)", in R. Pretagostini ed., *Tradizione e innovazione nella cultura greca da Omero all'età ellenistica, scritti in onore di Bruno Gentili* I, Roma 1993, 61-68.
Segal Ch., *Singers, Heroes and Gods in the 'Odyssey'*, Ithaca London 1994.
Sévryns A., *Le cycle épique dans l'école d'Aristarque*, Paris 1928.
Snodgrass A., *Archaic Greece, The Age of Experiment*, London 1980.
Spaltenstein F., "Continuité imaginative et structure des Argonautiques", in H.J. Tschiedel ed., *Ratis omnia vincit, Untersuchungen zu den* Argonautica *des Valerius Flaccus*, Hildesheim Zürich New York 1991, 89-100.
Stanford W.B., *The Odyssey of Homer*, London (2)1965.
Stanley K., *The Shield of Homer, Narrative Structure in the Iliad*, Princeton 1993.
Steinrück M., "Der Bericht des Proteus", *QUCC* 71, 1992, 47-60.
——— *Rede und Kontext. Zum Verhältnis von Person und Erzähler in frühgriechischen Texten*, Bonn 1992.
——— *Kranz und Wirbel*, Hildesheim 1997.
——— "Roi et tyran dans l'imaginaire grec archaïque", *Gaia* 3 1998, 27-35.
——— "Wie entsteht der epische Schein bei Homer (eine Alternative)?", *Poetica* 31 1999, 324-338.
——— "Neues zur Blemyomachie", *ZPE* 126 1999, 99-114.
——— "Comment faire l'éloge d'une femme?: tuer et mettre au monde dans les Ehées", *Métis* 11 [1996] 2000, 25-36.
——— *Iambos, Studien zum Publikum einer Gattung in der frühgriechischen Literatur*, Hildesheim 2000.
——— *La pierre et la graisse, Lecure dans l'intertexte grec antique*, avec une préface de P. Pucci, Amsterdam 2001.
——— "*Gender* ou initiation", forthcoming in *Actes du VIIIe Congrès des Historiennes* (Genève 27-28. 96).
——— "Sur le parfum tragique des côla métriques chez Aristophane", in C. Calame ed., *Poétique et langue d'Euripide en dialogue, Etudes de lettres* 4 2004, 59-70.
Steinrück M, Lukinovich A., *A quoi sert la métrique? interprétation littéraire et analyse des formes métriques grecques:une introduction*, Grenoble 2007.
Suter A., "Paris and Dionysos, Iambus in the Iliad", *Arethusa* 26 1993, 1-18.
Thalmann W., *The Swineherd and the Bow, Representation of Class in the Odyssey*, Ithaca London 1998.
Treu M. ed., *Archilochos*, München 1959.
Ulf Ch., *Die homerische Gesellschaft*, München 1990.
Van Leeuwen J. Mendes de Costa M.B., *Homeri carmina cum prolegomenis et annotatione critica*, Leyden 1887.

Van Wees H., "The Homeric Way of War: The 'Iliad' and the Hoplite Phalanx I + II", *G & R* 41 1994, 1-18, 131-155.
Vernant J.-P., "À la table des hommes. Mythe de fondation du sacrifice chez Hésiode", in M. Detienne J.-P. Vernant edd., *La cuisine du sacrifice en pays grec*, Paris 1979, 37-132.
Vian F. ed., *Les Argonautiques Orphiques*, Paris 1987.
Viret Bernal F., *Au fil de la lame*, Paris 2007.
Voigt Ch., *Überlegung und Entscheidung*, Meisenheim/Glan 1972.
West M.L. ed., *Iambi et elegi graeci ante Alexandrum cantati*, voll. I+II, Oxford 1971, I 1992.
―― *Studies in Greek Elegy and Iambus*, Berlin New York 1974.
―― "The Ascription of Fables to Aesop", *Entretiens Hardt* 30 1983, 105-128.
―― *The Hesiodic Catalogue of Women*, Oxford 1985.
―― "Simonides Redivivus", *ZPE* 98 1993, 1-14.
―― *The East Face of Helicon, West Asiatic Elements in Greek Poetry and Myth*, Oxford 1997.
West S., "Archilochus' Message Stick", *CQ* 38 1989, 42-47.
Wilamowitz U.v., *Aeschylus-Interpretationen*, Berlin 1914.
William A. P. III, *Pederasty and Pedagogy in Archaic Greece*, Urbana Chicago 1996.
Woodhouse W.J., *The Composition of Homer's Odyssey*, Oxford 1930.
Yamagata N., "Young and Old in Homer and in Heike Monogatari", *G&R* 40 1993, 1-10.
Zielinski T., "Die Behandlung gleichzeitiger Ereignisse im antiken Epos", *Philologus Suppl.* 8 1899-1901, 407-449.
Zirmunskij V. ed. L. Pen'kovskij vert., *Alpamys po variantu Juldasa Fazyla*, Moskva 1958.

Index

Achilles 20,
  and the Suitors 69f.
Acta Theclae 34.8 Lipsius 79 n.5
Aegisthus 75, 84
Aelianus *N.A.* 4.56 79 n.5, 6.39.8 38 n.32
Aeschylus *Ag.* 36f. 62 n.7, *Ag.* 48ff. 46 n.15, *Ag.* 1125f. 62 n.6, *Septem* 10f. 68 n.18
Aesopus 12, 39, fab. 32 (I) Hausrath 12 n.28, *fab.* 83 (I) Hausrath 43 n.4, 2.17 45 n.14
Agamedes, 123
Agamemnon 68f., 96
Age Trojan War 17, time of marriage 15, legend of Ages 27, adult Iron Age 27
aggression 8, against girls 12, aggression-rituals 8
akroteriasmos 91, 93
Alcaeus fr. 119.16 Voigt 12 n.28, fr. 129 L 89 n.33
Alcibiades 28
Alcman fr. 1.50, 59 Calame 13 n.37, fr. 1.60 Calame 13 n.37, fr. 5.2 II 22 Calame 57
Alexis fr. 264.1-7 K.-A. 9 n.15
ἀλλύω 97
Alpamysh 29, 33f.
Anacreo 8, fr. 13 Gentili 44 n.6
Ananius 8
Anaxilas fr. 67 K.-A. 12 n.26
ancestors 27 cf. heroes
Anchises 79
andres 55, 86, cf. husband
Anthologia Palatina 5.19, 12.205 12 n.28, 7.351, 7.71 8 n.9 + 11 n.24
Antinous 92f., 125
Anti-Odyssey 135
Antiphanes fr. 164 K.-A. 9 n.14
ants 70 + n.27
Aphrodite 46f., 79f., 132-134
Apollo 16f., 133f.
Apollodorus *bibliotheke* 99, 3.12.6 13 n.38
Archenactides 54f.
Archilochus fr. 10.10 W 7 + 7 n.4, fr. 19 W 52, fr. 21-22 W 16 n.62, fr. 23.16 W 70 n.27, fr. 25 W 53 n.36 + 56 n.44, fr. 26 W 17 n.66 + 93 n.42, fr. 34 93 n.42, fr. 109, 114 8 n.8, fr. 115 W 52 n.33, fr. 122 W 54 + 95 + 111, fr. 133 W 14 n.45 + 15 n.49, fr. 168 W 94, fr. 172 W 44, 172ff. W 94, fr. 177 W 56, fr. 179 W 56, fr. 182-184 W 16 n.65, fr. 185 ff. W 18f. + 43, fr. 196a.14 W 63 + n.11, frr. 196 and 196a 80 n.6 + 12 n.27, fr. 196a.3 96, fr. 215 W 7, fr. 276 W 93 n.42, fr. 279 W 77 n.2, fr. 286 W 17 n.68,
Arctinus fr. 16 Bernabé 7 n.3
Argonautica 82f.,
  Argonautica orphica 639ff. 82 n.14, 83,
  Apollonius Rhodius 1.1187ff. 82 n. 17,
  Valerius Flaccus 82, 3.545 82 n 17
Aristarchus 47
Aristophanes *Lys.* 360f. 87 n 31, Schol. Ad. Lys. 645 13 n.37, *Nub.* 1ff. 44 n.6, Schol Ad Ar., Nub. 508a 114.7 Holwerda 136 n.8, *Eccl.* 1015, 63 n.11, *Ran.*1190 8 n.18, *Ran.*1133 7, *Ves* 289, 8 n.18,
Aristophanes of Byzantium 8 n.5, 47
Aristoteles *Poet.* 1448a19-28 107 n.8, *Poet.* 1460a 5-11 107 n.8, *Cat.* 6B30 115 n.33, *Rhet.* 1418b28 18 n.74, *Rhet.* 1418b23 52 n.31 + 52 n.34, *Hist. an.*592b 5-6, *Hist. an.*619b 23-25 46 n.17, *Hist. an.*619a 27-31, 45 n.10, *Hist. an.*620a 1-5 45 n.11
army 50, 68, the young and the old 68
Athena 38, 46, 61-64, 84, 124
Athenaeus 10.412d 136, 148A 109
audience 17 n.69, 36-39,
  epic audience of husbands and wives 39, 80, 90, 100f.,
  colonial audience 133,
  twofold relationship the epic audience 28,
  same audience for iambus and elegy? 8,
  lectrices in fabula 86,
  lector in fabula 125,
  theater-audience 28
Augia 136

Bacchylides 5.173 S-M. 93 n.43
Bachtin 84 n.23, 106 n.6, 107
baldness 94f., 137 n.9
Bally 107 n.7
Battus 133
beautiful battle death 14

beggar-mask 90
belly 19, 58, 89-91, 95, 136,
　Odysseus' belly 136,
　belly-monster 20
Berend 108
biography of the author 8,
　biographistic explanation 8,
　of a group 9,
　cosmic biography 24
blame - praise 3 n.2
Bou(e)chetos 88,
　bougaios 88,
　Boupalos 88
bow-contest 29. 34, 99, 117
box-fighting 88f., 91,
　between the youngster and the older father 67f.
Bupalus 9
burden of the arable land 132

Callimachus 62, *Iamb*. 1.1-4 Pf. 62 n.9, *Aitia* 3.5 79 n.5
Callinus 15, fr. 1 W 15 n.47 + 68 n.19
Calypso 20, 35, 84
Candaules 77, 80
catalogues 17 n.70
centaur 92f., 126, 133, cf Hesiodus
Cercyo 135
channels 38
characters 32, 110,
　character-point of view 120, 131,
　character-speech 32, 110, 127,
　freedom of 109,
　indirect speech 108
Circe 31, 34, 81f., 84f., 135
Clemens of Alexandria 21, *Paed.* 1.7 (55.2) 38 n.32
colonization 8, 15f., 37, 86 n.26,
　image of a 134,
　as a marriage substitute 37,
　image of wedding 15,
　colonization-stories 21,
　ἀποικία 15, 15 n.52
Commencini 48 n.22
companions 21, 31, 34,
　losing them 34 + 39,
　abandoning them 35
composition 27, 33,
　Telemachy 48,
　two halves of the *Odyssey* 34,
　Serbian epic stories 29,
　τέλος 47

concomitance 32
Critias 28, fr. 4 W 28 n.3, 88b44 D.K. 28 n.3
Cyclops 30, 133
Cypria 23 and 48 49 n.23, 49, 57, T 14.5
　Davies 57 n.45, fr. 9. Bernabé 13 n.38.
Cyrene 37, 134

Dascylus 78
death of young men 34, 35
Deianira 93
deixis of relations 131, 124 cf. identication markers
Demodocus 85, 118, 125, 134
dialogue 90
Digenis Akritas 105
dihegetes 28
Dio Chrysostomus 60.1 93 n.42, Euboean speech 83 n.19
Diodorus 4.31.7 61 n.2, Sic. 8 fr.23.2 16 n.56
Diomedes metricus (1, 477, 9 Keil) 7 n.3
Diomedes 68 n.21
Dionysius of Halicarnassus *De com* 23.151ff. 119 n.38, 119
dog throttler 80, cf. Candaules + Hermes
doors in 76, 79, 85, 95
Dostoevsky 106
doves 13 n.37

eagle 44f.,
　eagle for *father* 45,
　phene 46f.
ecphrasis 136
ἐγγύη of δειλοί 134 cf. Hephaestus
Ekhetos 91- 99
elegy 14, 68
Elpenor 83
énonciateur 31, 106 n.5 cf. Narrator
entering the present 30
ephebes 61, 66
epos justifying the status of husbands and wives 22,
　epic style 19
erotic adventure 21, 75, 79 cf. iambus
Eteocles 68
ethos 52f., 52 n.31, 94,
　adynata 52
Eugammon 135
Eumaeus 61, 117

INDEX   147

Euripides *Hec.* 547ff. 68 n.16, *Hippol.* 629 15 n.52, Schol. Eur. Andr. 687 13 n.38, *Med.* 232f. 10 n.17
Eurycleia 30, 121-124
Eurymachus 95
Eurytus 99f.
Eusebius *Praeparatio evangelica* 5.32.2 8 n.9 + 12 n.26
Eustathius In Od. 1.363.38 38 n.32, In Od.1.395.17 (1669.48) 13 n.36, In Od. 2.117.20 137 n.10

fat 89 + n.34
fathers 36, 40, 43, 47, 77-79, 88, 95, 99, 134f.,
 father of gods and men 79, 84
 father-iambus 93,
 father Zeus' βουλή 71,
 Father Lycambes 44, 55,
 should not kill other fathers 50,
 unwilling bride-father 95,
 father Zeus 15, 56,
 πατὴρ ἀνδρῶν τε θεῶν τε 51,
 realm of the fathers 49
Fazyl 34
female positions
 and aristocratic positions 44,
 iambic story 81, 91,
 viewpoint 66,
 female takes the male as wife 16
fertilization of the mother-city 38 cf. canal, cf. tyrannos
focalizer 106 n.5, 111
fox 12, 43f., 58, 91, fox for *young man* 57

geese 46
Geistesgeschichte 127
gender 14, 27 n.1, 44 n.5, 57, 64, 66, 71, 80,
 gender-polemics 81,
 solidarity 64,
 stag-hunting 82f.
 domination between wives and husbands 28,
 δοῦμος 13,
 ἀφροδίσιοι λόγοι 13,
 initiation-dance group 13,
 παρθένοι and γυναῖκες 66, cf. husband, young men
genre 14 n.43
γέροντες 69 *Il.* 2.266 69, 89, 91, 96, 117,
 παλαιὰ εἰδώς 67,
 προγενέστερος 63 cf. husband

gods of the νέοι 17, cf. Hermes, Herakles
ground to cultivate 36, 62, 134
Gyges 52, 77

hedgehog 44 n.5
Hekabe 67
Helena 46
Heliodorus 106
Hephaestio *De Poem.* 7.2 (71 Consbruch) 19 n.76
Hephaestus 86, 134, ἀμφιγυήεις 134
Herakles 17, 61f., 82f., 99f., 99 n.49 + n.50
Hermes 17, 52, 70, 75, 84, 79f., 83f., 85 n.25, 99, 99 n.49, 125, 135,
 "killer of the dog Argos" 85
Hermogenes *De id.* 2.1.57 106 n.4
Herodas 1.70 13 n.40.
Herodotus 1.8.3-1.12.2 78 n.3, 1.146.2 37 n.26, 6.107.2 38 n.31
heroes 35, Heroic Age 17 + 28,
 heroic style 19,
 hero non-adult 28f., 36
Hesiodus 27, *Catalogue of women* 71,
 fr.1.12f. M.-W. 105 n.1, fr. 43a.41-43 M.-W. 43 n.3, fr. 43a.41-43 M.-W. 81 n.10, fr. 43, 31 13 n.37, fr. 204.120 M-W. 16 n.60, *Op.* 406 15 n.54, *Op.* 59ff. 56 n.43
Hippias 38
Hippocrates *De articulis*, 32.11 87 n.30
Hipponax 20. n.79, 38, fr. 1 W 16 n.63, fr. 2a W 78, fr. 3a W 78, fr. 4 W 16 n.65, fr. 12.1-2 38 n.32, fr. 30 W= Hesych. 4.2256 13 n.41, frr. 32f., 36 8 n.8, fr. 70.8 W 44 n.5, fr. 70.7ff. 38 n.32, fr. 79 W 86f., fr. 84.10ff. 75, fr. 84, 104 W 12 n.27, fr. 104 W 75f., fr. 128 W 19, 22, fr. 129 W 20
Homeric Hymn
 HCer 13, *HCer* 82ff. 86 n.28, *HCer* 202-204 13 n.40,
 hBacc 81,
 hM 52, 85,
 hV 22ff. 56 n.41
homophily 14 n.44, 14, 132
Horatius *epod.* 2.67 52 n.34, *epod.* 11 80 n.6, *epod.* 11 97, *epod.* 6.11 ff. 11 n.24, *epist.* 1.19.23ff. 8 n.9+ 11 n.24, *epist.* 1.19.26. 8 n.6, Pseudoakron (1.404 Keller) ad Hor. *epod.* 6.11 ff. 8 n.9
horses 13 n.37
husbands 14, 21, 77, 81, 88f., 92f., 96,
 husbands and wives 69, 81, 105,
 Agamemnon 70,

human husband 36,
ἀνήρ = husband 10,
ἄνδρες 64, 89,
ἀνάλειπτοι 89

iambic adespota 14 W 134 n.4, fr. 146 W 98 (Archilochus?), fr. 148 W, fr. 158 W 97
iambus 7f., 71, 17-19
   cathartic prevention of misbehavior 9,
   soupspoon 137,
   καλή μάχη 62,
   donkey-woman 13,
   catalogue of wives 56,
   audience 21, 58,
   burglar-stories 93,
   attacks against reluctant fathers of nubile girls 12,
   ambush-story 76, 79, 97,
   Sapphic iambus 13 n.42,
   pun 88,
   attacking seers 16,
   alexandrian edition 8 n.5,
   style 19,
   attacking fathers 11,
   stock-character 11,
   Orodocides 11,
   ψόγος and ἔπαινος 8,
   κερτομέω 94
identification- markers
   πόσις 112, 120,
   φίλον πόσιν, 113f.,
   αὔριον 109, 115,
   ξένος 120f,
   ἠῶθεν 109,
   tomorrow 108, 109,
   tonight 107,
   relation-marker 116 n.34, 117,
     title 117,
   ἄναξ 115, 117f,
   ἄνακτες and δέσποιναι 127,
   δέσποινα 117
identification-reader 105, 117, 121f., 125, 131,
   absence of necessary 127
Iliad 20, 1.505 70, *Il.*2.260 50, *Il.*4.339-355 55 n.40, *Il.*4. 356f. 55 n.40, *Il.*19.86-138 99 n.50, *Il.*19.215 91 n.38, *Il.* 19.225 91 n.38, Schol. Il. 1.5 = F 1 Davies 57 n.46, Schol in Il. 1.36b 115 n.33, Il. Schol. Il. 1,349 19 n.78, Schol. Il. 19.5 19 n.78
illusion (epic) 108, 111,
   κηληθμός 89, 111,

Tarzan-flight 111,
thelgein 106,
   kelein 106
imitator Homeri 82
incest 16 n.64
infanticide 10,
   demographic records 10,
   ἐγχυτρισμός 10 n.18
intertext 3, 13, 21, 80, 90,
   between the *Iliad* and the *Odyssey* 91,
   polemic intertext 17, 90, 100,
   attacks from the female side 21,
   self-justification for killing young men 21,
   catalogue of Heroines 17
inversion 94f.,
   inverted iambic stories 79-82, 91,
   ideological inversion 132
Iole 99
Iphitus 100
Iron-Age 58,
   Iron-Age-adults 91,
   age of husbands and wives 17
irony 64, 117
Irus 88, 93, 125f.

Jason 82

Kazantzakis 135
king 39, 38 n.30, 44, 65, 92, 94
knocked-out teeth 86f.,
   waxen 87
knowledge 92, 117, 120

Laertes 49, 57
Lapiths 92
laughter 54, 87, 94f., 125
lie 122
Lithika 82 n.16
λόγοι ἀφροδίσιοι 86
Lotophages 106
Lucanus 9.902-906 45 n.11
Lycambes 11, 99
Lysanias of Cyrene 8 n.5
Lysias *or.* 1 93

Margites 12f., 43, 44 n.5, 81, fr. 4 W 13 n.36
Marius Victorinus, *Ars grammatica* IV, 141ff. Keil VI. 19 n.76
marked - unmarked 3 n.2
marriage 14, 30f., 35, 38, 79, 81, 105,

INDEX

marriage refusal 100,
married-unmarried. 70,
woman-located marriage 15, 37, 134,
unmarried Phoenix 70,
re-marriage of Odysseus 71,
marriage-rites 15-17,
virilocal wedding 15 n.56,
status of her husband's "daughter" 15,
ἔχων 93,
Hektor 93,
expensive wedding gifts 10,
ὄμφαξ 12
master and slave 115, 118, 131
Medea 82
Medon 62
Melanthius 93
Melantho 94
Meleager *AP* 352 8 n.9 + 11 n.24
Méliès 32
Menandrus, *Sam.* 389 10 n.18, *Sam.* 727f. 52 n.32, *Samia*, 741f. 62 n.4
Mestra 13, 13 n.37, 81
metaphor 54, 70,
    lion 81,
    snake-hero 50 n.25,
    earth's burden 16,
    weasel-woman 13,
    wedding-metaphors 15
μῆτις 12
metonymy 91
metre 8, 19,
    trimeter 19 n.75,
    synizesis 20,
    stikhos epoidos 19 n.76,
    iambeîa 7,
    epic verse 19
Mimnermus 8
Minucius Felix 106
muse 32
Musil 110 n.16, 110

narrative patterns 29, 32, 34,
πέρας and "end" of the *Odyssey* 47f.
triplets 113 n.24,
parallelism 34
revenge story 48,
Telemachus-story 48,
Odysseus-story 48,
husband at his wife's wedding 29
hic et nunc" 107,
loud 125,
Locutor/Narrator 106 n.5,

discours indirect libre 106,
control 109,
embedded focalization 116, 124,
analepse 32,
    external 32, 110, 122,
    false internal 123,
narrative style 38
    hyptiotes 106 n.4,
    skaz 52,
Narrator 31f., 106 n.5, 111f., 120 - 123, 131, 134,
    narrator 1 31, 106 n.5,
    narrator 2 31, 106 n.5,
    Narrator/Locutor 106 n.5 111, 122, 131,
    Narrator's point of view 108,
    objective Narrator 107,
    Narrator apologizes 71,
    implied poet 106 n.5
Nausicaa 84
Neoboule, 81
neos νέος ἀνήρ 63, 66 n.15, 66f.,
    νέοι 15, 89,
    νεώτεροι 67, 82,
    νεανίσκαρχος 70, cf. young men, cf. gender
Nestor 70
nostalgia 105
nothoi 16 n.58 cf. young men
nymph 13 n.38,
    first νύμφη 31,
    second νύμφη 31,
    third νύμφη 31, 85
    Nausicaa 31, 36,
    νύμφη 84f.

oar breaking 82-84
Odysseus: 86, 91, 105, 131,
    as a young man 82,
    ridiculed 137,
    like an eagle 49,
    Iliadic Odysseus 50
Odyssey proem 110, *Od.* 1.6 71, *Od.* 1.32 71, *Od.*1.42f. 84, *Od.* 1.108 61, *Od.* 1.116f. 63, *Od.* 1.226 94, *Od.* 1.249 96, *Od.* 1.325 126, *Od.* 1.328-366 113 n.24, *Od.* 1.358 64, *Od.* 1.360 127, *Od.* 1.365f. 127, *Od.* 1.392 65, *Od.* 1.394f. 65, *Od.* 2.28f. 63, *Od.* 2.40 64, *Od.* 2.151 45 n.13, *Od.* 2.188f. 67, *Od.* 2.293 65, *Od.* 3.162ff. 46 n.16, *Od.* 4.443 79, *Od.* 4.655 110 n.19, *Od.* 5.8 57, *Od.* 5.99 84, *Od.* 6.142 113, *Od.* 7.241ff. 33, *Od.* 8.266ff.

134, *Od.* 8.306 57, *Od.* 8.338ff. 17 n.67, *Od.* 8.491 119, *Od.* 10.230f. 81, *Od.* 10.392 82, *Od.* 10.410 62, *Od.* 11 133, *Od.* 11.235ff. 17 n.71, *Od.* 12.70 82, *Od.* 12.357ff. 61 n.1, *Od.* 13.222 66, *Od.* 14.7-9 115f., *Od.* 14.36 116, *Od.* 14.185-359 43, *Od.* 14.450 116, *Od.* 15.141ff. 46 n.18, *Od.* 15.480 79 n.5, *Od.* 15.557 119, *Od.* 16.136 53, *Od.* 17.71ff. 120, Od. 17.107ff. 48, *Od.* 17.193 + 282 53, *Od.* 17.294 66, *Od.* 17.502 66, *Od.* 18.1ff. 91, *Od.* 18.6 66, *Od.* 18.27ff. 88, *Od.*18.30f. 88, *Od.* 18.34 89, *Od.* 18.35 125, *Od.* 18.51 125, *Od.* 18.51ff. 89, *Od.* 18.61 90, *Od.* 18.94 125, *Od.* 18.100 126, *Od.* 18.111 126, *Od.* 18.155 126, *Od.* 18.178 122 n.45, *Od.*18.184 127, *Od.* 18.193 122 n.45, *Od.* 18.212 127, *Od.* 18.281 p 122f., *Od.* 18.349f. 94, *Od.* 18.351ff. 95, *Od.* 18.385 95, *Od.* 19.53-604 113 n.24, *Od.* 19.62 121, *Od.* 19.209 114, *Od.* 19.392 121 n.43, *Od.* 19.393ff. 121, *Od.* 19.468 121 n.43, *Od.* 19.479 125, *Od.* 19.536ff. 46, *Od.* 20.11 119 n.36, *Od.* 20.216 116 n.34, *Od.* 20.351 53, *Od.* 20.375 121 n.40, *Od.* 21.9 117 *Od.* 21.13f. 99, *Od.* 21.27 100, *Od.* 21.83 118, *Od.* 21.289ff. 92, *Od.* 21. 295ff. 92, *Od.* 21.393 117, *Od.* 21.395 117, *Od.* 21.430 34, *Od.* 22.119 118, *Od.* 22.362-364 62 n.8, *Od.* 23.62 112 n.22, *Od.* 23.85ff. 113, *Od.* 23.86 114f., *Od.* 23.94 113, *Od.* 23.121f. 70, *Od.* 23.296 47, *Od.* 24.121ff. 48, *Od.* 24.125ff. 96, *Od.* 24.131ff. 96, *Od.* 24.139f. 97, *Od.* 24.145 97, *Od.* 24.351 57, *Od.* 24.514f. 49, *Od.* 24.538 47, Schol. Od. Hypoth. 85.16 H.Œ. 93 n.45, Schol. Q 11.128 137
Oenomaus 99
Olympiodorus 105
optativus obliquus 110
oracular discourse 137, oracular hexameters 54
Orphic Argonautica 82
Ortilochus 100
Oxen = husbands 61f.,
    ox like Agamemnon, 62
    Clytaemestra as a cow 62

papyri
    Dubl. 193a = T 10 Tarditi 18 n.73, 11 n.24,
    Oxy. 2174.4 87
parechesis 54
parody 17, 20,
    parody of epic style 16
party 7,
    τερπωλή 89 cf. iambus
past 27,
    of the Heroes 105,
    escaping the past 30
Pelike of the Villa Giulia 48238, ARV(2) 287, 27 137 n.9
Penelope 30, 35, 64, 96, 99, 105, 113, 117, 122-124, 126f., 131f., 135
Phaeacians 21, 34, 85f., 124, 133, 86 n.26
Phemius 126
Philoetius 118
Pindarus 17, 28 n.2, 134, *Pyth.* 2.44 93, *Pyth.* 4 134, *Pyth.* 9 133, Schol. Pind. Ol. 1.9 17 n.68
Piraeus 120
Pisistratus 38
Pittacus 89
Plato 15, 68 n.22, *Legg.* 658d7 96 n.47, *Legg.* 682d 3 n.1, *Legg.* 708b. 10 n.21, *Legg.* 736a1f. 8 n.7, *Legg.* 776ab 16 n.56, *Legg.* 923 15 n.50 + 37 n.26, *Resp.* 392d 107 n.8, *Phaedr.* 243a 112 n.22, *Plt.* 293d 37 n.28, *Sym* 212d3ff. 28 n.3
Plinius *NH* 10.6, 10.10 45 n.11, *NH* 10.13. 46 n.17
plotting of the couple 29 cf. composition
Plutarchus *Coniug. praec.* 142d 32 110 n.17, *De tranqu. an.*471B1ff. 44 n.6, *Cleom.* 23 [2].4 15 n.49
point of view 111, 123,
    group-perspective. 127,
    hindering perspective 123,
    negative point of view of a group 112, 123,
    quiet perception 124f.,
    of the Suitors 131,
    ich-origo 124,
    stealing point of view 124,
    two different viewpoints 39,
    avoiding patterns 39
Pollux, *Onom.* 3.34ff. 37 n.26
Polyxena 67, 68 n.17
Poseidon 134
Proclus 136
Prohaeresius 37
Proteus 79, 85
Ps.-Hdt. *Vita Hom.* 30 22 n.84

INDEX

Pseudo-Longinus *De subl.* 9.10 55 n.39, 109

queen 117 cf. king
Quintus Smyrnaeus 82

recognition-scene 124
return 36, 39 105, *Returns* 126, theme of return 36
Rhesos 87
ring composition 15 n.48, 50f., 50 n.27, 104 n.35,
δίνη 45 n.13

sacrifice 49, performed by the νέοι 68
Sappho 8, 132, fr. 1 Voigt 111, fr. 5 Voigt 13 n.42, fr. 16 Voigt 13 n.42, fr. 31 Voigt 13 n.42, fr. 105a Voigt 12 n.30, fr. 160 94, Sappho's iambi 13
sausage 91 cf. belly
scholars quoted: Ahl 30 n.7, 35 n.21, Ameis 115 n.25, Andrewes 38 n.30, Arend 33 n.19 Assunçâo 14 n.46, Baldick 29 n.6, Beck 50 n.27, Bérard 115, Bertman 51 n.30, Berve 38 n.30, Birge 82 n.12, Bodson 12 n.33, Bona 43 n.2, Bonanni 66 n.13, Bowra 12 n.33, Braswell 86 n.29, Brelich 10 n.16, 28 n.2, Brown 8 n.11 + n.12, 13 n.40, Büchner 122 n.44, Burkert 44 n.7, Burnett 52 n.31, Calame 13 n.40, 14 n.43+n.44, 15 n.51, 31 n.12, 36 n.25, 133 n.3, Carlier 38 n.30, Casevitz 15 n.52, Ceccarelli 80 n.3, Chadwick 29 n.6, Chantraine 109 n.15, Clay 85 n.24, 115 n.28, Contiades-Tsitsoni 36 n.26, Cook 35 n.22, 39 n.36, 75 n.1, Da Cunha Corrêa 98 n.48, Danek 29 n.6, 32 n.15, De Jong 106 n.5, 107 n.9, 113 n.24, 115 n.29, 120 n.39, 124 n.47, Deger 38 n.30, Detienne 12 n.34, 15 n.51, 36 n.25, Doherty 17 n.69, Dougherty 15 n.51 + 56, 36 n.25, Dover 11 n.22, Dräger 82 n.13, Drews 38 n.30, Durand n.1, Erbse 47, 47 n.21, Finkelberg 14 n.46, Forbes 9 n.13, Ford 29, Foucault 47 n.20, Fränkel 52 n.34, Gallant 10 n.19, Garnsey 91 n.39, Genette 110, 110 n.18, Gerber 55 n.38, Germain 32 n.18, Giangrande 38 n.29, Graf 99 n.49, Graham 36 n.26, Greimas 45 n.12, Haase 36 n.26, Hainsworth 50 n.26 + n.27, Halleux 82 n.16, Halperin 14 n.44, Hamburger 108, 108 n.10. 108 n.12, Henrichs 105 n.2, Herter 50 n.27, Heubeck 114 n.27, Hunter 83 n.20, Hurst 50 n.27, Jakob 12 n.32, Kahil 13 n.37, Kahn 85 n.25, Kantzis 7 n.4, Katicic 50 n.27, Katz 115 n.28, Kirk 69 n.26, Knight 83 n.20, Krischer 34, 34 n.20, Lacombrade 7 n.1, Lambin 30 n.8, Lang 38 n.34, Lasserre 52 n.31, Latacz 30 n.8, 69, 69. n.24, 70 n.28, Lateiner 63 n.10, Leduc 10 n.17, 16 n.55, 27 n.1, Lehrs 47 n.21, Lennartz 7 n.2, Létoublon 37 n.27, 106 n.3, 133 n.3, Livrea 82 n.15, Lloyd-Jones 13 n.37, Lohmann 15 n.48, Loraux 13 n.37, Louden 33 n.19, Lukinovich 19 n.75, Mader 109 n.14, Malkin 36 n.24, Marcozzi 99 n.50, Marzullo 20 n.81, Mendes de Costa 115 n.30, Meuli 82 n.13, Minchin 17 n.70, Miralles 8 n.5, 8 n.12, 11 n.23, 20 n.79, 81 n.9, Mösch-Klingele 37 n.26, Mossman 68 n.17, Muchnova 109 n.15, Müller 50 n.27, Nagy 3 n.1, Nünlist 32 n.15, Ogden 38 n.30, 68 n.20, Page 12 n.31, Papadopoulou-Belmehdi 31 n.10, 32 n.23, Pazdernik 21 n.82, 35 n.21, Pellizer 8 n.12, Peradotto 84 n.23, Pichler 78 n.3, Poland 99 n.49, Pomeroy 10 n.19, 15 n.53, Pòrtulas 8 n.5, 8 n.12, 11 n.23, 20 n.79, 81 n.9, Powell 33 n.19, Pralon 99 n.50, Pratt 47 n.19, Pucci 2, 3 n.5, 90 n.35, 89 n.34, 90f, 91 n.36, Quincy 12 n.25, Rabel 106 n.5, 124 n.47, Radermacher 53 n.35, Rankin 6. n.8+10, Reece 43 n.2, Rengakos 32 n.15, Rieu 49 n.24, Roisman 30 n.7, 35 n.21, Rosen 20 n.80, Roy 108 n.11, 108 n.10, Ruschenbusch 10 n.21, Russo 43 n.2, Rutherford 92 n.41, Schamp 82 n.16, Schear 12 n.35, Scheid-Tissinier 3 n.1, Schindler 12 n.29, Schmidt 47 n.21, Schmied 50 n.27, Schubert 21 n.83, 39 n.36, Schwartz 123 n.46, Schwyzer 110, Seeck 32 n.15, Segal 30 n.9, 31 n.11, 43 n.1, 69 n.23, 84 n.21, 105, Sévryns 68 n.21, Snodgrass 10 n.21, Spaltenstein 83 n.20, Stanford 115 n.31, Stanley 15 n.48, Steinrück 3 n.4, 13 n.36, 15 n.48, 17 n.72, 19 n.75, 32 n.15 + 16, 38 n.35, 44 n.5, 51 n.29, 79 n.4, 82 n.15, 83 n.18, 89 n.34, 111 n.21, 121 n.42 , Suter 3 n.1, Thalmann 3 n.3, 92, 92 n.40, Treu 12 n.33, 52 n.31, Ulf 63 n.11, Van Leeuwen

115 n.30, Van Wees 70 n.28, Vernant 12 n.34, 17, 61 n.1, Vian 83 n.18, Viret-Bernal 62 n.5, Voigt 114 n.25, West 12 n.28, 14, 14 n.43, 15 n.48, 17 n.70, 44 n.9, 70 n.27, West S. 19 n.77, Wilamowitz 50 n.27, William 132 n.2, Woodhouse 123 n.46, Wray 12 n.25, Yamagata 63 n.10, Ziegler 50 n.27, Zielinski 32 n.14, 121, Zirmunskij 29 n.6
seal 79 n.5, 79
seer 21, 83,
    Halitherses 67,
    Batusiades 17 n.65, 53 n.36,
    Theoclymenus 53,
    Kikon 17 n.65
Semonides 13, 17f., 38, 55 n.40, 56, 81, fr. 1.17ff. 8. n.8, frr. 2-3 W 14 n.45, 15, fr. 7.114 W 93 n.46, fr. 7, 22f. W 56 n.42, fr. 7.68 W 93 n.46, fr. 7.90 W 86 n.27, fr.16 W 79, fr. 40 W 95
Seneca *Tro.* 343. 69 n.25
shortage (food) 45, 57, 91, land-shortage 10 n.21
Sirens 106
skyphos of Thebes (priv. coll. cf. *JHS* 84 1964, pl. 5-6) 13 n.39
slave: good slave 66 cf. Eumaeus
solidarity 83
Solo 8, fr. 19 W 86 n.26, fr. 25 W 14 n.44
son: better 136,
    legitimate son 135 cf. nothos
song as a drug 106
Sophocles *Ichn.*366f. 17 n.67
spartan 28 n.2, 44, 68f.
Stesichorus fr. 192 Davies 112 n.22
Strabo, 6.3.2 67 n.20
Suda 2.665.16 Adler 16 n.63, 4.360.7 Adler 16 n.61
Suitors 132,
    ignorance 126,
    viewpoint 111, 127, 132,
    good, Amphinomus 126,
    Suitors' stories 92,
    sacrificial rite 68,
    their own fault 35, 81, 83,
    their own stories 80,
    murder of the Suitors 34,
    Suitors = iambic audience 21,
    title of Suitors 21
swine 62, 81 cf. inverted iambus
symposium 89, 94

Telegonia 135, l. 3 Davies 135 n.6, T 2A Davies 135 n.5,
Telegonus 135f.
Telemachus 64f., 90, 93, 105, 126
Terent. Maurus 2456ff. *Gramm.Lat.* 6.398 8 n.6
Thales 55
Themis 57
Theognis of Megara 14
θυμός 90
Trophonius 136
Turgenev 110
tyrannos 16, 38 n.30, 38f.,
    sleeping with their mother 38,
    Oedipus 38
Tyro 17 n.71
Tyrtaeus 15, fr.10W 15 n.47, 68, fr. 10 W 68 n.19
Tzetzes *Alleg. Hom.* Il. 24.125ff. 7 n.4

Vergilius *Aen* 1.184ff. 82 n.11
vulture 46

wheat-shovel 83
wives 81, 127, *wife and husband* 131
wolves 81, walks like 11 n.22
wooden horse 30

ξενία 100
Xenophanes 8, fr. 1.21-24 W 93 n.44
Xenopho *Res Lac.* 3.4 28 n.2, *Mem.* 1.2.35 9 n.13

young and the old 63, 66,
    young old have strife 88, 124, 126, 134,
    in the army 67,
    young and old "kings" 65,
    ships 66,
    two councils 66
young men 9, 22, 31, 40, 63, 63 n.10, 81-85, 93, 99,
    Achilles 99 n.50, 121,
    death of 71,
    like-gods, 105 n.1,
    young men's enlightenment-ideology 67,
    younger than they were before 67,
    young but married warrior 69,
    Tyrtaean νέοι 70,
    νόθος 85, 136,
    γνήσιος 85, 136,
    mêtis of young men 44,
    corporations of νέοι 17, 70,

young cows 62,
young man killed by his own fault 71,
wall of the city 70,
Socrates and his νέοι 70,
Stenka Razin 35,
Partheniai 68,
young men as the audience of the iambus 9,
age by 20-30 years 9,
Ares 134,

peeping 126,
subject of laughter in Attic comedy 9,
unwillingly bachelors 10
younger epic poets : νεώτεροι 137

Zenodotus 47
Zeus 16, 84,
as a father 56,
Athena accuses her father 57